Culture and Abortion

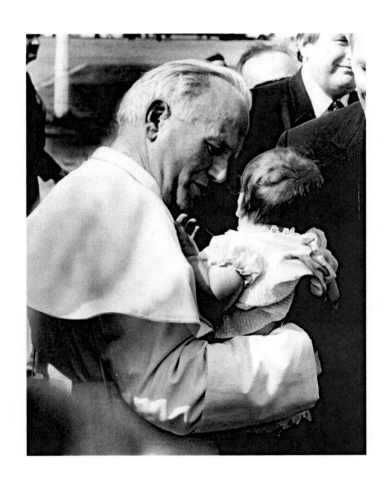

Culture and Abortion

Edward Short

For ~~Jaqueline~~ With affectionate best wishes Edward 19 Aug. 2013

Gracewing

First published in England in 2013
by
Gracewing
2 Southern Avenue
Leominster
Herefordshire HR6 0QF
United Kingdom
www.gracewing.co.uk

ISBN 978 085244 820 5

Typeset by Gracewing

Cover design by Bernardita Peña Hurtado

Cover painting: John Henry Fuseli, *Lady Macbeth* (1784),
Musée du Louvre, Paris

For
Sophia Thérèse Mariana

Διά τὸ θαυμάζειν ἡ σοφία

CONTENTS

List of Illustrations

Lady Macbeth Sleepwalking (1784) by Henry Fuseli (Courtesy of Louvre Museum)

Pope John Paul II (Public Domain)

Matthew Arnold (1881) by Frederick Anthony Augustus Sandys (Courtesy of British Museum)

Anne Ridler (Courtesy of Perpetua Press)

Jonathan Swift (1718) by Charles Jervas (Courtesy of British Museum)

Joanna Baillie (1851) by Sir William John Newton (Courtesy of British Museum)

Penelope Fitzgerald (Public Domain)

Prof. John and Mrs. Nuala Scarisbrick (Courtesy of Prof. J. J. Scarisbrick)

Walker Percy as a Boy of 11 (Public Domain)

William Wilberforce (1828) after Sir Thomas Lawrence (Courtesy of British Museum)

Nathaniel Hawthorne and Rose Hawthorne (Courtesy of Dominican Sisters of Hawthorne)

Pope Paul VI (Public Domain)

Charles Dickens (late 1850s) by John and Charles Watkins (Public Domain)

G. K. Chesterton and his Wife Frances (1922) (Courtesy of G. K. Chesterton Library Trust)

Pope John Paul II, New York City (1979) (Public Domain)

PREFACE

M ANY GENEROUS PEOPLE gave me critical support while I was writing *Culture and Abortion*. First and foremost, I should like to thank Mr. Tom Longford of Gracewing for his belief in the project when it was still evolving and his persevering good counsel once it began to take shape. Sister Mary Joseph, OSB, Librarian of the Venerable English College in Rome, kindly gave me the benefit of her crack editorial smarts, as did Rev. Dr. Paul Haffner, Theological and Editorial Director of Gracewing. Mrs. Anne Conlon and Mrs. Maria McFadden of the *Human Life Review* were also forthcoming with their kind assistance. I am particularly grateful to Mrs. Conlon for urging me to take my melancholy theme and fashion it into a book. Then, again, I am pleased to express my abounding thanks to Prof. and Mrs. J. J. Scarisbrick, who shared with me the good work of their far-flung pro-life organization, LIFE, which has pregnancy care centers, fertility clinics, hospices, and education offices throughout the United Kingdom, the Republic of Ireland, Sri Lanka, Uganda and Nigeria. There are many others to whom I am indebted. Prof. Jo Anne Sylva was unstinting in her sympathetic support. Mrs. Stella Becker gave me the grace of her prayers and best wishes. Miss Kaitlin Walter kept me abreast of the younger generation. Father Dermot Fenlon of Newman's Oratory gave me his keen critical support. Father Aquinas Guilbeau, OP, introduced me not only to Mother Mary Francis and the Hawthorne Sisters but to Sister Sylvia Enriquez and the Servants of Mary, all of whom helped me to understand the culture of life and love. Dr. Tracey Rowland once again came to my rescue from occasionally sunny Melbourne. Robert Crotty, Esq. gave me the benefit of his good counsel and good company. John Forry, Esq. was another source of vital support. Miss Madeleine Beard pointed out to me that the mother of Margot Fonteyn had sought to have the great ballerina aborted. Monsignor Austin Bennett of the Church of St. Rita was another source of great support, as were Mr. and Mrs. William Law from faraway Wisconsin. Prof. Mary Ann Glendon of Harvard Law School impressed upon me how the evil of euthanasia now threatens America's public health system. Monsignor George Bardes inspired me with his stalwart pro-life witness, as did Mrs. Frances O'C. Hardart. The Right Honorable William Hague sharpened my understanding of the parallels between the pro-life movement and William Wilberforce's campaign to abolish slavery. Mrs. Charlotte Allen of *The Weekly Standard* helped me to understand the full evil of Planned Parenthood. And Miss Caroline Van Horn of Line Designs gave me brilliant help with the images that grace my cover and chapters.

Lastly, I am grateful to my wife Karina and our obstreperous newborn Sophia, both of whom have helped me to understand the preciousness of life, which makes the Golgotha at the core of this book all the more distressing.

Edward Short
Feast of St. Cyril of Jerusalem
18 March 2013
Astoria, New York

"Man is called to a fullness of life which far exceeds the dimensions of this earthly existence, because it consists in sharing the very life of God. The loftiness of this supernatural vocation reveals the greatness and the inestimable value of human life even in its temporal phase. Life in time, in fact, is the fundamental condition, the initial stage and an integral part of the entire unified process of human existence. It is a process which, unexpectedly and undeservedly, is enlightened by the promise and renewed by the gift of divine life, which has its full realization in eternity."

Pope John Paul II, *Evangelium Vitae* (1995)

"The supreme adventure is being born."

G. K. Chesterton, *Heretics* (1905)

"Man's life comes from God; it is his gift, his image and imprint, a sharing in his breath of life. God therefore is the sole Lord of this life; man cannot do with it as he wills."

Pope John Paul II, *Evangelium Vitae* (1995)

Matthew Arnold

INTRODUCTION

O NE OF THE people I had in mind when I was writing *Culture and Abortion* was Matthew Arnold (1822– 88), whose *Culture and Anarchy* (1869) continues to generate keen interest in a society where we seem to have so much of the latter and so little of the former. Yet if Arnold believed that culture could somehow enable his combustible society to prevent anarchy, I wished to argue in my book that false notions of culture could actually foment anarchy, not only the sort that leads people to engage in street fighting and the like, but the rather more consequential sort that prevents people from distinguishing good from evil. That so much of what constitutes the culture of our own social order promotes abortion turns Arnold's original contention on its head. Whether we choose to see the wreck of our culture as stemming from the noisome influence of the State or the universities or the chattering classes, or what Cardinal Newman once called "the great *apostasia*," many of those who set themselves up as custodians of culture now uniformly subscribe to the notion that killing babies in the womb redounds to the well-being and indeed the dignity of women. As Nathaniel Hawthorne had his narrator remind his readers in *The House of the Seven Gables* (1851): "the influential classes … those who take upon themselves to be leaders of the people are fully liable to all the passionate error that has ever characterized the maddest mob."[1]

What I sought to do in *Culture and Abortion* was to see if some aspects of culture—which is to say works of poetry, history, criticism, fiction, and the encyclicals of popes—

---

[1] N. Hawthorne, *The House of the Seven Gables* (Folio Society, 2012), p. 5.

could help make sense of this life-destroying notion,
though another and perhaps more important purpose was
to argue that in order to end the evil of abortion we need
a revival of culture, true culture, not the travesty of culture
that Arnold recommends.

Having said this, I must also say that in many ways
Arnold is a sympathetic figure. He had a delicious sense of
humor, derived in large measure from growing up with his
father, the famous headmaster of Rugby, who seems to have
had no sense of the ridiculous whatsoever. We can get a
good example of the son's humor in *Friendship's Garland*
(1867), where Arnold describes showing his imaginary
Prussian hero Arminius the English legal system in action.
When they arrive at the magistrate's court where a poacher
is being tried, Arminius asks whether the two justices in
attendance, Lord Lumpington and Mr. Hittal, gained anything from their time at Oxford, to which Arnold replies:

> Well ... during their three years at Oxford they were
> so much occupied with Bullingdon and hunting that
> there was no great opportunity to judge. But for my
> part I have always thought that their both getting
> their degrees at last with flying colours, after three
> weeks of a famous coach for fast men, four nights
> without going to bed, and an incredible consump-
> tion of wet towels, strong cigars, and brandy-and-
> water, was one of the most astonishing feats of
> mental gymnastics I ever heard of.[2]

In addition to his charming sense of fun, Arnold was a
dutiful husband and a doting papa. He wrote an elegant,
bantering, ironical English. He could be an inspired poet
and an insightful critic. Towards the end of his life, when
London society began to lionize him, he wrote scoffingly
to one of his friends, "People think I can teach them style.

---

[2]   M. Arnold, *Friendship's Garland* (London, 1903), p. 50.

What stuff it all is! Have something to say, and say it as clearly as you can. That is the only secret of style."[3]

These were the winning aspects of the man. But when he proceeded to lecture his contemporaries on culture he showed what mischief ensues when trifling men—George Meredith called Arnold "a dandy Isaiah"—take it into their heads to conceive of culture in terms that have nothing to do with God or man's longing for God.[4] It also has to be said that elitism played a certain part in the formation of Arnold's notions of culture, as it does in so many of those who adopted these notions after him. He was something of what Thackeray might have called a "literary snob." Convinced that his own extensive reading put him at the center of the universe, he tended to look down his nose at anyone outside this blessed plot. Indeed, in discussing the requirements of culture, he turned the thing itself into a most unsympathetic snob.

> Culture says: "Consider these people, then, their way of life, their habits, their manners, the very tones of their voice; look at them attentively; observe the literature they read, the things which give them pleasure, the words which come forth out of their mouths, the thoughts which make the furniture of their minds; would any amount of wealth be worth having with the condition that one was to become just like these people by having it?" And thus culture begets a dissatisfaction which is the best possible value in stemming the common tide of men's thoughts in a wealthy and industrial community, and which saves the future, one may hope, from being vulgarized, even if it cannot save the present.[5]

[3] G. W. E, Russell, *Collections and Recollections* (London, 1903), p. 136.
[4] G. Meredith, *Fortnightly Review* (July 1909).
[5] M. Arnold, *Culture and Anarchy* (London, 1903), p. 16.

By contrast, Shakespeare, Johnson and Chesterton, the most egalitarian of our writers, positively rejoiced in concurring with this "common tide of men's thoughts," especially when it accorded with ancient, unfashionable, unbiddable truth. Arnold could only bring himself to deplore the thoughts of ordinary men. Indeed, the nihilist in him could be strangely impatient with life itself.

There is a striking example of this in the preface to his first series of critical essays, where he notes how "the *Saturday Review* maintains that our epoch of transformation is finished; that we have found our philosophy; that the British nation has searched all anchorages for the spirit, and has finally anchored itself, in the fullness of perfected knowledge, on Benthamism.

> This idea at first made a great impression on me; not only because it is so consoling in itself, but also because it explained a phenomenon which in the summer of last year had, I confess, a good deal troubled me. At that time my avocations led me to travel almost daily on one of the Great Eastern Lines,—the Woodford Branch. Every one knows that the murderer, Müller, perpetrated his detestable act on the North London Railway, close by.[6] The English middle class, of which I am myself a feeble unit, travel on the Woodford Branch in large numbers. Well, the demoralisation of our class,— the class which (the newspapers are constantly saying it, so I may repeat it without vanity) has done all the great things which have ever been done in England,—the demoralisation, I say, of our class,

---

[6]   On July 9, 1864, Thomas Briggs, a bank clerk, was murdered in his first-class compartment by Max Müller, a German tailor, while traveling on the North London Railway between Bow and Hackney-wick. Müller murdered Briggs for his gold watch and chain. See *The Illustrated London News* (16 July 1864).

> caused by the Bow tragedy, was something bewil-
> dering. Myself a transcendentalist (as the *Saturday
> Review* knows), I escaped the infection; and, day
> after day, I used to ply my agitated fellow travellers
> with all the consolations which my transcenden-
> talism would naturally suggest to me.

Of course, the reference here to his "transcendentalism"
was facetious. Arnold had no transcendentalism of any
stripe. His definition of religion could have been borrowed
from Julian the Apostate: "The true meaning of religion is
... not simply morality, but morality touched by emotion."[7]
It was G. K. Chesterton who first called attention to the
pagan statism to which Arnold's views on religion and
culture incline.

> He seems to have believed that a "Historic
> Church," that is, some established organisation
> with ceremonies and sacred books, etc., could be
> perpetually preserved as a sort of vessel to contain
> the spiritual ideas of the age, whatever those ideas
> might happen to be. He clearly seems to have
> contemplated a melting away of the doctrines of
> the Church and even of the meaning of the words:
> but he thought a certain need in man would always
> be best satisfied by public worship and especially
> by the great religious literatures of the past. He
> would embalm the body that it might often be
> revisited by the soul—or souls ... But while Arnold
> would loosen the theological bonds of the Church,
> he would not loosen the official bonds of the State.
> You must not disestablish the Church: you must
> not even leave the Church: you must stop inside it
> and think what you choose. Enemies might say that
> he was simply trying to establish and endow
> Agnosticism. It is fairer and truer to say that

---

[7]   M. Arnold, *Literature and Dogma* (London, 1873), p. 21.

> unconsciously he was trying to restore Paganism:
> for this State Ritualism without theology, and
> without much belief, actually was the practice of
> the ancient world. Arnold may have thought that
> he was building an altar to the Unknown God; but
> he was really building it to Divus Caesar.[8]

In an essay called "Democracy" in his *Mixed Essays* (1879),
Arnold elaborates on his statist views of culture by claim-
ing how, "the very framework and exterior order of the
State ... is sacred ... because of the great hopes and designs
for the State which culture teaches us to nourish." As to
exactly what these "great hopes and designs" are, Arnold
is not altogether clear, though he is convinced that they
bind us to the State in profound ways, for "believing," as
he says, "in right reason, and having faith in the progress
of humanity towards perfection, and ever labouring for
this end, we grow to have clearer sight of the ideas of right
reason, and of the elements and helps of perfection, and
come gradually to fill the framework of the State with
them, to fashion its internal composition and all its laws
and institutions conformably to them, and to make the
State more and more the expression, as we say, of our best
self, which is not manifold, and vulgar, and unstable, and
contentious, and ever-varying, but one, and noble, and
secure, and peaceful, and the same for all mankind ..."[9]
Now that our own State culture insists on regarding
abortion as a form of healthcare and calls for a redefinition
of marriage that will not only degrade marriage but
corrupt and abuse children on an unprecedented scale,
Arnold's confidence in the ability of the State to embody
right reason looks distinctly delusional.

---

[8]   G. K. Chesterton, *Collected Works: Chesterton on Dickens* (San
Francisco, 1989), XV, pp. 453–454.
[9]   M. Arnold, *Mixed Essays* (New York, 1903), p. 43.

Moreover, Arnold's pseudo-religion led him to take a view of his fellows that could be strikingly callous. The "consolations" that he relates sharing with his fellow train travelers are tell-tale.

> I reminded them how Caesar refused to take precautions against assassination, because life was not worth having at the price of an ignoble solicitude for it. I reminded them what insignificant atoms we all are in the life of the world. "Suppose the worst to happen," I said, addressing a portly jeweler from Cheapside; "suppose even yourself to be the victim; *il n'y a pas d'homme nécessaire.* We should miss you for a day or two upon the Woodford Branch; but the great mundane movement would still go on, the gravel walks of your villa would still be rolled, dividends would still be paid at the Bank, omnibuses would still run, there would still be the old crush at the corner of Fenchurch Street." All was of no avail. Nothing could moderate, in the bosom of the great English middle-class, their passionate, absorbing, almost blood-thirsty clinging to life. At the moment I thought this over-concern a little unworthy; but the *Saturday Review* suggests a touching explanation of it. What I took for the ignoble clinging to life of a comfortable worldling, was, perhaps, only the ardent longing of a faithful Benthamite, traversing an age still dimmed by the last mists of transcendentalism, to be spared long enough to see his religion in the full and final blaze of its triumph. This respectable man, whom I imagined to be going up to London to serve his shop, or to buy shares, or to attend an Exeter Hall meeting, or to assist at the deliberations of the Marylebone Vestry, was even, perhaps, in real truth, on a pious pilgrimage, to

> obtain from Mr. Bentham's executors a secret bone
> of his great, dissected master.[10]

This shows Arnold at his most playfully witty and yet if we attend to what he is actually saying we can see that there is something like real despair beneath the playfulness.

First, Arnold's view of life did not significantly differ from that of the Utilitarians. Of course, he wanted his contemporaries to pay more attention to the literature of the Continent and less to English newspapers; he wanted the new industrial middle-classes to acquire better manners and less objectionable tastes; he certainly wished the Catholics in his midst to leave off insisting that the Humpty-Dumpty of orthodox Christianity be put back on his wall; but other than that his own brand of secularism had more in common with Benthamism than he cared to admit. After all, he might gently mock the fact that Benthamism nears "the full and final blaze of its triumph," but he does not take issue with it. On the contrary, he shared Bentham's view that "perfected knowledge" should be the object of culture. As he claims in *Culture and Anarchy* "culture is, or ought to be, the study and pursuit of perfection ..." Moreover, he was convinced that when it came to the "perfection as pursued by culture ... sweetness and light are the main characters."[11] This is an abstract, impersonal idea of culture, fit perhaps for Empedocles, whom Arnold describes in his laboriously despondent poem as "Nothing but a devouring flame of thought ... a naked, eternally restless mind" but not for human beings with hearts as well as minds.[12]

---

[10] M. Arnold, *Essays in Criticism: First Series* (London, 1920), p. 3.

[11] *Culture and Anarchy*, p. 40.

[12] M. Arnold, "Empedocles on Aetna," *The Poems of Matthew Arnold 1840–1867*, ed. A. T. Quiller-Couch (Oxford, 1913), p. 122.

Secondly, there is something a little chilling in this
otherwise jocular passage. He is saying that the middle-
class passengers on the train should not worry whether
the train murderer returns and kills them because *"il n'y
a pas d'homme nécessaire."* Coming from any one else this
would sound a banal enough jest. But Arnold took his
nihilism seriously; he really did believe that we are all
"insignificant atoms in the life of the world." When he tells
his companions that they should be reconciled to the
prospect of their own extinction he is giving a foretaste of
that contempt for life which was not separate from his
views on culture. After all, he borrowed his very definition
of culture from one of Swift's satires, *The Battle of the
Books* (1704) in which the Dean has his ancients defend
their culture against the moderns by likening it to that of
bees, for, "Instead of dirt and poison we have rather chosen
to fill our hives with honey and wax; thus furnishing
mankind with the two noblest things, which are sweetness
and light." How the rhetorician in Arnold could have
thought that such an allusion strengthened his case is
baffling; but then in likening men to bees he was keeping
true to his pagan, denigratory view of human life. After all,
Arnold really did not care for people. His inadequate
definition of culture stemmed from an inadequate understanding of the *caritas* on which true culture must be
based. One can see his distaste for his fellows in a famous
piece that he wrote in defense of Lord Byron.

> As the inevitable break-up of the old order comes,
> as the English middle-class slowly awakens from
> its intellectual sleep of two centuries, as our actual
> present world, to which this sleep condemned us,
> shows itself more clearly—our world of an aristoc-
> racy materialised and null, a middle-class purblind
> and hideous, a lower class crude and brutal—we
> shall turn our eyes again, and to more purpose,

upon this passionate and dauntless soldier of a
forlorn hope ...[13]

Needless to say, anyone who had somehow convinced
himself that the only person worth paying any mind to in
early nineteenth-century Britain was Byron, had hardly
the wide-ranging sympathies necessary to pronounce on
something as necessarily catholic as culture. It is also
worth noting that most of the literary Modernists who
shared Arnold's cultural elitism, including Pound, Eliot
and Yeats, also shared this low view of ordinary men. Eliot
was particularly saturnine on this score, writing his
brother after his father's death, "I feel that both he and
mother in spite of their affection were lonely people, and
that he was the more lonely of the two—he hardly knew
himself ... in my experience everyone except the fools
seem ... warped or stunted."[14]

Lord Annan, the sybaritic don and intellectual historian, also betrayed the hollowness of Arnold's idea of
culture when he noted how "Matthew Arnold was the first
modern critic ... to declare that people could be consoled,
healed, and changed by reading literature and therefore
that their awakening depended on understanding which
was the finest literature. He was the first to argue that the
spiritual health of a society such as England depended on
there being a sufficient number of civilized human beings
devoted to the ideal of spreading Culture."[15] Newman's

---

[13] M. Arnold, "Byron," *Essays in Criticism: Second Series* (London, 1888), p. 202.

[14] T. S. Eliot to Henry Eliot (27 February 1919), *The Letters of T. S. Eliot*, ed. Hugh Haughton and Valerie Eliot (London, 2011), I, p. 324.

[15] N. Annan, Introduction to *Matthew Arnold: Selected Essays* (Oxford, 1964), p. vii. Of Lord Annan, David Cannadine wrote in the *Oxford Dictionary of National Biography*: "As the foremost spokesman of his generation he cared passionately about educa-tion, culture, and the intellect, 'everything else was secondary.'"

response to this sort of mandarin culture, of which both Arnold and Annan were such ardent proponents, was unsparing: "If we attempt to effect a moral improvement by means of poetry, we shall but mature into a mawkish, frivolous and fastidious sentimentalism."[16] Then, again, twenty-eight years before the publication of *Culture and Anarchy*, Newman had argued against the strictly secular view of culture in a series of letters to *The Times* which he later collected in a brilliant piece called "The Tamworth Reading Room" (1841). In one of the letters, he wrote how

> It does not require many words, then, to determine that, taking human nature as it is actually found, and assuming that there is an Art of life, to say that it consists, or in any essential manner is placed, in the cultivation of Knowledge, that the mind is changed by a discovery, or saved by a diversion, and can thus be amused into immortality,—that grief, anger, cowardice, self-conceit, pride, or passion, can be subdued by an examination of shells or grasses, or inhaling of gases, or chipping of rocks, or calculating the longitude, is the veriest of pretences which sophist or mountebank ever professed to a gaping auditory. If virtue be a mastery over the mind, if its end be action, if its perfection be inward order, harmony, and peace, we must seek it in graver and holier places than in Libraries and Reading-rooms.[17]

Nevertheless, Arnold was unpersuaded. He wrote *Culture and Anarchy*, as he said, "to recommend culture as the great help out of our present difficulties; culture being a pursuit of our total perfection by means of getting to know, on all the matters which most concern us, the best which

---

[16]   J. H. Newman, "Tamworth Reading Room," *Discussions and Arguments* (London, 1872), p. 275.

[17]   Ibid., p. 268.

has been thought and said in the world, and, through this knowledge, turning a stream of fresh and free thought upon our stock notions and habits, which we now follow staunchly but mechanically, vainly imagining that there is a virtue in following them staunchly which makes up for the mischief of following them mechanically."[18] If anyone should object that this was rather a narrow prospectus for any cultural agenda, Arnold was prepared to supplement it with afflatus of a higher order. "More and more mankind will discover that we have to turn to poetry to interpret life for us, to console us, to sustain us," he declared in a famous essay. "Without poetry, our science will appear incomplete; and most of what now passes with us for religion and philosophy will be replaced by poetry."[19]

This was the culture of knowledge for which Arnold intended poetry to act as a kind of surrogate religion. A variation of this culture continues to wield great influence, particularly among our political, educational and cultural elites, though now the knowledge on which it is based is technocratic rather than literary and the pantheism of the environmentalists supplies the necessary surrogate religion. What should be of interest to anyone interested in protecting vulnerable life is that the culture of knowledge spurns conscience and regards the weak, the dying and those struggling to be born with a utilitarian ruthlessness on which Bentham himself could hardly improve. Set this idea of culture up in any society and sooner or later abortion on demand will follow; euthanasia will follow. This is what happened in England in 1967; this is what happened in America in 1973; and this is what has happened nearly everywhere else in the world since. Hats off

---

[18] *Culture and Anarchy*, p. viii.
[19] M. Arnold, "The Study of Poetry," *Essays in Criticism: Second Series* (London, 1888), p. 3.

to the Maltese for bucking this atrocious trend but they are in a very distinct minority.

My book is not only a criticism of abortion: it is a criticism of the false notions of culture that make abortion possible. In this regard, I do not believe that the culture of knowledge and all its death-dealing variations can remedy abortion any more than it can remedy anarchy. The great tragic irony with respect to Arnold is that, although he might have set out to extol culture, in trying to base culture on the conviction that God and the heart's desire for God were somehow obsolete he actually put in place a culture that is profoundly antagonistic to culture. To defend life—and to bring about that culture of love which Pope John Paul II so prized—we must renounce this false Arnoldian notion of culture and reaffirm true culture, which is necessarily based on the Source of Life, the Giver of Life, the God of Life.

In *Culture and Abortion* I celebrate the Creator of Life by celebrating the work of some of His most life-affirming creatures. Hence, there is a chapter on the marvelous poet Anne Ridler, who still has not received her proper due. There is a chapter on the work of Prof. John J. Scarisbrick and his worldwide pro-life organization, LIFE, which is bringing the Gospel of Life to those who need it most. There is a chapter on the writer and critic Walker Percy, who tells his readers in his mock self-help book, *Lost in the Cosmos,* of the identity crisis that is at the heart of my chapter as well, "You live in a deranged age, more deranged than usual, because in spite of great scientific and technological advances, [you have] not the faintest idea of who [man] is or what he is doing."

The pages that follow also include a brief chapter on a magnificent short story by Penelope Fitzgerald, the niece of Ronald Knox, who had something of her uncle's genius for precise and witty prose. They include a chapter on the great prophet Pope Paul VI and one on the great liberator William Wilberforce. They include interrelated chapters on Dickens and Chesterton, both in their own ways staunch defenders of life. For Dickens, it was being condemned to Warren's blacking factory at 30 Hungerford Stairs, just off the Strand, when he was scarcely twelve years old, after the imprisonment of his father in the Marshalsea for debt that made him so appreciative of the vulnerability of children.[20] And it was largely the champion of children in Dickens that inspired Chesterton's great love of the man and his work, which he expressed so brilliantly in his incomparable critical essays. Dickens rarely spoke of his harrowing experience at the factory, though he made an exception with his first biographer, John Forster, with whom he shared an autobiographical fragment towards the end of his life in which he confessed how:

> It is wonderful to me how I could have been so easily cast away at such an age. It is wonderful to me, that, even after my descent into the poor little drudge I had been since we came to London, no one had compassion enough on me—a child of singular abilities, quick, eager, delicate, and soon hurt, bodily or mentally—to suggest that something might have been spared, as certainly it might have been, to place me at any common school ... The blacking warehouse was the last house on the left-hand, the blacking side of the way at old Hungerford-stairs. It was a crazy, tumble-down old house, abutting of course on the river and literally overrun with rats. Its wainscotted rooms, and its rotten floors and staircase, and the old grey rats

---

[20] According to Michael Slater, the greatest of living Dickensians, Dickens was in the blacking factory for thirteen or fourteen months—"an eternity for a twelve-year-old." See M. Slater, *Charles Dickens* (New Haven, 2009), p. 24.

swarming down in the cellars, and the sound of
their squeaking and scuffling coming up the stairs
at all times, and the dirt and decay of the place, rise
up visibly before me, as if I were there again ... My
work was to cover the pots of paste-blacking; first
with a poor little piece of oil-paper, and then with
a piece of blue paper; to tie them round with a
string; and then to clip the paper close and neat,
all round, until it looked as smart as a pot of
ointment from an apothecary's shop. When a
certain number of grosses of pots had attained this
pitch of perfection, I was to paste on each a printed
label; and then go on again with more pots. Two
or three other boys were kept at similar duty down
stairs on similar wages. One of them came up, in a
ragged apron and a paper cap, on the first Monday
morning, to show me the trick of using the string
and tying the knot. His name was Bob Fagin; and
I took the liberty of using his name, long afterwards, in *Oliver Twist.*[21]

Here, it is essential to compare Dickens' "pitch of perfection"
with the perfection that so beguiled Bentham and Arnold
because it bespeaks an understanding of the realities of our
imperfection, without which culture is vain and superficial.

My book also includes a chapter on Nathaniel Hawthorne's daughter, Rose, later Mother Alphonsa, who is
destined to have a greater impact on American culture
than all the sages of New England put together, even
though many in America, let alone the world beyond,
scarcely know who she is. Then, again, there is a chapter
on some little-known, though superb poets of the eighteenth century whose philoprogenitive verse is a welcome
rebuke to the manifold distortions of that most ahistorical
thing, feminist history.

---

[21] John Forster, *Life of Charles Dickens* (New York, 1899), I, pp. 25–26.

Finally, I have a chapter on how certain historians have handled the subject of abortion and in this I quote some lively passages from Henry James' great travelogue, *The American Scene* (1905) to try to put the mad unreality of abortionism into some historical context. Much more work needs to be done to share with readers just how remiss our historians have been with respect to this issue which, in its way, dominates the twentieth and twenty-first centuries as tragically as slavery dominated the nineteenth. In his life of Addison, Dr. Johnson noted how "It was [Addison's] practice when he found any man invincibly wrong to flatter his opinions by acquiescence, and sink him yet deeper in absurdity."[22] When it comes to abortion, many of our historians have been doing something similar to this for decades, the only difference being that they do not regard the pro-abortion authorities as "invincibly wrong" and the deeper these authorities sink in absurdity the more sincere becomes our historians' flattery. It is a piece of folly that would have provoked unmerciful scorn from Swift, who related the anecdote about Addison to his dear friend Stella.

What do all of these chapters add up to? What is my conclusion? If false culture led us into this shambles, true culture can help extricate us from it. And the grounds for that new culture must be humility, without which true respect for life is not possible. And that is why we must share with others the wisdom of Pope John Paul II's *Evangelium Vitae*, in which he wrote of the scourge of abortion with such consummate charity. Here, in closing, is a passage from that encyclical in which the great pope addresses "a special word to women who have had an

---

[22]   S. Johnson, *Lives of the English Poets*, ed. G. B. Hill (Oxford, 1935), II, p. 124.

abortion," though obviously what he has to say applies to men who have connived in abortion as well.

> The Church is aware of the many factors which may have influenced your decision, and she does not doubt that in many cases it was a painful and even shattering decision. The wound in your heart may not yet have healed. Certainly what happened was and remains terribly wrong. But do not give in to discouragement and do not lose hope. Try rather to understand what happened and face it honestly. If you have not already done so, give yourselves over with humility and trust to repentance. The Father of mercies is ready to give you his forgiveness and his peace in the Sacrament of Reconciliation. To the same Father and his mercy you can with sure hope entrust your child. With the friendly and expert help and advice of other people, and as a result of your own painful experience, you can be among the most eloquent defenders of everyone's right to life. Through your commitment to life, whether by accepting the birth of other children or by welcoming and caring for those most in need of someone to be close to them, you will become promoters of a new way of looking at human life.[23]

This is the sort of practical humility that we must exemplify if we are to revive our culture. What we need is not Matthew Arnold's "pursuit of perfection" but the gift of contrition.

---

[23] Pope John Paul II, *Evangelium Vitae*, 57.

Anne Ridler

1

ANNE RIDLER AND
THE POETRY OF LIFE

WHEN ONE STOPS to consider the various ways in which one might move hearts and minds in the often intransigent debate over abortion, poetry might not seem the most persuasive means. William Butler Yeats, who spent so much time trying to bring round the Irish to his various points of view had no illusions about the efficacy of verse for his own polemical proposes. What are those memorable lines of his?

> The rhetorician would deceive his neighbors,
> The sentimentalist himself; while art is but a vision of reality.[1]

Well, reality is at the heart of the abortion debate and even if poetry can only offer "a vision of reality," it can still identify the abstractions that often falsify the debate.

One poet whose work is ideal for this purpose is Anne Ridler. Born in Warwickshire in 1912, the only daughter of Henry Christopher Bradby, a housemaster at Rugby, and his wife, Violet Milford, Ridler went to Downe House (where Elizabeth Bowen was schooled), spent six months in Florence and Rome and then took a diploma in journalism at King's College, London in 1932.[2] Between 1935 and 1940,

---

[1] This is from Yeats' poem *"Ego Dominus Tuus,"* (1917) from *Collected Poems of W. B. Yeats* (London, 1956), p. 157.

[2] Bowen wrote a witty essay about her school days at Downe House, which she attended from September, 1914. Speaking of her young self and her classmates, she says: "We cannot really have been emotional girls; we were not highly-sexed and any attractions had

she worked at Faber and Faber as T. S. Eliot's secretary. In her posthumous *Memoirs* (2004), she recalled his saying after reading through a pile of manuscripts, "Sometimes I feel I loathe poetry."[3] She also recalled the Fabers' butler telling her how Vivienne would often deliberately humiliate her husband when they came to dinner "by breaking the string of her beads so that he had to crawl all over the floor looking for them."[4] In 1938, Anne married Vivian Ridler, the last printer to the University of Oxford, with whom she had two daughters and two sons. In bringing up her rambunctious children with the help of a number of European nannies, some good, some not so good, she was naturally given a deal of contradictory counsel, which she memorialized in a charming piece of doggerel:

> O drink for the sake of your health, dear,
> Refrain for the sake of your child;
> And whatever the midwife adwises,
> Perform it, and answer her mild.
>
> O stand on your head in the bed, dear,
> But not on your feet on the floor;

---

an aesthetic, snobbish, self-interested tinge. Conversations over the radiator were generally about art, Roman Catholicism, suicide, or how impossible somebody else had been. At nine o'clock a bell rang from the matron's room and we all darted back to our bedrooms and said our prayers." Later, when she returned to the place, she was dismayed to find that it had been turned into a shrine to Charles Darwin (he had lived in the house and died there before it became a school). "I have never liked scientific people very much," Bowen confessed, "and it mortifies me to think of them trampling reverently around there on visiting days, thinking of Charles Darwin and ignorant of my own youth." See *The Mulberry Tree: Writings of Elizabeth Bowen*, ed. H. Lee (New York, 1987).

[3] A. Ridler, *Memoirs* (London, 2004), p. 110.

[4] Ibid., p. 122.

And remember that bearing a babe, dear,
Is as easy as shutting the door.[5]

Throughout her married life in Oxford, Ridler and her family attended the University Church of St Mary the Virgin, where Newman gave his great Anglican sermons. She published eleven volumes of poetry over nearly fifty years; she also wrote verse dramas and translated librettos. For thirty years, she sang in the Oxford Bach Choir. She was also a peripheral member of the Inklings, the group surrounding C. S. Lewis, which included J. R. R. Tolkien and Charles Williams. The chief contemporary influences on her work were Eliot, Auden, Louis MacNeice and Williams. She was also influenced by Donne, Marvell, and the devotional poets of the seventeenth century, Herbert, Traherne and Vaughan. In fact, she edited a very good edition of Traherne's verse for Oxford University Press. The themes of her own poetry are varied, rooted as they are in the life of the family, and range from love and separation to the power of place, faith in God, marriage, the birth of children and something that does not figure so much as it did once in poetry: the eternal. She died in 2001.

After her death, the literary biographer Grevel Lindop wrote of how "She had the clearest and best-balanced poetic intelligence I had ever met. She was also a fine, understated raconteuse, with a perfect ear for dialogue and a neat sense of comic self-deprecation."[6] Something of her sense of humor can be seen in a passage from her memoirs, where she recalled a childhood trip to Italy when the family's minimal Italian became problematic. "Father," Ridler recalled, "who knew the language well for reading purposes, was tongue-tied when he tried to speak; Mother, who

5 Ibid., p. 132.
6 *The Guardian* (15 October 2001).

actually knew rather less, employed her vocabulary with great panache, though occasionally falling into traps as when, conducting a railway conversation about Protestant beliefs, she assured our fellow-passenger that we believed in Jesus 'ma non nelle Pape ('but we do not believe in breasts')."[7]

Her critical reception was mixed. Eliot was always full of encouragement, telling her when she showed him her first poems, "I should go on," which she prized, knowing how disinclined he was to "facile praise or cowardly half-truths."[8] Philip Larkin, on the other hand, reviewed her collection *A Matter of Life and Death* (1959) and found it "stodgy" and "tuneless," even quoting a passage from it and remarking: "The reader may judge ... whether or not he shares my deafness."[9]

I have to say I do not share his deafness. The lines Larkin quotes have precisely the music of spoken conviction that characterizes the best verse of Thomas Traherne, of whose work Ridler was so fond.

> Yes, on the face of the new born,
> Before the soul has taken full possession,
> There pass, as over a screen, in succession
> The images of other beings:
> Face after face looks out, and then is gone.
>
> Nothing is lost, for all in love survive.
> I lay my cheek against his sleeping limbs
> To feel if he is warm, and touch in him

---

[7]   *Memoirs*, p. 66.

[8]   Ibid., p. 111.

[9]   In taking Larkin's strictures into account, we should also keep in mind that when asked which book he would take on a desert island, Larkin plumbed for the collected works of Bernard Shaw because, as he said, Shaw was "such a sane and light-hearted writer and so free of self-pity." Nothing could more plainly expose the limitations of his critical judgment. See P. Larkin, *Further Requirements* (London, 2001), p. 110.

> Those children whom no shawl could warm,
> No arms, no grief, no longing could revive.

What Larkin may have disliked about Ridler's poem is its implied criticism of his own "An Arundel Tomb" (1956), in which he wrote of how the tomb of the Earl of Arundel and his second wife, Eleanor of Lancaster, perpetuated what Larkin regarded as the "untruth" of marital fidelity:

> Time has transfigured them into
> Untruth. The stone fidelity
> They hardly meant has come to be
> Their final blazon, and to prove
> Our almost-instinct almost true:
> What will survive of us is love.

Living fidelity, by contrast, was one of Ridler's great themes. Then, again, in her poem "For a Child Expected," she tilled ground largely passed over in English poetry, which, in any case, it is unlikely that Larkin would have appreciated.[10]

> Lovers, whose lifted hands are candles in winter,
> Whose gentle ways like streams in the easy summer,
> Lying together
> For secret setting of a child, love what they do,
> Thinking they make that candle immortal, streams forever flow,
> And yet do better than they know.
> So the first flutter of a baby felt in the womb,
> Its little signal and promise of riches to come ...

The poem captures the hopes that crowd the threshold of birth.

> ... whatever we liked we took:
> For its hair, the gold curls of the November oak
> We saw on our walk;

---

[10] All quotations from Ridler's poems are from A. Ridler, *Collected Poems* (Manchester, 1997).

Snowberries that a Milky Way in the wood
For its tender hands; calm screen of the frozen flood
For our care of its childhood.

But the birth of a child is an uncontrollable glory;
Cat's cradle of hopes will hold no living baby,
Long though it lay quietly.
And when our baby stirs and struggles to be born
It compels humility; what we began
Is now its own.

This celebration of the joys and obligations of pregnancy
is radically different from what one encounters at Planned
Parenthood, where pregnant women are counseled "to
compare the benefits, risks, and side effects of each of your
options. For example, both medication abortion and early
vacuum aspiration are extremely safe. But current data
suggest that medication abortion may carry a higher risk
of death than early vacuum aspiration abortion. Even so,
both procedures are much safer than abortion later in
pregnancy or carrying a pregnancy to term." *Medication
abortion, vacuum aspiration* ... One has to wonder
whether those who routinely use such language recognize
that we have a moral obligation to eschew false witness.
Eliot, with Dante in mind, said that one charge of poetry
is "to purify the dialect of the tribe/And urge the mind to
aftersight and foresight."[11] Advocates of abortion use
language to mask their assault on the unborn. Ridler's
poetry uses ordinary language with extraordinary precision to show how all our history and all our future unite
in the unborn, how the birth of a child fuses foresight and
aftersight.

Time and hope and moral responsibility necessarily
figure in her understanding of these things. In "Christmas

---

[11]   This is from "Little Gidding" (1942), one of the *Four Quartets*
which Eliot composed between 1936 and 1942.

and Common Birth," Ridler considers why we celebrate the birth of Christ in December, a time usually associated with death.[12]

> Christmas declares the glory of the flesh:
> And therefore a European might wish
> To celebrate it not at midwinter but in spring,
> When physical life is strong,
> When the consent to live is forced even on the young,
> Juice is in the soil, the leaf, the vein,
> Sugar flows to movement in limbs and brain.

To stress the strangeness of midwinter for such a celebration, Ridler describes what mothers-to-be experience, when

> ... before a birth, nourishing the child
> We turn again to the earth
> With unusual longing—to what is rich, wild,
> Substantial: scents that have been stored and strengthened
> In apple lofts, the underwash of woods, and in barns;
> Drawn through the lengthened root; pungent in cones
> (While the fir wood stands waiting; the beech wood aspiring,
> Each in a different silence), and breaking out in spring
> With scent sight sound indivisible in song.

Yet Ridler sees in the paradox of Christ's birth at what she calls "the iron senseless time" home truths that many choose to reject.

> It is good that Christmas comes at the dark dream of the year
> That might wish to sleep ever.
> For birth is awaking, birth is effort and pain;
> And now at midwinter are the hints, inklings

---

[12] Clement of Alexandria ventured 20th May as the date of Christ's birth; the 25th of December was only settled on in the later fourth century. For a trenchant look at the history of the Nativity, see G. K. Chesterton's "The History of Christmas," which first appeared in *G. K.'s Weekly* on December 26, 1935.

(Sodden primrose, honeysuckle greening)
That sleep must be broken.
To bear new life or learn to live is an exacting joy:
The whole self must waken; you cannot predict the way
It will happen, or master the responses beforehand.
For any birth makes an inconvenient demand;
Like all holy things
It is frequently a nuisance, and its needs never end ...

One of the first needs of a child is the need for a name. In naming our children, we name our hopes and our dreams; we commemorate our dearest memories; we invoke the heroism of the saints and the wisdom of the prophets; we unite the living and the dead. In her poem, "Choosing a Name," Ridler shows how names are a kind of poetry, a making—and, for the children they christen, a launching into history—which children remake.

My little son, I have cast you out
 To hang heels upward, wailing over a world
 With walls too wide.
My faith till now, and now my love:
 No walls too wide for all you hide.

I love, not knowing what I love,
 I give, though ignorant to whom
 The history and power of a name.
I conjure with it, like a novice
 Summoning unknown spirits: answering me
 You take the word and tame it.

Ridler is no nominalist: she recognizes the reality of the material world and affirms the "glory of the flesh." In this, she reminds one of the Rembrandt of the incomparable *Bathsheba*, whose "expression of reverie," as Kenneth Clark brilliantly pointed out, is "so complex that we follow her thought far beyond the moment depicted: and yet those thoughts are indissolubly part of her body, which speaks to us in its own language as truthfully as Chaucer and Burns." Indeed, for Clark, her "ample stomach" and "heavy practical hands and feet" attain "a nobility far greater than the ideal form of, shall we say, Titian's *Venus of Urbino*."[13] To epitomize how the nude of Western art embodied the body's thoughtful dignity, Clark turned to Edmund Spenser for one of his epigraphs: "For soule is forme, and doth the bodie make," a profound truth which all of Riddler's poetry affirms.

Similarly, names for Ridler are not epistemological fictions but tokens of our faith and love.

> Even as the gift of life
>> You take the famous name you did not choose
>> And make it new.
> You and the name exchange a power:
>> Its history is changed, becoming yours,
>> And yours by this: who call this, calls you.

Maternal solicitude has rarely been given more moving expression. Where else in all our English poetry is there a prayer like this?

> Strong vessel of peace, and plenty promised,
>> Into whose unsounded depths I pour
>> This alien power;
> Frail vessel, launched with a shawl for sail,
>> Whose guiding spirit keeps his needle-quivering
>> Poise between trust and terror,
> And stares amazed to find himself alive;
>> This is the means by which you say *I am*,
>> Not to be lost till all is lost,
> When at the sight of God you say *I am nothing*,
>> And find, forgetting name and speech at last,
>> A home not mine, dear outcast.

---

[13] K. Clark, *The Nude: A Study in Ideal Form* (Folio Society, 2010), p. 250.

Besides this cry of love, the legalism of the advocates of "choice"—an impudent euphemism for the violent rejection of life—is more than a little inhuman. To appreciate Ridler's poems about children and childbirth we have to step back and see them in some context.

When we think of English poetry about children we tend to think of Blake and Wordsworth. Ridler was influenced more by the childhood poems of Traherne and Vaughan.[14] A century before Rousseau's *Emile* (1762), which began the vogue of treating childhood as a happy hunting ground for theory, Traherne urged that "We must disrobe ourselves of all false colors and unclothe our souls of evil habits; all our thoughts must be infant-like and clear: the powers of our soul free from the leaven of this world, and disentangled from men's conceits and customs."[15] Vaughan echoed this in one of his most famous poems, "The Retreat," in which he wrote:

> Happy those early days! When I
> Shin'd in my Angel-infancy.
> Before I understood this place
> Appointed for my second race,
> Or taught my soul to fancy aught
> But a white, Celestial thought ...[16]

Traherne and Vaughan took their view of childhood not from theorists but from Scripture. As Traherne wrote: "Our Savior's meaning ... [that] he must be born again and

---

[14] It might be helpful to furnish dates for these different poets. Henry Vaughan (1621–95); Thomas Traherne (1637–74); William Blake (1757–1827); and William Wordsworth (1770–1850).

[15] T. Traherne, *Poems, Centuries and Thanksgivings*, ed. A. Ridler (Oxford, 1966), p. 266. This quotation comes from "The Third Century," one of his long meditative prose poems.

[16] H. Vaughan, *The Works of Henry Vaughan*, ed. L. C. Martin (Oxford, 1957), p. 419.

become a little child that will enter the Kingdom of Heaven is deeper far than is generally believed." When Wordsworth and the Romantics began extolling the spiritual acuity of childhood in the early nineteenth century they were adopting the rather less reverent ideas of Rousseau, who saw children not so much as creatures made in the image of their Creator but as *tabulae rasae*, laboratory mice that could validate his educational theories.[17] Lord Byron took the Swiss writer's measure rather unsparingly when he called him "the self-torturing sophist, wild Rousseau." Samuel Johnson was no kinder, calling him "a rascal, who ought to be hunted out of society."[18] No one can read Rousseau's *Confessions* (1782–89) without rec-

---

[17] To be fair, Rousseau's ideas on education were not entirely bad. As R. G. Collingwood pointed out, "Rousseau's conception of education depends on the doctrine that the child, undeveloped though he may be, has a life of his own, with his own ideals and conceptions and that the teacher must understand and sympathize with this life, treat it with respect, and help it to develop in a way proper and natural to itself. This conception, applied to history, means that the historian must never do what the Enlightenment historians were always doing, that is, regard past ages with contempt and disgust, but must look at them sympathetically and find in them the expression of genuine and valuable human achievements. Rousseau was so much carried away by this idea as to assert (in his Discourse on the Arts and Sciences) that primitive savagery is superior to civilized life [hence my charge that the effect of his theories was to sentimentalize children]; but that primitive savagery he later withdrew ...", though not before the damage had already been done in terms of his influence. One can clearly see that influence in multiculturalism's refusal to discriminate between the savage and the civilized, or to exalt the savage and denigrate the civilized. See R. W. Collingwood, *The Idea of History* (Oxford, 1994), p. 87.

[18] See J. Boswell, *Life of Johnson*, ed. G. Birbeck Hill and L. F. Powell (Oxford, 1934), II, p. 12. Rousseau *was* hounded out of France and given sanctuary in England by David Hume, with whom, however, he eventually quarreled.

ognizing that the man most responsible for turning children into sentimental abstractions was something of a
hypocrite. In 1745, he set up house in a Paris hotel with a
chambermaid with whom he proceeded to have several
children, all of whom he summarily deserted. No sooner
were they born than he sent them off to foundling hospitals, despite the protests of their mother.[19] It was not from
these that he derived his theories about the inherent
goodness of children.

Notwithstanding Rousseau's theorizing and Wordsworth's "Intimations of Immortality" (1807), with its
famous claim that "The Child is Father of the Man," the
Victorians rejected the notion that children were the
source of all goodness. In rejecting one fallacy, however,
they adopted another. Max Beerbohm gives a vivid picture
of the Victorian nursery. "Children were not then recognized as human creatures. They were a race apart; savages
that must be driven from the gates; beasts to be kept in
cages; devils to whose voices one must not listen. Indeed,
the very nature of children was held to be sinful. Lies and
sloth, untidiness and irreverence ... were taken to be its
chief constituents. And so nurseries ... were the darkened
scene of temporal oppression, fitfully lightened with the
gaunt reflections of hell-fire."[20] The novels of Dickens
corroborate this, as do Samuel Butler's *The Way of All
Flesh* (1903) and Sir Edmund Gosse's *Father and Son*
(1907). And yet what chilling significance Beerbohm's
words have acquired! *"Children were not then recognized
as human creatures ..."*

---

[19]   See P. Johnson's essay on Rousseau in his brilliant book, *Intellectuals* (New York, 1988), 1–27.
[20]   M. Beerbohm, "A Cloud of Pinafores" in *More* (New York, 1922),
p. 195.

Upper-class nurseries might have had something of the penal about them but they were little paradises compared to what awaited children of the slums. Lady Violet Bonham Carter (1887–1969), the daughter of the Liberal Prime Minister Asquith, and one of the last standard-bearers of English Liberalism, wrote about "the tortures of commercial exploitation to which the children of the poor were mercilessly sacrificed in the mills and in the mines during the Industrial Revolution, little more than a hundred years ago." (She was writing in 1947.) Children from the slums and workhouses of London were sent up to the mill-owners in cartloads from the age of seven and put at the mercy of their masters until they were twenty-one. Lady Violet found these odious practices hard to credit.

> That many of the enlightened philanthropists, humanitarians, and reformers who had fought for the abolition of slavery in the British Dominions, should have tolerated and defended the slavery of children in the factories and mines of England appears to us to-day fantastically inexplicable. We must, I suppose, accept the explanation that they were deluded fatalists, bowing to what they believed to be melancholy economic necessity. They were convinced that poverty was inevitable and incurable and that any interference with economic processes could only result in disaster for all mankind. This belief may explain their callous acceptance of industrial suffering in the factories and mines. It cannot explain their refusal to protect the child chimney-sweeps—the 'Climbing Boys'— whose fate Lord Shaftesbury declared to be ten times worse than that of the factory children ... It was not until 1875 ... that Lord Shaftesbury at last

succeeded in carrying this bill which brought these horrors to an end.[21]

With these unedifying proceedings lodged in her mind, Lady Violet might have become an influential defender of children, especially when their very survival was endangered by the abortion bill that David Steel introduced into the House of Lords in 1967. Instead, she chose a different course, as her diary proves.

> Monday 17 July: Went to H. of L. Abortion alas! Comes on Wed ... Met Frank (Longford) who is passionately against it & engaged me in an argument about it ... Appalled at David Steel producing a foetus (half an inch long) in the H. of C.! 'What wld your father have felt?' I said he wd have been deeply interested. I have never seen Frank so near real anger! ...

According to Mark Pottle, the editor of Bonham Carter's diaries: "Steel produced the seven week-old embryo when moving the third reading of the Medical Termination of Pregnancy (Abortion) bill, after an all-night sitting of the Commons 13–14 July 1967. He used it to emphasize the point that the bill allowed for abortion only at an early stage in pregnancy, before the embryo could be said to have a human form: 'This is what we are weighing against the life and welfare of the mother and family.'[22] Yet *pace* Lady Violet, what made Steel's show-and-tell appalling was its moral obtuseness, not its grisliness, though the diaries exhibit this obtuseness at every turn.

---

[21] This is from an essay entitled "Childhood and Education" that Bonham Carter contributed to a book of essays edited by the once famous (now largely forgotten) intellectual historian Ernest Barker called *The Character of England* (Oxford, 1947), p. 221.

[22] *Hansard*, vol. 750, col. 1347.

Wednesday 19 July: Abortion debate. Opened by
Lord Silkin ... Then (a body blow) my dear Arch-
bishop [Michael Ramsey]. He began by saying that
the present laws of Abortion were shockingly
bad—& urgently needed reform. But there were
certain features of the present Bill he cld not
support & he therefore felt obliged to abstain on
the second reading. [Later, Lady Violet was quoted
in the *Daily Mail* as telling Ramsey, "Michael, I
never thought of you as a moral coward."] I felt
despair because his leadership in this issue is so
vital ... However, to my amazement and relief
when the division was called it did go through—
overwhelmingly! It had been a thinnish House
throughout & the majority of the speakers had
either had fierce indictments from the R.C. lobby
(who turned out and spoke in force) or critical and
half-hearted support ... Of the R.C.'s Frank Longford made the most violent & the worst speech I
thought. He usually lacks indignation to a fault—
but this Bill really inflamed him & he dragged in
Euthanasia & all sorts of other irrelevancies ...[23]

To compare these entries with Lady Violet's earlier
passage decrying Victorian heartlessness is to be reminded
of Mrs. Jellyby, the reformer in Dickens' *Bleak House*
(1852–3), who is so busy interfering in the lives of other
people's children that she neglects her own.[24] If Lady
Violet was so appalled by the treatment doled out to the
children forced to sweep chimneys—Charles Lamb called

---

[23] *Daring to Hope: The Diaries and Letters of Violet Bonham Carter
1946–1969*, edited by M. Pottle (London, 2000), pp. 318–319.

[24] It is typical of Dickens' optimism that he should have drawn Mrs.
Jellyby's eldest daughter Caddy, who bears the brunt of her
mother's madcap philanthropy, as the quintessential survivor.
Chesterton called her "by far the greatest, the most human, and
the most really dignified of all the heroines of Dickens."

them "these dim specks, poor blots, innocent
blacknesses"—why could she not see the far more horrifying treatment that legalized abortion would dole out to
the unborn?[25] The Victorians had no monopoly on moral
blindness. Legalized abortion in England and America
shows the callousness of our own attitude towards children, which, for all our protesting otherwise, links us more
than we care to admit to the oppressors of children of
Victoria's age.

This is why Anne Ridler matters as a poet. She reminds
us of truths that have been forgotten by those who
continue to see children in unreal, abstract, expendable
terms. In "For a Christening," Ridler celebrates the reality
of love in the life of the newborn. If she is prepared to
affirm reason's ability to grasp reality, she is not oblivious
to the mysteriousness of life. Addressing the newborn, she
says:

> You are our darling and our foreign guest;
> We know all your origins, and this is to know nothing.
> Distinguished stranger to whom we offer food and rest;
> Yet made of our own natures; yet looked for with such longing.
> Helpless wandering hands, the miniature of mine,
> Fine skin and furious look and little raging voice —
> Your looks are full human, your qualities all hidden:
> It is your mere existence we have by heart, and rejoice.
> The wide waters of wonder and comprehension pour
> Through this narrow weir, and irresistible their power.
> The rainbow multiple glory of our humanity cannot pierce
> As does the single white beam of your being.
> This makes your presence so shattering a grace,
> Unsheathed suddenly from the womb; it was none of our intending
> To set in train a miracle; and yet it is merely
> Made palpable in you, missed elsewhere by diffusion.

---

[25]   C. Lamb, "The Praise of Chimney-Sweepers" in *Essays of Elia and
Last Essays* (Oxford, 1961), p. 157.

Therefore we adore God-in-our-flesh as a baby:
Whose Being is His Essence, and outside It, illusion.
Later, the fulfillment, the example, death, misprision —
Here the extraordinary fact of Being, which we see
Stripped and simple as the speechless stranger on my knee.

The close attention she pays her growing boy in her poem,
"A Matter of Life and Death" reinforces the sense of
mystery that children nurture in all of us.

Down the porphyry stair
Headlong into air
The boy has come: he crouches there
A tender startled creature
With fawn's ears and hair-spring poise
Alert to every danger
Aghast at every noise ...
And perfect as his shell-like nails,
Close as are to the flower its petals,
My love unfolded with him.
Yet till this moment what was he to me?
Conjecture and analogy;
Conceived, and yet unknown;
Behind this narrow barrier of bone
Distant as any foreign land could be.

The wonder of children is their perennial gift:

His smiles are all largesse,
Need ask no return,
Since give and take are meaningless
To one who gives by needing
And takes our love for granted
And grants a favor even by his greed.
The ballet of his twirling hands
His chirping and his loving sounds,
Perpetual expectation
Perpetual surprise—

This wonder is instructive of a far greater wonder. It prompts Ridler to consider how the lives of children recover our own lost life and herald the life to come.

> ... what can ever restore
> To these sad and short-coming lives of ours
> The lovely jocund creatures that we were
> And did not know we were?
> What can give us at once
> The being and the sense?
>
> Why, each within
> Has kept his secret for some Resurrection:
> The wonder that he was
> And can be, which is his
> Not by merit, only by grace.
> It comes to light, as love is born with a child ...

The wonder of our being is deepened by time. In her epigraph to her poem "2 October 1983," Ridler quotes Thomas McFarland on Coleridge: "The eyes looking out from our time-eroded bodies are the lights of a soul that does not change." Ridler's sense of the sanctity of life is always uppermost in her sense of its preciousness. Addressing her husband after forty years of marriage, she writes

> Once I recalled in a poem
> Your hopeful infant gaze repeated
> In the lover whom I cherished,
> But could not see old age.
> Seeing it now, I wonder
> At the joyful mystery
> That a man's life should age him
> Yet leave him still the same,
> And cherished, honored, ever.

What the writer of this poem would have thought of any "hopeful infant gaze" being denied life to make way for 'reproductive rights' is not difficult to imagine. But then

Ridler must have found much that was dismaying in a world where to honor and to cherish had become empty vows. Here we encounter again the theme of words. They meant a good deal to the woman who took the rigorous Eliot as her mentor. The double-talk behind the arguments for abortion could only have been anathema to her. In this, she concurred with Ben Jonson who recognized that "wheresoever manners and fashions are corrupted, language is. It imitates the public riot. The excess of feasts and apparel are the notes of a sick state; and the wantonness of language of a sick mind."[26] The force of Ridler's poetry inheres in its precision. Most of us discover that love is knowledge by the grace of God; here the discovery is expressed with a radiant succinctness.

> Where are the poems gone, of our first days?
> Locked on the page
> Where we for ever learn our first embrace.
> Love come of age
> Takes words as said, but never for granted
> His holy luck, his pledge
> That what is truly loved is truly known.
> Now in that knowledge
> Love unillusioned is not love disenchanted.

I will end with a poem about another christening which epitomizes the power of this unjustly neglected poet. The careful attention that Anne Ridler pays to language is emblematic of the care she showed life.

> Choir, candles, kindred faces,
> Isobel goes in a gaggle of children,

---

[26] B. Jonson, *The Complete Poems*, ed. G. Parfitt (London, 1975), p. 403. This is from a long discursive prose piece that Jonson wrote called *Timber: Or Discoveries* about poetry, language, society and other related matters, drawn from his reading. See also I. Donaldson, *Ben Jonson: A Biography* (Oxford, 2012).

'Issued from the hand of God'
To a plentiful drench of holy water,
Unprotesting, unperturbed.
Tiny chrysalis, lapped in shawl,
So parceled, signed, and answered for.
But heart to heart against my shoulder
What I hold is something different:
Life beating with secret purpose;
What I see, face to face,
Is recognition,
Spark of the eternal light.

IONAT. SWIFT S.T.P. & Decan. S¹ Patric: Hib.

Non Pareil

Jonathan Swift

2

WHAT ENGLISH LITERATURE
WOULD BE LIKE IF PRO-ABORTION

"HISTORY," HUGH TREVOR-ROPER told his students in his valedictory to the Oxford History School in 1980, "is not merely what happened; it is what happened in the context of what might have happened."[1] Trevor-Roper was not a particularly good historian—he made a terrible ass of himself when he insisted on the authenticity of those obviously forged Hitler diaries—but he was right about the importance of might-have-beens for any true understanding of how and why events unfold. To ignore such lively possibilities is to subscribe to historical determinism. For years Marxist historians claimed that the impact of the individual on events was negligible because impersonal trends, not people drove history. It has only been fairly recently that historians have begun repudiating that immense fallacy. Might-have-beens are crucial to this task because historians can only measure an individual's impact by asking what history might have looked like without this or that individual. The case of Churchill vividly illustrates this. If Lord Halifax instead of Churchill had become prime minister in June 1940, after France had fallen and the invasion of England seemed imminent, it is questionable whether Halifax would have pushed for total victory to rid the world of Nazism. His fondness for appeasement

---

[1]   H. Trevor-Roper, "History and Imagination," A Valedictory Lecture delivered before Oxford, 20 May 1980 (Oxford, 1980), p. 15.

throughout the 1930s suggests that he would have done a deal, sparing his compatriots Churchill's blood, toil, tears and sweat but in the process allowing Nazism an indefinite triumph. What might have been, had there been no Churchill, is rather horrifying.[2]

One of the might-have-beens that has always intrigued me is what English literature might look like if the different societies for which it was written had agreed with the pro-abortion view that abortion is not only defensible but actually humane. The first thing that strikes one in considering this possibility is that it would almost certainly have resulted in fewer authors. How many of those that were unwanted or simply unplanned would have survived is, of course, impossible to say. But a world favorable to abortion would probably not have been favorable to the survival of Swift, Samuel Johnson, Coleridge, De Quincey, the Brontes, Dickens, Thackeray, Kipling, or Saki—to name just a few English authors.

Swift is a good case in point. It requires some suspension of disbelief to imagine the parents of Swift reasoning that the most humane alternative to an inconvenient birth might be abortion. The Anglo-Irish were a peculiar people—they drank a lot, gambled a lot, built houses they could never afford to finish, and loved suing each other -- but they were never known to care a pin for the sort of theoretical thinking that would later lead to the French Revolution, which, in turn, produced the moral relativism that animates the pro-abortion position. Still, we are speaking of contra-factual history and if, somehow, pro-abortion views had obtained in eighteenth-century Dublin, Swift might never have seen the light of day.

---

[2]   Cf. A. Roberts, *The Holy Fox: A Biography of Lord Halifax* (London, 1991).

As it was, Swift claimed that he had been born in his father's house at Number 7 Hoey's Court, a smart residence before it succumbed, like so many of Dublin's Georgian houses, to disrepair. But in her lively biography Victoria Glendinning asserts that "Such a house could not have belonged to Swift's impecunious father, [who was] clinging on to a less than glorious legal career ..."[3] The house probably belonged to Swift's uncle, Godwin, a prosperous businessman, who took young Jonathan in after his father's death. Swift's father died in his twenties after siring five daughters and six sons. About Swift's mother Abigail, we know little other than that she took no part in her youngest son's upbringing. The one time she returned to Dublin to visit her grownup son, she stayed in a boarding house where she told the landlady that she had come to town "to receive the addresses of a lover and under that character received her son ..."[4] Mother and son clearly shared the same droll sense of humor. In all events, if Georgian Dublin had subscribed to the tenets of Planned Parenthood it is questionable whether that partcular tryst would ever have taken place. And without Swift we should never have had "A Modest Proposal" (1729), which provides one of the greatest of all critiques of the pro-abortion mentality by satirizing the arrogance and the ruthlessness of those who treat human life as though it were nothing more than a matter of base expedience.

The peculiar solicitude that advocates of so-called 'reproductive rights' show women—their contention, for example, that aborting babies somehow redounds to the dignity of women—is of a piece with the philanthropy of Swift's projector who, deploring the number of poor Irish mothers, "followed by three, four, or six children, all in

---

[3]   V. Glendinning, *Jonathan Swift* (London, 1998), p. 17.

[4]   Ibid., p. 30.

rags, and importuning every passenger for alms" observes that "whoever could find out a fair, cheap and easy method of making these children sound and useful members of the commonwealth, would deserve well of the public."[5] The solution he proposes has nothing if not a certain elegant finality. "A young healthy child well nursed is at a year old, a most delicious nourishing and wholesome food, whether stewed, roasted, baked, or boiled; and I make no doubt that it will equally serve in a fricassee, or a ragout."[6] The solution to the problem is cannibalism, the benefits of which Swift's projector sets out with studied reasonableness. It will decrease the number of papists (as much a nuisance for the Anglo-Irish as unwanted black children were for Margaret Sanger, the founder of Planned Parenthood); provide poor tenants with money to pay their rent; enhance the national cuisine; free parents of the burden of supporting costly children; give the owners of taverns something new to offer their customers; and improve relations between husbands and wives.

If readers adopted his proposal, Swift's projector insists, "Men would become as fond of their wives, during the time of their pregnancy, as they are now of their mares in foal, their cows in calf, or sows when they are ready to farrow, nor offer to beat or kick them (as is too frequent a practice) for fear of miscarriage."[7] Addressing parents, the projector suggests further uses for their children: "Those who are more thrifty (as I must confess the times require) may flay the carcass; the skin of which, artificially dressed, will make admirable gloves for ladies and summer boots for fine gentlemen."[8] If there is any difference between that

---

[5]   *Satires and Personal Writings of Jonathan Swift* (Oxford, 1932), p. 21.

[6]   Ibid., p. 23.

[7]   Ibid., p. 28.

reasoning and the reasoning that says that aborted babies can serve the interests of scientific research by furnishing the means for life-enhancing stem-cell research, I don't see it.

If we try to imagine an English literature informed by the pro-abortion view, what do we see? We would not see the attention that the literature we actually have pays to children, especially to children fighting for their lives against cruel and uncaring adults. We would not see David Copperfield, Pip, Jane Eyre, or Heathcliff. Dickens would never have written *Oliver Twist* (1838) because his pro-abortion audience would never have stood for Oliver's mother dying so that Oliver might live. If one writes in a culture convinced that bad odds in life should be obviated by killing off the potentially unfortunate, one will not expend much energy trying to understand the struggles of unwanted or unloved or inconvenient children. In such a society, the abortionists will step in and relieve the world of such struggles. So the great comic tradition in the English novel, beginning with Fielding's *Tom Jones* (1749) would not have materialized. After all, Tom, as Fielding says, "was certainly born to be hanged" and no abortionist would stand for that.[9] Nor, for that matter, would we have the children of Saki or the motherless Bertie Wooster. Or that most wretched of all wretched children, Punch, the exiled hero of Kipling's great story, "Baa, Baa, Black Sheep" (1892). The brilliant critic V. S. Pritchett once remarked that "Saki did not suffer as Kipling suffered, but we hear of an aunt whom his sister described as a woman of 'ungovernable temper, of fierce likes and dislikes, imperious, a moral coward, possessing no brains worth speaking of and a primitive disposition.' "[10] In a pro-abortion world

---

[8]   Ibid., p. 25.

[9]   H. Fielding, *Tom Jones* (Folio Society, 1959), p. 61.

keen on keeping the unhappy unborn, no one would have
to suffer the barbarisms of aunts.

If literature were pro-abortion, we would never have
seen the great heroines of Henry James, not only the
fiendishly abused Maisie Farange in *What Maisie Knew*
(1897) but Isabel Archer in *The Portrait of a Lady* (1882)
and Milly Theale in *The Wings of the Dove* (1902)—all
heroines who reminded James of something George Eliot
had once said, that "In these frail vessels is borne onward
through the ages the treasure of human affection."[11] In a
world built on pro-abortion assumptions the survival of
these vessels would have been dubious. The pro-abortion
mind abominates frailty. Indeed, it is convinced that the
difficulties that make for frailty should not so much be
overcome as simply removed.

Yet James, like Yeats, was fascinated by the difficult. He
deliberately immersed his heroines in its trammels. "To
see deep difficulty braved is at any time, for the really
addicted artist, to feel almost even as a pang the beautiful
incentive, and to feel it verily in such sort as to wish the
danger intensified. The difficulty most worth tackling can
only be for him, in these conditions, the greatest the case
permits of."[12] So Isabel Archer should not only be given a
precarious start in life but a labyrinthine bad marriage.
Why? Because only such difficulties would allow us to see
"a certain young lady affronting her destiny"[13]—and
forming her moral sense, which becomes part and parcel
of her eventual strength. James concentrates the action in
his heroine's consciousness so that the reader can see the

---

[10]   V. S. Pritchett, "The Peforming Lynx," *Complete Collected Essays*
       (New York, 1992), p. 644.

[11]   H. James, Preface to *The Portrait of a Lady* (Oxford, 1981), p. xxxiii.

[12]   Ibid., p. xxxiv.

[13]   Ibid., p. xxxii.

formation of that sense in all its richness. The dignity that this conception of fiction accords the difficult is a dignity that the mean economies of the abortionists simply cannot afford. In fine, in Isabel Archer, we have a pro-life heroine *par excellence*, who could scarcely have emerged from a culture favorable to abortion.

It does not take much to imagine how ill-advised, imprudent and indeed irresponsible the pro-abortion mind would regard the birth of Samuel Johnson. His parents were both elderly—his father Michael was fifty-two and his mother Sarah was forty. In these two unhappy people the advocates of 'reproductive rights' would probably see a wretched pair doomed to give birth to wretched children, and they would be right. Johnson's parents were the prototypical Darby and Joan. His mother married beneath her and never left off regretting it. His father was a failed bookseller who found his querulous wife an intolerable penance. Johnson's only brother Nathaniel, whom he described as a "lively, noisy man," was a failed bookbinder who died young and miserable—possibly by his own hand.[14] Johnson himself was a wretched child and an even more wretched adult. As he later recorded in a fragment of autobiography, "I was born almost dead, and could not cry for some time."[15] Later, he would tell Boswell that his had been a "life radically wretched." Nonetheless, at his birth, the male midwife, George Hector, looked down at the grotesque pock-marked child, held him up before the exhausted mother and cried: "Here is a brave boy."[16] Yet despite all of their shared sorrows, had anyone ever suggested to Sarah and Michael that they should abort their sickly, querulous, hideous child, they would

---

[14] W. J. Bate, *Samuel Johnson* (London, 1978), pp. 160–162.

[15] Ibid., p. 5.

[16] Ibid.

have looked upon him with scorn as not only cowardly but
wicked.

The cowardice of the abortionists has not been inconsequential. C. S. Lewis once pointed out that, "Courage is
not simply one of the virtues but the form of every virtue
at the testing point."[17] Johnson, echoing Aristotle, put the
matter even more categorically: "Sir, you know courage is
reckoned the greatest of all virtues; because, unless a man
has that virtue, he has no security for preserving any
other."[18] No one who grasps this can be surprised by the
disrepute into which the very concept of virtue has fallen
since our court legalized abortion.

Walter Jackson Bate, one of the better biographers of
Johnson, observed that, "The reason why Johnson has
always fascinated so many people of different kinds is not
simply that he is so vividly picturesque and quotable ...

> The deeper secret of his hypnotic attraction ... lies
> in the immense reassurance he gives to human
> nature, which needs—and quickly begins to val-
> ue—every friend it can get. To begin with, there is
> the moving parable of his own life ... As in the
> archetypal stories in folklore, we have a hero who
> starts out with everything against him, including
> painful liabilities of personal temperament—a
> turbulent imagination, acute anxiety, aggressive
> pride, extreme impatience, radical self-division and
> self-conflict. He is compelled to wage long and
> desperate struggles, at two crucial times of his life,
> against what he feared was the onset of insanity.
> Yet step by step, often in the hardest possible way
> he wins through to the triumph of honesty to
> experience that all of us prize in our hearts ... [19]

---

[17]   See C. Connolly, *The Unquiet Grave* (London, 1944).

[18]   *Boswell's Life of Johnson*, ed. by G. B. Hill and L. F. Powell (Oxford,
       1934), II, p. 339.

This shows why for Johnson "The only end of writing is to enable readers better to enjoy life, or better to endure it ..."[20] The uses of difficulty were not lost on him.

With no Johnson, we would have no "Life of Richard Savage" (1744), one of Johnson's finest works, which he later included in *The Lives of the English Poets* (1779-81). When Johnson met Savage he commiserated with the proud, down-at-heels poet and saw in him a type of frustrated talent. Savage claimed to be the illegitimate son of the fourth Earl Rivers and Lady Macclesfield—a claim which was later discredited, though Savage had grounds for believing it to be true. In all events, Savage was no saint—he was a spendthrift, drank recklessly, and even killed a man in self-defense outside a Charing Cross coffee-house by running him through with his sword—but he nonetheless confirmed Johnson's conviction that "there has rarely passed a life of which a judicious and faithful narrative would not be useful." In trying to sum up his unfortunate friend's life, Johnson indulged in a fair amount of special pleading, writing in one memorable passage:

> He lodged as much by accident as he dined, and passed the night sometimes in mean houses, which are set open at night to any casual wanderers, sometimes in cellars, among the riot and filth of the meanest and most prolifigate of the rabble; and sometimes, when he had not money enough to support even the expenses of these receptacles, walked about the streets till he was weary, and lay down in the summer upon a bulk or in the winter with his associates in poverty among the ashes of a glasshouse ... On a bulk, in a cellar, or in a glass-

---

[19] W. J. Bate, *Samuel Johnson* (London. 1978), pp. 3–4.

[20] S. Johnson, "Review of Soame Jenyns' *A Free Inquiry into the Nature and Origins of Evil*," *Johnson: Prose and Poetry*, ed. Mona Wilson (London, 1970), p. 366.

> house among thieves and beggars, was to be found
> the author of *The Wanderer*, the man of exalted
> sentiments, extensive views, and curious observa-
> tions; the man whose remarks on life might have
> assisted the statesman, whose ideas of virtue might
> have enlightened the moralist, whose eloquence
> might have influenced senates, and whose delicacy
> might have polished courts.[21]

This is warmly partial. Yet Johnson was never reluctant to extend the partiality of compassion. As he said in his conclusion, "Those are no proper judges of his conduct, who have slumbered away their time on the down of plenty; nor will any wise man presume to say, 'Had I been in Savage's condition, I should have lived or written better than Savage.' "[22] Here is a might-have-been with a useful moral: we are none of us entitled to make pharisaical comparisons.

However, for pro-abortion readers, the whole question of Savage's life would be moot because for them it would be a life that need never have been lived in the first place. After all, to their way of thinking, one of the great benefits of abortion is that it spares the world of drunkards and wastrels, murderers and orphans. For Johnson, such a view would have been simply flagitious. Indeed, one of the reasons why he came to feel such love for Savage was precisely because the poet shared the same sense of fellow-feeling that Johnson prized above all else—fellow-feeling that the abortionists and their sycophantic histo-rians must condemn as wrong-headed and inexpedient.

> Compassion was indeed the distinguishing quality
> of Savage; he never appeared inclined to take advan-

---

[21] S. Johnson, *Lives of the English Poets*, ed. Arthur Waugh (Oxford, 1952), II, pp. 151–152.

[22] Ibid., p. 182.

tage of weakness, to attack the defenseless, or to press upon the falling: whoever was distressed was certain at least of his good wishes; and when he could give no assistance to extricate them from misfortunes, he endeavored to sooth them by sympathy and tenderness.[23]

Another eighteenth-century writer who might have written quite differently if he had grown up in a society convinced of the benefits of abortion is Thomas Gray. What would have been Gray's thoughts if while strolling through that country churchyard he had thought not of the obscure country dead but of the obscure country aborted? Would the *Elegy Written in a Country Churchyard* (1751) contain lines like these?

> Full many a gem of purest ray serene,
> The dark unfathomed caves of ocean bear:
> Full many a flower is born to blush unseen,
> And waste its sweetness on the desert air.
>
> Some village-Hampden, that with dauntless breast
> The little tyrant of his fields withstood;
> Some mute inglorious Milton here may rest,
> Some Cromwell guiltless of his country's blood.

What would have been the point? The mute inglorious Miltons, village-Hampdens and Cromwells guiltless of their country's blood would not have been in that country churchyard because they would never have been born. Apropos Gray himself, it is worth noting that he was the fifth of twelve children and the only one to survive infancy. Indeed, he nearly died himself. Had it not been for his mother, a milliner, having the presence of mind to grab a pair of scissors and slit open one of his veins when he was having one of his boyhood seizures, he would have died.

---

[23] Ibid., pp. 116–117.

It is not easy imagining this indomitable woman seeing anything defensible in the pro-abortion position.

Roe v. Wade argues that the child in the womb is not entitled to even the most rudimentary protection of the law because it is a legal nullity. Abortionists imagine this reasoning so persuasive that only religious fanatics can contend otherwise. Well, James Joyce was no religious fanatic. He was much too proud to be bound by religion. And yet in *Ulysses* (1922) he has Stephen Daedalus observe of a slow-witted schoolboy:

> Ugly and futile: lean neck and tangled hair and a stain of ink, a snail's head. Yet someone had loved him, borne him in her arms and in her heart. But for her the race of the world would have trampled him under foot, a squashed boneless snail. She had loved his weak watery blood drained from her own. Was that then real? The only true thing in life? ... *Amor matris*: subjective and objective genitive ...[24]

Would Joyce have clung to this most basic of realities if he had grown up in a society that regarded the child in the womb as a disposable parasite? Probably, not. The most fastidious of romantic apostates would have had nothing to cling to. As it was, the training he received from the Jesuits might not have convinced him of the indispensability of the sacraments but it helped him to recognize the primacy of love in a world all too ready to squash the weak and defenseless.

The pro-abortion reader might counter that the pro-abortion position is not concerned with the weak and defenseless but with the unwanted. Why should any woman be forced to bring a child into the world that she is not ready to rear? Why not simply terminate a pregnancy that might otherwise issue in an unwanted child?

---

[24] J. Joyce, *Ulysses* (London, 1992), p. 33.

So many unwanted children grow up to be criminals and drug addicts, vagrants and unemployables: why consign them to such a fate?

Here we might cite one of Yeats' late verses, "Among School Children (1925)," where he asks:

> What youthful mother, a shape upon her lap
> Honey of generation had betrayed,
> And that must sleep, shriek, struggle to escape
> As recollection or the drug decide,
> Would think her son, did she but see that shape
> With sixty or more winters on its head,
> A compensation for the pangs of his birth,
> Or the uncertainty of his setting forth?[25]

The difference between what Yeats is asking here and what the abortionist asks when he asks why we should not be at liberty to do away with unwanted children is that Yeats asks his question of a society that did not imagine that abortion was a warrantable option. It is a given that the youthful mother in these lines will have her child. That is what makes the question compelling. Given that women do endure the pangs and uncertainties of labor and motherhood for the love of a child, what would they say if they could see their children "with sixty or more winters on its head?" Yeats asks his question to prompt his readers to consider the nature of love. He is not asking the question to suggest that mothers should think twice before bringing children into the world that will only grow old and die. If his audience had been in the habit of simply ending troublesome pregnancies, there should be no point in Yeats putting his question. He could hardly expect them to recognize the sacrificial core of love if they were intent on treating the child in the womb as unreal. In rejecting that child, the pro-abortion mind rejects the sanctity of life and we can

---

[25] W. B. Yeats, *Collected Poems* (London, 1956), pp. 213–214.

see all too plainly the appalling child abuse, abuse of the old, and abuse of the infirm which that has caused.

Another lively writer of English who presents problems for the abortionist is John Ruskin. There are many passages in his work that exhibit his admirable solicitude for the weak and the oppressed. In "The Veins of Wealth," for example, from *Unto This Last* (1862), he recalls encountering servants in a rich man's kitchen who appeared "ill-dressed," "squalid," and "half-starved" and he concludes that the riches of any man who tolerates this level of want in his own household must be of a "very theoretical" character indeed. But then he goes on to make a much more fundamental point about the true nature of wealth, a point which the disciples of the culture of knowledge must always find profoundly embarrassing, especially those who put the dictates of feminist ideology before the life of children. Ruskin is one of the most eloquent of writers but here he outdoes himself.

> Since the essence of wealth consists in power over men, will it not follow that the nobler and the more in number the persons are over whom it has power, the greater the wealth? Perhaps it may even appear, after some consideration, that the persons themselves *are* the wealth—that these pieces of gold with which we are in the habit of guiding them, are, in fact, nothing more than a kind of Byzantine harness or trappings, very glittering and beautiful in barbaric sight, wherewith we bridle the creatures; but that if these same living creatures could be guided without the fretting and jingling of the Byzants in their mouths and ears, they might themselves be more valuable than their bridles. In fact, it may be discovered that the true veins of wealth are purple—and not in Rock, but in Flesh—perhaps even that the final outcome and consum-

mation of all wealth is in the producing as many as possible full-breathed, bright-eyed, and happy-hearted human creatures. Our modern wealth, I think, has rather a tendency the other way...[26]

What our abortionists think when they read that is anyone's guess but surely they cannot claim to have had any part in increasing the true *purple* veins of wealth. On the contrary, they are guiltier than anyone of depleting that wealth, so much so that now we are poorer demographically than ever.[27]

Recently a speaker at a pro-life dinner in New York predicted that the days of Roe v. Wade were numbered. Why? Since 1973, we have become a nation of infanticides—over 50 million children, after all, have been killed in the womb since then—and our collective guilt has become insupportable. We must repeal Roe v. Wade to begin to expiate that guilt. And this reminded me of the scene in the final act of *Macbeth* when a Doctor of Physic is called to Dunsinane to attend to the sleepwalking Lady Macbeth. How nicely it captures our own insomniacal guilt!

Enter Lady Macbeth, with a taper

Gentleman:	Lo you! Here she comes. This is her very guise; and, upon my life, fast asleep.
Doctor:	How came she by that light?

---

[26] *Unto This Last and Other Writings by John Ruskin*, ed. C. Wilmer (Penguin, 1985), pp. 188-189. Byzants, or bezants, were gold coins struck at Byzantium and common in England until supplanted by the noble of Edward III's reign. Sir Walter Scott mentions byzants in *Ivanhoe*: "Here, Isaac, lend me a handful of byzants." See note to Volume 17 of Ruskin's *Collected Works*.

[27] See Jonathan V. Last, *What To Expect When No One's Expecting: America's Coming Demographic Disaster* (New York, 2013).

Gentleman:	Why, it stood by her: she has light by her continually; 'tis her command.
Doctor:	You see, her eyes are open.
Gentleman:	Ay, but their sense are shut.
Doctor:	What is it she does now? Look, how she rubs her hands.
Gentleman:	It is an accustom'd action with her, to seem thus washing her hands ...
Lady M.:	Yet here's a spot.
Doctor:	Hark! She speaks. I will set down what comes from her ...
Lady M.:	Out damned spot! Out I say! ... What need we fear who knows it, when none can call our power to accompt? Yet who would have thought the old man to have had so much blood in him? ...
Doctor:	Go to, go to: you have known what you should not.
Gentleman:	She has spoke what she should not, I am sure of that: Heaven knows what she has known.
Lady M.:	Here's the smell of the blood still: all the perfumes of Arabia will not sweeten this little hand. Oh! Oh! Oh! ...
Doctor:	This disease is beyond my practice ...
Lady M.:	Wash your hands, put on your night-gown; look not so pale.—I tell you Banquo's buried: he cannot come out on's grave.
Doctor:	Even so?
Lady M.:	To bed, to bed: there's knocking at the gate. Come, come, come, come, give me your hand. What's done cannot be undone ...
Doctor:	Foul whisp'rings are abroad. Unnatural deeds Do breed unnatural troubles: infected minds To their deaf pillows will discharge their secrets. More needs she the divine than the physician. — God, God forgive us all![28]

---

[28] *Macbeth*, Act 5, Sc. 1, lines 18–72.

In Dostoyevsky's *Crime and Punishment*, before Raskolnikov murders his landlady, he resolves that he will not succumb to what he calls the "disease" of guilt. "So far as he was concerned," Dostoyevsky writes, "there could be no question of his suffering from the symptoms of this disease ... there was consequently no danger of reason or will-power being in any way affected during the carrying out of his plan, simply because what he intended to do was 'not a crime.' "[29] No one could have subscribed more confidently to Raskolnikov's dismissive contempt for the very notion of crime than Lady Macbeth, and yet her guilt becomes every bit as harrowing as his. Macbeth is rather different. He fully acknowledges the living hell to which his murders banish him and when he pleads for some cessation of his guilty torment there can be no question as to the reality of crime.

> Canst thou not minister to a mind diseased,
> Pluck from the memory a rooted sorrow,
> Raze out the written troubles of the brain,
> And with some sweet oblivious antidote
> Cleanse the stuffed bosom of that perilous stuff
> Which weighs upon the heart?[30]

The Doctor responds that "the patient must minister to himself." Well, what should we do with our own "rooted sorrow"? Like Lady Macbeth, we have light continually by us: the light of reason and the light of faith. We have the light of conscience. We also have the light of literature, which, thank God, is not pro-abortion but resoundingly pro-life. We must use this light to acknowledge the "unnatural deeds" that have bred "unnatural troubles" in our "sickly weal" and continue to denounce the murder of the innocent.

---

[29] F. Dostoyevsky, *Crime and Punishment*, trans. D. Magarshack (Penguin, 1951), p. 90.
[30] *Macbeth*, Act 5, Sc. 3, lines 40–45.

Joanna Baillie

3

"THE RICH INHERITANCE OF LOVE": MOTHERHOOD IN GEORGIAN ENGLAND

I N HIS *LIFE of Johnson*, Boswell recalls Johnson arguing with a "pertinacious gentleman," who, after talking "in a very puzzling manner," turned to the old sage and said, "I don't understand you, Sir," whereupon Johnson threw up his hands and replied "Sir, I have found you an argument … I am not obliged to find you an understanding."[1]

Anyone who has ever endeavored to convince a hardened abortionist of the inviolability of unborn life will know the exasperation Johnson felt. The reasoning necessary to recognize that destroying unborn life is indefensible is not abstruse. Grasping the golden rule is sufficient: we must not do unto others what we would not have others do unto us. When Ronald Reagan said, "I've noticed that everybody that is for abortion has already been born," he was refuting the case for abortion with the same appeal to common sense with which Johnson refuted Bishop Berkeley's theory of the non-existence of matter, when, kicking a large immovable stone, he declared: "I refute it thus." Yet to many abortionists common sense makes no appeal. For them, the child in the womb, like that immovable stone, is simply unreal.

This refusal to accept the testimony of common sense is characteristic of certain feminist history. In her highly

---

[1]   J. Boswell, *Life of Johnson*, ed. Hill and Powell (Oxford, 1934), IV, p. 313.

acclaimed book, *The Gentleman's Daughter: Women's Lives in Georgian England* (1998), Amanda Vickery depicts her upper-class female subjects as noble victims, resigned to "the symbolic authority of fathers and husbands, the self-sacrifices of motherhood and the burdensome responsibility for domestic servants, house-keeping and family consumption." Moreover, for Vickery, their very victimization led to their acquiescing in their fate—"rebelling against roles that appeared both prehistoric and preordained would profit nothing."[2] If common sense suggests that her subjects became mothers and managed households out of love and a concomitant sense of responsibility, common sense is mistaken: they assumed such roles because they had no choice but to assume them.

For Vickery, if eighteenth-century women had their way they would have rebelled against these "prehistoric and preordained" roles. Like their feminist successors, they would have revolted against the authority of fathers and husbands, refused the self-sacrifices of motherhood and let others manage the servants and the household accounts. Vickery's book abounds in scholarly evidence. She has pored over county record offices and immersed herself in journals and miscellanies. But rather than let the evidence speak for itself she misrepresents it to support prejudices that would have been unfathomable to her subjects. In this chapter I shall chart the ways in which she advances her blatant feminist agenda at the expense of the reality of her subjects.

One can see this agenda in the way she treats the subject of childbirth. For Vickery and other feminist historians, the question of how past women viewed childbirth must necessarily present embarrassing challenges to feminist

---

[2]   A. Vickery, *The Gentleman's Daughter: Women's Lives in Georgian England* (New Haven, 1998), p. 278.

orthodoxy, particularly as this relates to abortion. Of course, there were no pro-abortion women in the eighteenth century or in any other century prior to the late twentieth century: they were all categorically (the feminist historian might say "benightedly") pro-life. Yet what is remarkable is how this never seems to disconcert feminist historians. It certainly never deters Vickery from saddling her philoprogenitive subjects with attitudes hostile to the very idea of childbirth.

If the evidence shows that women assumed the responsibilities of motherhood bravely and, on the whole, uncomplainingly, despite the considerable perils of childbirth in an era without the benefit of obstetrics, Vickery must always insist that this is a sign of "acquiescence," never of choice, never of preference, and certainly never of self-sacrificial love. If one objects that motherhood was an inalienable part of female identity in the eighteenth as in any other century, Vickery has her answer ready:

> Linked to the celebration of marriage was the growing sentimentalisation of motherhood. Of course, the veneration of the mother is at least as old as the Madonna. Elizabeth I would hardly have represented herself as the Mother of her People if the role did not evoke positive associations, and the Puritans did much to promote the honour of breastfeeding in the elite. However, what distinguishes the eighteenth-century discourse of motherhood from its predecessors is the overlaying of secular hosannahs on the ancient religious solemnizations. Breastfeeding became an ultra-fashionable practice eulogized in the most gushing manner in the novels of Samuel Richardson. But for all the sugariness of the proliferating representations of motherhood, the experience for most was not one of undiluted sweetness. Being a mother, against a background of

disease and debility, remained a bloody, risky, uncontrollable and often gut-wrenching experience, such that a painting of a cherub chasing a butterfly, or a description of a blushing nursing mother, spoke only intermittently and even then superficially to the powerful feelings evoked. The Bible, and in particular the book of Job, still had more to say than most. The self-representation commonest among genteel mothers was not that of a sighing, contented Madonna, it was rather that of a self-made pillar of fortitude and resignation, built to withstand the random blows of fate.[3]

The object here is to diminish motherhood, to argue that an intolerable reality—"a bloody, risky, uncontrollable and often gut-wrenching experience"—has been somehow falsified and glossed over by sentimentality and bad art. She may concede that, "Of course, the veneration of the mother is at least as old as the Madonna ..." Yet this is a concession that does scant justice to the immense creative influence of Our Lady on the formation of Western civilization, a fact which even Henry Adams could appreciate. From the ruins of Wenlock Abbey in Shropshire, Adams wrote in 1891 of how "Progress has much to answer for in depriving weary and broken men and women of their natural end and happiness; but even now I can fancy myself contented in a cloister, and happy in the daily round of duties, if only I still knew a God to pray to, or better yet, a Goddess; for as I grow older I see that all the human interest and power that religion ever had, was in the mother and child ..."[4] In *Mont-Saint Michel and Chartres* (1904), Adams looked at the influence of the Virgin Mary on the civilization of thirteenth-century

---

[3]   Ibid., pp. 279–280
[4]   H. Adams quoted in E. Samuels, *Henry Adams* (Harvard, 1989), p. 270.

Europe and found that it had made for cultural unity, coherence and confidence. Adams, of course, was no Roman Catholic but in showing the Catholic world of the Middle Ages such objective sympathy he proved himself capable of precisely the sort of intellectually honest, unprejudiced history that feminists have shown themselves incapable of producing.

Apropos Vickery's use of "Madonna," G. K. Chesterton makes an interesting observation in his essay, "Mary and the Convert" from *The Well and the Shallows* (1935): "I was brought up in a part of the Protestant world which can be described by saying that it referred to the Blessed Virgin as the Madonna," Chesterton writes. "Sometimes it referred to her as *a* Madonna; from a general memory of Italian pictures. It was not a bigoted or uneducated world; it did not regard all Madonnas as idols or all Italians as Dagoes. But it had selected this expression, by the English instinct for compromise, so as to avoid both reverence and irreverence. It was, when we come to think about it, a very curious expression. It amounted to saying that a Protestant must not call Mary "Our Lady," but he may call her "My Lady." This would seem, in the abstract, to indicate an even more intimate and mystical familiarity than the Catholic devotion. But I need not say that it was not so. It was not untouched by that queer Victorian evasion of translating dangerous or improper words into foreign languages ..."[5] For all of the zeal she exhibits to appear a proper progressive, Vickery is an unsuspecting legatee of this Victorian tradition.

Nevertheless, Vickery is doubtless right when she points out that, for the Georgian English, Elizabeth I was the more

---

[5]   *The Collected Works of G. K. Chesterton, Vol. III: The Catholic Church and Conversion; Where All Roads Lead; The Well and the Shallows; and others* (London, 1990), p. 460.

compelling source of the veneration of motherhood:
English mothers were venerated not because Our Lady gave
birth to the Son of God, but because a political virgin liked
to fancy herself the "Mother of her People." Yet here one
can see how Vickery's own hostile view of motherhood
stems directly from the tragic loss among the English of any
understanding of the Virgin Mother whose consent at the
Annunciation and her own motherhood, as Pope Paul II
reminds his readers, "stand at the very beginning of the
mystery of life which Christ came to bestow on humanity."
To explain his point further, John Paul quotes from Blessed
Guerric of Igny, who spoke of Mary as "the mother of the
Life by which everyone lives, and when she brought it forth
from herself she in some way brought to rebirth all those
who were to live by that Life."[6]

Vickery is on shaky ground when she charges Samuel
Richardson with sentimentalizing motherhood, for when
it came to paying close attention to the often overlooked
quotidian aspects of motherhood and marriage Richardson was a pioneer. Lady Mary Wortley Montagu might
have thought that he "should confine his pen to the
amours of housemaids, and the conversation of the stew-
ard's table," and Sir Horace Walpole might have considered Clarissa and Sir Charles Grandison "pictures of high
life as conceived by a bookseller ... romances ... spiritual-
ized by a Methodist teacher," but these were the objections
of snobbery.[7] For Lady Mary and Sir Horace it was
inconceivable that a joiner's son could know anything
about society. Nevertheless, many more readers, including
Samuel Johnson and Sir Walter Scott agreed with
Macaulay when he gave it as his opinion that "No writings,

---

[6]   Pope John Paul II, *Evangelium Vitae*, 164.
[7]   M. Wortley Montagu, *Letters* (New York, 1992), p. 471 and H. Walpole,
        Letters (Oxford, 1903–05), VI, p. 163.

Shakespeare excepted, show more profound knowledge of the human heart."[8] No less a critic than V. S. Pritchett had only the most discriminating praise for *Clarissa*: "In the sheer variety of their styles the letters in this novel are astonishing. The bovine uncles, the teasing parenthetical Miss Howe, the admonitory Belford, the curt Colonel Morden, heading for his duel, the climbing neurotic brother whose descendants were no doubt in the British Union of Fascists, all have their styles, as they are as distinctive as Lovelace's or Clarissa's. Richardson is the least flat, the most stereoscopic novelist of an age which ran the plain or formal statement to death ..."[9]

Something of his knowledge of the heart can be gleaned from a passage in *Sir Charles Grandison*, where one of the characters remarks, "A feeling heart is a blessing that no one, who has it, would be without; and it is a moral security of innocence, since the heart that is able to partake of the distress of another, cannot willfully give it."[10] Again, we encounter the golden rule. Only the hard-hearted would regard such fellow-feeling as sentimental.

Yet what really annoys Vickery about Richardson is not that he was sentimental but that he acknowledged many more positive aspects about marriage and motherhood than she and her feminist friends are prepared to concede. His character Clarissa Harlowe, for example, first rebels against the political marriage arranged by her father with Roger Solmes because she recognizes that personal freedom is indispensable to the proper equality of mar-

---

[8]   T. B. Macaulay, "Speech on Copyright", *Speeches* (London, 1854), p. 241.

[9]   V. S. Pritchett, *The Complete Collected Essays* (New York, 1992), p. 159.

[10] S. Richardson, *History of Sir Charles Grandison* (London, 1754), III, Letter 32.

riage. In this sense, Clarissa might seem unobjectionable
enough and least of all to women. But, in feminist eyes,
she throws away whatever credibility she has when she
freely elopes with the monstrous Lovelace. Worse, after
she rebels against Lovelace, she commits the supreme
feminist sin by submitting to an altogether more patriarchal master. Apropos this submission, the English critic
Patrick Parrinder is perceptive:

> In opposition to Lovelace's tyranny, Clarissa ceases
> to appear as the rebellious slave she had been at
> home and becomes, instead, both a queen and a
> saint. Lovelace compares her to Mary Queen of Scots
> at the mercy of Elizabeth I (iv. 31). ... She renounces
> her father, too. When at the end she states that she
> is "setting out with all diligence for my father's
> house" (iv. 157), the father she means to return to is
> God himself. Not only has she refused to allow Mr.
> Harlowe to delegate his patriarchal authority to
> James [her brother], but she is no longer willing to
> recognize delegation from a heavenly to an earthly
> father. Clarissa's final "coming of age," which is
> marked by her decision to devote herself to God
> alone, is the means of her victory over Lovelace ...[11]

Submission to God requires submission to a natural order:
this is why Richardson must repulse feminist critics. One
can see Vickery's distrust of this natural order in her
handling of motherhood. In a chapter about childbirth
and maternity, aptly entitled "Fortitude and Resignation,"
Vickery goes to great lengths to depict Georgian motherhood as not only oppressive but nightmarish. What she
calls the "sentimental prestige of parenthood" and "the

---

[11]   P. Parrinder, *Novel and Nation: The English Novel from its Origins
   to the Present Day* (Oxford, 2006), p. 112.

celebration of the pet-like appeal of the progeny" carries no weight with her.[12]

Referring to children as having "pet-like appeal" is oddly demeaning. What could have compelled Vickery to use such language? She pinched it from the historian Roy Porter. In his Penguin history of Georgian England, Porter observed how "Ladies were beginning to make more time for their children ... From the mid-century it became the done thing for well-bred ladies to interest themselves with nursing babies and training toddlers—more with the exquisite delight of discovering a new pet under one's nose than with the dutifulness of the Victorian matriarch ..."[13] It is a shame that Georgian women cannot somehow be summoned to answer this charge. Their testimony, I suspect, would make mincemeat of the polemical conjectures of Porter and Vickery. In any case, the claim that Porter makes here and that Vickery accepts is that Georgian motherhood was the result of cultural conditioning; there was nothing natural in the solicitous love that Georgian women showed their children; and yet neither historian produces a scrap of evidence to support the claim.

The aspect of motherhood that most interests her is "the sheer blood and guts of bearing and raising children." Accordingly, she presents motherhood as inherently nasty. She also claims that it is unsafe, unpredictable, and unhealthy. "When a woman conceived she was launched on a roaring wave of fate. No one could predict how easily she would bear pregnancy, how safely she would deliver, how robust would be her infant, or how long and healthy the life of the child."[14] Lest her readers somehow miss the

---

[12] *Gentleman's Daughter*, p. 98.
[13] R. Porter, *England in the Eighteenth Century* (London, 1982), p. 44.
[14] *Gentleman's Daughter*, p.98.

point, Vickery is careful to drive it home with a suitably macabre example. "In June 1739 Anne Gossip laboured in agony for forty-nine and a half hours, and with a stoicism barely imaginable suffered her dead baby to be torn within her and removed in pieces."[15] And of course it was a male midwife who attended.

If this does not dissuade her readers from cherishing any positive feelings toward motherhood, Vickery reminds them that even if her subjects and their newborns survived childbirth, their troubles had only begun. Begetting children, she insists, then, as now, kept women from doing anything else. "For fertile women, motherhood could absorb almost all reserves of physical and emotional energy for at least a decade, and was an anxious backdrop for a lifetime."[16] Breastfeeding presented additional problems. "Bessy Ramsden nursed her four children—Billy, Betsy, Tommy and Dick—her self. 'As I am a nurse,' she reported in 1768, 'I take great care of myself and drink porter like any fishwoman.' But breastfeeding was not without its difficulties and side-effects. Dame Bessy suffered headaches, loss of concentration and diminishing sight."[17] (The readiness here to link breastfeeding with adverse side-effects should be compared to contemporary feminists' refusal to concede the link between abortion and breast cancer, not to mention post-abortion trauma.)

Notwithstanding these negative consequences, Bessy's ordeal had a silver lining. Breastfeeding, she was convinced, prevented her from being "in an increasing way," which prompts Vickery to comment: "Either she drew on the widespread belief in the contraceptive power of prolonged lactation, or she acknowledged the conservative prohibition

---

[15]   Ibid., p. 106.
[16]   Ibid., p. 99.
[17]   Ibid., p. 113.

against intercourse while breastfeeding. Either way, she registered a desire to delay weaning and control her own fertility."[18] Bessy, in other words, was (dimly) aware of 'reproductive rights'—the great grail of all feminist history.

Still, this did not change the fact that "Once embarked upon a maternal course, married women had only limited time and creative energy to invest in anything beyond household and kin …"[19] Hence, "As new mothers, genteel women became less mobile and their time for company was radically reduced."[20] Then, too, children in the eighteenth century were always coming down with life-threatening illnesses. The whooping cough and small pox were particularly lethal. "Maternal preoccupation with sick children and the sinister stirrings of infection in the locality were … standard themes of women's letters and diaries."[21] Indeed, for Vickery, "a mother's role was interchangeable with that of a sick-nurse."[22] In 1776, one smallpox epidemic alone killed seventy children. "To be a parent," Vickery recognizes clearly enough, "was to be keenly exposed to the vagaries of fate"—though it was mothers, not fathers, who were held most responsible for keeping children healthy.[23] So the patriarchal defendant remains in the dock.

What is interesting about Vickery's book, however, is that, despite her readiness to pander to every feminist prejudice, she is clear-sighted enough to recognize that "Motherhood was not a discrete event, or the work of a day, it was the quintessential labour of love which knew

---

[18] Ibid., p. 117.
[19] Ibid., p. 117.
[20] Ibid., p. 118.
[21] Ibid., p. 123.
[22] Ibid., p. 120.
[23] Ibid., p. 124.

no clock and spent itself in endless small services ... In its boundless details, mothering swamped genteel matrons even as it defined them."[24] What she does not acknowledge is the all-important *voluntary* nature of this "labour of love." Women willingly made sacrifices for their children, out of love, not because of that stalest of feminist bugbears, patriarchal social conditioning.

For a truer understanding of how Georgian women viewed motherhood and childbirth we can turn to the poetry they wrote. In a poem called "A Mother to Her Waking Infant," Joanna Baillie (1762–1851), wrote about the mother and child relationship with unsentimental authority.

> Now in thy dazzling half-oped eye,
> Thy curled nose and lip awry,
> Thy up-hoist arms and noddling head,
> And little chin with chrystal spread,
> Poor helpless thing! what do I see,
>   That I should sing of thee?
>
> From thy poor tongue no accents come,
> Which can but rub thy toothless gum;
> Small understanding boasts thy face,
> Thy shapeless limbs nor step nor grace;
> A few short words thy feats may tell,
>   And yet I love thee well ...
>
> Each passing clown bestows his blessing,
> Thy mouth is worn with old wives' kissing;
> E'en lighter looks the gloomy eye
> Of surly sense, when thou art by;
> And yet I think whoe'er they be,
>   They love thee not like me ...[25]

---

[24] Ibid., p.126.
[25] J. Baillie, "A Mother to her Waking Infant" (1790) from *Women Poets of the Eighteenth Century*, ed. Roger Lonsdale (Oxford, 1989), p. 442.

Vickery writes sneeringly of the "pet-like appeal of the progeny," as though maternal love were somehow analogous to the fondness that one might feel for a pet. Baillie proves, if we need proving, that there is a fundamental difference between the two. It was Baillie's realism that appealed to Byron, not the Byron who spent so much of his short life chasing after other men's wives but the Byron who loved his daughter so much that he insisted on her being brought up by nuns because, as he told one correspondent, "What with incense, pictures, statues, altars, shrines, relics, the real presence, confession, [and] absolution, there is something sensible to grasp at."[26] Similarly, it was Joanna Baillie's sensibleness that led him to put her on a par with Walter Scott and George Crabbe, Thomas Moore and Thomas Campbell.[27]

There are other female poets besides Baillie whose work refutes Vickery's dismal view of Georgian motherhood. In "To a Little Invisible Being Who is Expected Soon to Become Visible" (surely a problematic title for any pro-abortion editor), Anna Laetitia Barbauld (1743–1825) addresses the unborn with matter-of-fact solicitude:

> Germ of new life, whose powers expanding slow
> For many a moon their full perfection wait—
> Haste, precious pledge of happy love, to go
> Auspicious borne through life's mysterious gate.[28]

In his excellent anthology of eighteenth-century verse by female poets, Roger Lonsdale notes how Barbauld grew

---

[26]   Byron quoted in F. McCarthy, *Byron: Life and Legend* (London, 2002), p. 391.

[27]   Lord Byron, *Selected Letters,* ed. L. Marchand (London, 1982), p. 258.

[28]   A. L. Barbauld, "To a Little Being Who is Expected Soon to Become Visible" (1795) from *Women Poets of the Eighteenth Century*, pp. 307–308.

up in a family of bright boys, which might have made her
diffident in society but which gave her intellectual powers
an admirable confidence. An adoptive parent, she wrote
the popular *Lessons for Children* (1778) and *Hymns in
Prose for Children* (1781), both of which went through
many editions. She also edited Richardson's letters. In
addition to winning the praise of Coleridge and Wordsworth, she was friendly with Hannah More, Maria Edgeworth, Lady Mary Wortley Montagu, and Walter Scott.
Yet when Lady Mary urged her to join a proposed academy
for women, Barbauld balked. As Lonsdale remarks, "she
saw no point in producing *femmes savants* rather than
'good wives or agreeable companions.' "[29] She never
considered herself merely a writer and poured scorn on
those who even suggested that she might wish to be known
as a female writer. In 1804 she wrote a number of letters
to Maria Edgeworth and her husband in which she made
it clear, to quote Lonsdale, "that she had little sense of a
tradition of women's writing, felt no common cause with
other literary women ('There is no bond of union among
literary women'), and believed that it would be pointless
to 'provoke a war with the other sex.'"[30] These opinions
are not likely to endear her to contemporary feminists.
Nor are her musings on the life of the unborn.

> What powers lie folded in thy curious frame,—
> Senses from objects locked, and mind from thought!
> How little canst thou guess thy lofty claim
> To grasp at all the worlds the Almighty wrought!
>
> And see, the genial season's warmth to share,
> Fresh younglings shoot, and opening roses glow!
> Swarms of new life exulting fill the air, —
> Haste, infant bud of being, haste to blow! ...

---

[29]   *Women Poets of the Eighteenth Century*, p. 300.
[30]   Ibid.

Come, reap thy rich inheritance of love!
Bask in the fondness of a Mother's eye!
Nor wit nor eloquence her heart shall move
Like the first accents of thy feeble cry.

Haste, little captive, burst thy prison doors!
Launch on the living world, and spring to light!
Nature for thee displays her various stores,
Opens her thousand inlets of delight.

If charméd verse or muttered prayers had power
With favouring spells to speed thee on thy way,
Anxious I'd bid my beads each passing hour,
Till thy wished smile thy mother's pangs o'erpay.[31]

There is nothing here or in Baillie's poem about the oppressiveness of pregnancy or the nastiness of childbirth. There are no complaints against the unfair demands of motherhood, nor any foreshadowing of 'reproductive rights'. Vickery would doubtless counter that these were *acquiescent* women, resigned to what they could not change. But were they? What evidence, after all, does she uncover to substantiate that eighteenth-century women found motherhood anything other than joyful and life-affirming? However much one might admire the research behind Vickery's book, it is inveterately filtered through her own feminist prejudices and falsified. If we go to primary sources, we find a very different story. Isabella Kelly (1759–1857) addresses her unborn child with a solicitude that no amount of feminist polemics can discredit. Here is the real voice of Georgian motherhood.

To an Unborn Infant

Be, still, sweet babe, no harm shall reach thee,
    Nor hurt thy yet unfinished form;
Thy mother's frame shall safely guard thee

---

[31] Ibid., pp. 307–308.

From this bleak, this beating storm.

Promised hope! expected treasure!
    Oh, how welcome to these arms!
Feeble, yet they'll fondly clasp thee,
    Shield thee from the least alarms.

Loved already, little blessing,
    Kindly cherished, though unknown,
Fancy forms thee sweet and lovely,
    Emblem of the rose unblown.

Though thy father is imprisoned,
    Wronged, forgotten, robbed of right,
I'll repress the rising anguish,
    Till thine eyes behold the light.

Start not, babe! The hour approaches
    That presents the gift of life;
Soon, too soon thou'lt taste of sorrow
    In these realms of care and strife.

Share not thou a mother's feelings,
    Hope vouchsafes a pitying ray;
Though a gloom obscures the morning,
    Bright may shine the rising day.

Live, sweet babe, to bless thy father,
    When thy mother slumbers low;
Slowly lisp her name that loved him,
    Through a world of varied woe.

Learn, my child, the mournful story
    Of thy suffering mother's life;
Let thy father not forget her
    In a future, happier wife.

Babe of fondest expectation,
    Watch his wishes in his face;
What pleased in me mayst thou inherit,
    And supply my vacant place.

> Whisper all the anguished moments
>> That have wrung this anxious breast:
> Say, I lived to give thee being,
>> And retired to endless rest.[32]

Some might argue that this is unrepresentative. Not all Georgian women would have been faced with crisis pregnancies—though Isabella Kelly herself suffered a crisis that must have seemed as stressful as any crisis pregnancy when she was left with two small children after her husband, a major in the British army, went missing in Madras.[33] Nevertheless, the poem nicely captures the intensity of maternal love, despite all the difficulties that Vickery describes. Feminists dwell on such difficulties to insinuate that if women had been given more of a choice in such matters they would never have given birth so frequently. But this is not an insinuation that the primary sources corroborate. Eighteenth-century women were far tougher than present-day feminists imagine. They knew that giving birth to children required manifold sacrifice. They knew that keeping them healthy was often a Sisyphean struggle. They knew that giving their children life might imperil their own life. But there is nothing in their letters or their other writings to suggest that they would have agreed with the feminist claim that 'reproductive rights' trump the life of unborn children. No "anguished moments" would have led them to subscribe to that grave fallacy.

---

[32]   I. Kelly, "To an Unborn Infant" (1794) from *Women Poets of the Eighteenth Century*, pp. 482–483.

[33]   Ibid., p. 482.

Penelope Fitzgerald

4

PENELOPE FITZGERALD'S
LIFE STORY

I N LOOKING TO literature for an affirmation of pro-life
principles one has to be careful. John Henry Newman
was right to remind his readers that

> One literature may be better than another, but bad
> will be the best, when weighed in the balance of
> truth and morality. It cannot be otherwise; human
> nature is in all ages and all countries the same ...
> Man's work will savour of man; in his elements and
> powers excellent and admirable, but prone to disor-
> der and excess, to error and to sin. Such too will be
> his literature; it will have the beauty and the fierce-
> ness, the sweetness and the rankness, of the natural
> man ...[1]

And yet pro-life principles animate even the most morally
dubious literature. After all, literature is only possible
because poets, novelists, playwrights, biographers and
historians recognize that life has intrinsic value, independent of any considerations of utility or expedience, and that
as such it merits not only being looked at but being looked
after—cared for, tended to, protected, *affirmed*. In this
essay, I shall look at how the work of one of our greatest
novelists exhibits pro-life principles in ways that are at
once unusual and compelling.

---

[1] J. H. Newman, *The Idea of a University*, ed. Martin J. Svaglic
(Oxford, 1976), p. 261.

Penelope Fitzgerald (1916–2000) was the daughter of the humorist and *Punch* editor, E. V. Knox, the niece of Dilly Knox, who helped the English foil Hitler by breaking the Enigma code, and Msgr. Ronald Knox, the Catholic convert, who was a close friend of Chesterton and Waugh and a master of English prose style. In 1977, Fitzgerald published a brilliant biography of the brilliant Knox brothers. In an autobiographical piece, she vividly described Hampstead in the Twenties where she lived as a child: "there were still sheep gracing on Hampstead Heath, chair menders, knife grinders, and muffin men in the streets (the muffin men, like the sheep were seasonal), lamplighters who walked at dusk from gas lamp to gas lamp, and small shops that sold pennyworths of licorice and Phillips soles, with which you repaired your own shoes. Milk came round in a pony cart. There were still plenty of horse-drawn vans." Her solicitude for the dead and gone, as this and indeed all of her work demonstrates was not unrelated to her solicitude for the unborn. Fitzgerald's mother—"a quietly spoken woman," as she remembered, "whom nothing defeated"—died the year she entered Somerville College, a loss which gave even Fitzgerald's funniest fiction a certain undertone of melancholy. After university, she married Desmond Fitzgerald, who was in the Irish Guards at the time, with whom she had two children. During the war she worked as an assistant at the BBC. Later, she wrote about her adventures at Broadcasting House in a novel called *Human Voices* (1980), which should be adapted for film: it is deliciously funny. She wrote her first novel, *A Golden Child* (1977), a mystery devised to beguile her dying husband, when she was sixty. Her second novel, *The Bookshop* (1978), a droll comedy of manners set in a small Suffolk village, won her well-earned comparisons to Jane Austen. *Offshore* (1979), her next novel, was based on the life she shared with her impecunious family aboard a barge called *Grace*, moored off the Thames. These were followed by four brilliant historical novels, most notably *The Gate of Angels* (1990), a philosophical romance set in Edwardian Cambridge and *The Beginning of Spring* (1988), a tale of marital betrayal set in pre-revolutionary Moscow. Her last novel, *The Blue Flower* (1995), was an international best seller based on the life of the Romantic poet, Friedrich Leopold von Hardenberg (1772–1801), otherwise known as Novalis. In his introduction to the Everyman edition, Frank Kermode reads the book terribly wrong. Fitzgerald also wrote good biographies of the poet Charlotte Mew (1869–1928), the Pre-Raphaelite painter Edward Burne-Jones (1833–98) and the Knox brothers.

Her posthumous book of short stories, *The Means of Escape* (2000), includes a wonderful pro-life story called "At Hiruharama." It is the story of a family's history. The narrator, Mr. Tanner, begins by telling how his grandfather and grandmother met and how the Tanner family got its start in New Zealand.

> Mr. Tanner was anxious to explain how it was that he had a lawyer in the family, so that when they all decided to sell up and quit New Zealand there had been someone they could absolutely trust with the legal business. That meant that he had to say something about his grandfather, who had been an orphan from Stamford in Lincolnshire and was sent out to a well-to-do family north of Auckland, supposedly an apprentice, but it turned out that he was to be more of a servant: he cleaned the knives, saw to the horses, waited at table and chopped the wood. On an errand to a dry goods store in Auckland he met Kitty, Mr. Tanner's grandmother. She had come out from England as a governess, and she too

> found she was really wanted as a servant. She was
> sixteen, and Tanner asked her to wait for three years
> while he saved his wages, and then to marry him.
> All this was at a Methodist social...[2]

When the newlyweds set about finding a place to live, they choose a deserted house north of Awanui where there are no churches or schools "but something you could give a thousand pounds for and not get, and that was a standpipe giving constant clear water from an underground well."[3] With this in hand, their future is set. "Tanner grew root vegetables and went into Awanui twice a week with the horse and dray. Kitty stayed behind, because they'd taken on two hundred chickens and a good few pigs."

Then something rather momentous happens. Tanner learns that his wife is pregnant. He takes the horse and cart into Awanui and asks the doctor what the life statistics are for the North Island.

> "Do you mean the death statistics?" the doctor asked.
> "They'll do just as well," said Tanner.
> "No one dies here except from drink or drowning. Out
> of three thousand people in Taranki Province there hasn't
> been a single funeral in the last sixteen months and only
> twenty-four six and infirm. You may look upon me as a
> poor man."

---

[2]   P. Fitzgerald, "At Hiruharama," from *A Means of Escape* (London, 2002), pp. 107–108.

[3]   Ibid., p. 108. Fitzgerald and the Tanners would have approved of this passage from Hilaire Belloc, *The Four Men* (London, 1911), p. 37: "I woke next morning to the noise, the pleasant noise, of water boiling in a kettle. May God bless that noise and grant it to be the most sacred noise in the world. For it is the noise that babes hear at birth and that old men hear as they die in their beds, and it is the noise of our households all our long lives long; and throughout the world, wherever men have hearths, that purring and that singing and that talking to itself of warm companionable water to our great ally, the fire, is home."

"What about women in childbirth?" asked Tanner

The doctor didn't have any figures for women dying in childbirth, but he looked sharply at Tanner and asked him when his child was due.

"You don't know, of course," the doctor said. "Well, don't ask me if it's going to be twins. Nature didn't intend us to know that ... Where are you living?"

"It's off the road to Houhora. You turn off to the right after twelve miles."

"What's it called?"

"Hiruharama."

"Don't know it. That's not a Maori name."

"I think it means Jerusalem," said Tanner.[4]

The doctor proceeds to ask Tanner if he has any neighbors. Yes, there is a fellow named Brinkman. Does he have a wife? No, he has always wanted one but he lives alone: you can't ask a woman to live in such an inhospitable place. "You can ask a woman to live anywhere," the doctor retorts. As he leaves, Tanner notices the other patients waiting to see the doctor.

> Some had empty medicine bottles for a refill. There was a man with his right arm strapped up, several kids with their mothers, and a woman who looked well enough but seemed to be in tears for some reason or other.—Well, you see life in the townships.[5]

On his way home, Tanner stops off and visits Parrish, a man who keeps racing pigeons. "Parrish had cut the entrances to the nests down very small, and every time a bird got home it had to squeeze past a bell on a string so that the tinkling sound gave warning. They were all Blue Checkers, the only kind, Parrish declared, that a sane man

---

[4] *AMOE*, pp. 109–110.
[5] Ibid., p. 111.

would want to keep. Tanner explained his predicament
and asked for the loan of two birds." When he had packed
the birds into his dray, he asked Parrish:

> "Have you got them numbered in some way?"
> "I don't need to. I know them all," said Parrish.[6]

When Tanner arrives home he surprises his wife with the
birds. "The Blue Checkers were the prettiest things about
the place." Then Kitty's pains begin and Tanner must send
the pigeons off to notify the doctor. He takes the basket
with the pigeons and walks out into the bright open air.

> He opened the basket, and before he could think
> what to do next they were out and up into the blue.
> He watched in terror as, after reaching a certain
> height, they began turning around in tight circles as
> though puzzled or lost. Then, apparently sighting
> something on the horizon that they knew, they set
> off strongly towards Awanui ...[7]

Then Brinkman turns up. And "of course ... as he'd come
eight miles over a rough road, he had to be asked to put
up his horse for a while and come in."

> Like most people who live on their own, Brinkman
> continued with the course of his own thoughts, which
> were more real to him than the outside world's commo-
> tion. Walking straight into the front room, he stopped
> before the piece of glass tacked over the sink and looked
> fixedly into it.
> "I'll tell you something, Tanner. I thought I caught
> sight of my first grey hairs this morning."
> "I'm sorry to hear that."
> Brinkman looked round. "I see the table isn't set."

---

6   Ibid., pp. 113–114.
7   Ibid.

"I don't want you to feel that you're not welcome," said Tanner, "but Kitty's not well ... Truth is, she's in labour." "Then she won't be cooking dinner this evening, then?" "You mean you were counting to have it here?" "My half-yearly dinner with you and Mrs. Tanner, yis, that's about it."[8]

Whereupon Brinkman recalls in fond detail all the delectable dishes Kitty had prepared and served the previous year. Still, he assures Tanner that he has returned this year not merely for the food but "for the sake of a woman's voice ..." The timing of this remark is richly ludicrous because:

> At that moment there was a crying, or a calling, from the next room such as Tanner had never heard before, not in a shipwreck—and he had been in a wreck—not in a slaughterhouse.

By the time the doctor arrives with his wife's widowed sister, Tanner has already delivered a baby girl. He comes out of the bedroom "covered with blood," looking like a butcher. He has wrapped the baby girl carefully in a washbasket. Then a stunned Brinkman appears and introduces himself by saying, "You may be wondering who I am ... I'm a neighbor, come over for dinner. I think of myself as one of the perpetually welcome." "Suit yourself," says the sister-in-law and pushes past him. Then the doctor emerges from the bedroom with unusual haste. "Please to go in there and wash the patient. I'm going to take a look at the afterbirth. The father put it out with the waste." There Tanner had made his one oversight. It wasn't the afterbirth, it was a second daughter, smaller, but a twin. —[9]

---

8   Ibid., pp. 114–115.
9   Ibid., pp. 116–117.

Here readers might wonder why Tanner, the narrator,
still has the last name Tanner if the two babies were girls.

> Well, the Tanners went on to have nine more
> children, some of them boys, and one of those boys
> was Mr. Tanner's father. That evening, when the
> doctor came in from the yard with the messy scrap,
> he squeezed it as though he were wringing it out to
> dry, and it opened its mouth and the colder air of
> the kitchen rushed in and she'd got her start in life.
> After that, the Tanners always had one of those
> tinplate mottoes hung up on the wall: *Throw
> Nothing Away* ... And this was the point that Mr.
> Tanner had been wanting to make all along: whereas
> the first daughter never got to be anything in partic-
> ular, this second little girl grew up to a lawyer with
> a firm in Wellington, and she did very well.
>
> All the time Brinkman continued to sit there by the
> table and smoke his pipe. Two more women born
> into the world! It must have seemed to him that if
> this sort of thing went on, there should be a good
> chance, in the end, for him to acquire one for
> himself.[10]

"At Hiruharama" is the best pro-life story in the language.
Muriel Spark liked to say that she wrote her fiction as though
it were poetry, taking care that each chapter, each line, each
word shaped the meaning of the whole in the dynamic,
organic way of poetry. Well, there is a wonderful coherence
and concision in Spark's fiction but I don't think that even
she came close to the poetic power that Fitzgerald achieves
in this brilliant story. It is a flawless piece of work, which
touches on all the great themes—history and family, love and
destiny, hope and resolution—with eloquent economy. But
most of all it celebrates life. There is indeed "something you

---

[10]   Ibid., p. 117.

could give a thousand pounds for and not get," which gives "constant clear water from an underground well." That underground well is the sacred well of life and it is God's gift to both the born and the unborn. In her defense of the dignity of that well—with its rousing motto *Throw Nothing Away!*—Penelope Fitzgerald crowned her career with a pro-life story for the ages.

Jack and Nuala Scarisbrick

5

J. J. SCARISBRICK AND THE PRO-LIFE SPECIAL RELATIONSHIP

Sreaking of "the special relationship" between Britain and America, Winston Churchill cited the things the two countries have in common in a speech to Harvard in 1943, "Law, language, literature—these are considerable factors. Common conceptions of what is right and decent, a marked regard for fair play, especially to the weak and poor, a stern sentiment of impartial justice, and above all a love of personal freedom ... these are the common conceptions on both sides of the ocean among the English-speaking peoples."[1]

What Churchill did not include in this list is what ought to be our shared commitment to the life of the unborn. I say "ought" because, of course, it is not universally shared. Many in America and Britain are persuaded that what are called 'reproductive rights' take precedence over the life of the unborn and that therefore abortion is defensible. (It is some relief to find that the dictionary of euphemisms recently compiled by R. W. Holder and aptly entitled "How Not to Say What You Mean" defines "reproductive freedom" as "the right to abort a healthy foetus.") As we all know, Britain's Abortion Act (1967) and America's Roe v. Wade ruling (1973) paved the way for an assault against unborn life that puts what Churchill referred to as our "marked regard for fair play" in a grotesque light. In Britain,

---

[1] W. Churchill quoted in Andrew Roberts, *A History of the English-Speaking Peoples Since 1900* (London, 2006), p. 641.

200,000 unborn children are killed each year; in America, the number is well over a million. Surely these are statistics that cry out for a renewed special relationship.

Fortunately, such a relationship has already been forged. J. P. McFadden, the founding editor of *The Human Life Review*, initiated cooperative partnerships with such British pro-lifers as Lynette Burrows and Mary Kenny. British pro-lifer Jack Scarisbrick is continuing that tradition by collaborating with many American pro-lifers, including Joel Brind, Professor of Human Biology and Endocrinology at Baruch College, City University of New York and Father Joseph Koterski, SJ, Professor of Philosophy at Fordham University and editor-in-chief of *International Philosophical Quarterly*. Prof. Brind has appeared at many LIFE conferences educating British pro-lifers on the abortion/breast cancer link (ABC) and Father Koterski, well known for his pro-life conferences in the US, recently addressed LIFE audiences in Exeter, Bristol, Gloucester and Bath, as well as conducting a seminar for LIFE Education Officers at Life's headquarters.

Prof. Scarisbrick came to the pro-life movement over forty years ago from a distinguished academic career. He was educated at the John Fisher School in Surrey, and, after serving in the RAF, at Christ's College, Cambridge, where he read History. He taught in the University of London, in Ghana and the USA, and from 1969 to 1994 was professor of History in the University of Warwick. Prof. Scarisbrick and his wife Nuala have two daughters and eight grandchildren. Together with Nuala, he founded LIFE, Inc. in 1970, a model pro-life agency that offers counseling, education, housing and natural fertility assistance to thousands of women and men each year. In addition to 33 LIFE houses, located throughout the UK, the agency operates Zöe's Place—Britain's and perhaps the world's first baby hospice, which provides 24-hour respite and terminal palliative care for children aged 0 to 5 with multiple specials needs. Currently, LIFE operates a Zöe's Place hospice in Liverpool, Middlesbrough and Coventry, though their goal is to have one operating in every major city in the UK.

Recently, I had the privilege to meet with Prof. Scarisbrick at his LIFE headquarters in Royal Leamington Spa, where he described the work that he and LIFE are doing to combat the scourge of abortion. My first introduction to his work, however, occurred years before when I was an undergraduate studying history and happened upon his magisterial biography of Henry VIII, a splendidly incisive account of the architect of the English Reformation. Nowhere else is the insatiable selfishness of the man more vividly presented. When Henry VIII dissolved the monasteries, he acquired a huge treasure trove of land and endowment. But rather than apply it to charitable works, to poor relief or education, he took most of it for himself and sold the rest to rapacious courtiers, about whom William Cobbett memorably observed: "For cool, placid, unruffled impudence, there have been no people in the world to equal the 'Reformation' gentry."[2] The divisions that Henry's confiscations caused affected all subsequent English history. But what struck me was something one of the men of that sad generation said after the consequences of Henry's vandalism became clear: "Our posterity will wonder at us ..."[3] For all who have witnessed the ravages of abortion, these are chilling words—but ones which must return us to the fight for life.

---

[2]   W. Cobbett, *A History of the Protestant Reformation in England and Ireland* (New York, 1896), p. 15.

[3]   J. J. Scarisbrick, *Henry VIII* (London, 1969), p. 461.

Prof. Scarisbrick and LIFE now fights for the unborn in a wonderful old assembly hall, which has an interesting history. It was originally built in 1906 for the Catholic Apostolic Church, an offshoot of the Methodist sect founded by Selina, Countess of Huntingdon (1707-91). Instrumental in introducing Methodism to England's upper classes, Lady Huntingdon formed her own group known as "the Countess of Huntingdon's Connexion" after breaking with John Wesley. Her preachers, according to the historian Paul Langford, "were seeking out sin, and not unreasonably thought it should be attacked most vigorously where it was strongest, in polite society. The early chapels of the Huntingdon Connexion were often in places of fashionable resort: Bath, Tunbridge, Margate, or at least in towns with assemblies, balls, and the regular attendance of the upper crust."[4] Hence, it would have been natural for her successors to set up shop in Leamington Spa, with its fashionable pump room. Prof. Scarisbrick gave me a tour of the new site when we met and it is impressive, with great timber beams and space galore for his education, counseling, and housing departments, as well as a clinical area for his LIFE Fertility Care Program. Now, Royal Leamington Spa is famous for more than Queen Victoria stopping here for lunch on her railway journeys to Balmoral or the future Napoleon III living briefly at 6 Clarendon Square or even Nathaniel Hawthorne living at 10 Landsdowne Parade with his young family in 1857, after serving as American consul at Liverpool. Now it is the place where Prof. Scarisbrick and LIFE helped bring about the end of abortion in Britain.

Prof. Scarisbrick and LIFE continue to make admirably dogged strides towards that end. Thanks to LIFE, over 26,000 active supporters throughout the UK and indeed

---

[4]   P. Langford, *A Polite and Commercial People: England 1727-1783* (Oxford, 1989), p. 253.

around the world now realize that there is a positive alternative to abortion, euthanasia, and the misuse and destruction of human embryos. By any measure, this is an impressive accomplishment, especially when one considers the power and the reach of the pro-abortion establishment.

How that establishment became so formidable is a melancholy tale. In 1967, David Steel's Abortion Act was passed ostensibly to clarify the 1861 Offences against the Persons Act and "stamp out backstreet abortions." In the intervening 40 years, the myth of "backstreet abortions" has given way to the reality of "abortion on demand." In September 2007, the aptly named Marie Stopes[5] International, a pro-abortion agency recorded its busiest month ever—6,000 abortions were performed in January 2007 alone.[6] Attempts to modify the 1967 Bill have almost universally failed.[7] In 1969, Norman St. John-Stevas,

---

[5]   Returning home from New York in 1924, Noel Coward met Marie Stopes on board the *SS Cedric*. At the time, Coward's first play, *The Vortex*, had just completed a successful run on the London stage. The play was about a debauched mother and her drug-addicted son, "trapped," as Coward put it, "in a vortex of beastliness." After seeing the play, Stopes wrote Coward an effusive fan letter suggesting that they team up and write a sequel. Coward wrote her back how, as he said, "I am afraid I never collaborate with anyone, and even if I did, it would not be over a sequel to *The Vortex*, as psychologically speaking, there is *no* sequel—unless of course the gardener's boy found the box of cocaine and gave it to his younger sister who took a boat to Marseilles and went into a bad house; one of those particularly bad houses for which Marseilles is justly famous." See *The Letters of Noel Coward*, ed. Barry Day (New York, 2007), p. 71.

[6]   *The Daily Telegraph*, "Clinic Reports busiest month for abortions," Sarah Womack, (9 September 2007).

[7]   I am indebted for this précis of the disappointments of the pro-life movement to Decca Aitkenhead and her piece in *The Independent*, "New Lease of LIFE the Struggle for Life," (11 August 1996).

Conservative MP for Chelmsford presented a Bill to amend the 1967 Act by requiring one of the certifying doctors necessary for an abortion to be a consultant gynecologist or doctor appointed by the Secretary of State. The government appointed the Lane Commission to investigate how the 1967 Act was working and reported back that it was working fine. In 1979, when Scottish Conservative and Unionist MP John Corrie presented a Bill designed to prohibit most abortions after 20 weeks and to limit the legal grounds for all abortions, the Trades Union Congress sided with the pro-abortion lobby and soundly defeated it. In 1980, another bill was introduced to prohibit abortions after 24 weeks but it failed. In 1982, Lord Robertson of Oakridge introduced a Bill similar to the one introduced in 1979 but the Lords rejected it. In 1987, Peter Bruinvels, Governor of the Church Commissioners, who once suggested that the BBC might wish to consider changing its name to the "Bolshevik Broadcasting Corporation," failed to pass a Bill that would have given putative fathers the right to be consulted before an intended abortion. In 1988, David Alton attempted and failed to establish a time limit of 18 weeks for abortions. In 1989, various Bills were presented attempting to amend the certifying clauses of the 1967 Bill and they were all rejected. In 1990, the Human Fertilisation and Embryology Act extended the scope of the 1967 Bill by permitting the use of human embryos for experimental purposes, establishing an upper limit of 24 weeks, instead of 28 weeks, for most abortions, and permitting abortion in certain multiple pregnancies. It also legalized the abortion up to birth of special-needs children—what Hitler called "*Vernichtung lebensunwerten Lebens*"—the "destruction of life not worth living."[8] Unlike our own culture of death, the Nazi variety could at least call a spade a spade.

The 1990 Bill had predictable consequences. In October 2004, a British high court judge ruled that Charlotte Wyatt, born three months premature, should be euthanized without further efforts to save her life. She had brain damage and injuries to her lungs and kidneys. Despite her condition, her parents requested doctors to continue doing everything possible to save the child. But, presiding Justice Hedley, citing "fundamental principles that undergird our humanity," ruled that her doctors should be allowed to discontinue treatment and, in effect, kill the child. In his ruling, Hedley said that it was in Charlotte's best interests that she be allowed to die "a good death."[9]

Nuala Scarisbrick categorically rejected this arrogant logic. "Doctors have no training in measuring 'quality of life.' No one has. It is a subjective and dangerous catch-phrase of the eugenics and euthanasia lobbies. Doctors have a duty to care for all patients, not to pick and choose according to some arbitrary and unscientific criterion."[10] American readers know the ruthlessness of such legal highhandedness from the Terry Schiavo case in which another court ruled against the quality of another life. Again, Nazi parallels are unavoidable. In 1936, a correspondent wrote to the SS paper, *Das Schwarze Korps* demanding that

---

[8]   Readers interested in comparative infamy might wish to see what Ian Kershaw has to say about the relationship between Nazi Germany's euthanasia program and the roots of the Holocaust. See Chapter 6, "Licensing Barbarism" in Ian Kershaw, *Hitler. Nemesis: 1936-1945* (New York, 2000), pp. 231-279. See also Scarisbrick, *Let There Be Life* (Leamington Spa), p. 30.

[9]   See *Lifenews.com*, "British High Court Judge Approves Euthanasia of Baby Charlotte," Steven Ertelt (8 October 2004).

[10] See *Lifenews.com*, "UK Judge Won't Overturn Order for Baby Charlotte's Euthanasia" (21 April 2005).

a law be passed permitting consenting parents to euthanize their mentally retarded children. The paper published the letter alongside commentary agreeing with the correspondent: a law should be passed "that helps nature to its right." If anyone should object that there is no morally defensible right to euthanize the mentally retarded, the paper "countered by saying that there was a hundred times less right to defy nature by keeping alive 'what was not born to life.' "[11] This makes Hedley's case better than his preening himself on bringing about "a good death." If he had simply said that the mentally retarded must be killed because they are unfit to live, his ruling would still have been contemptible but at least it would have been honest.

The high-handedness of the pro-abortion establishment is only matched by its callous irresponsibility. In January 2004, the British government announced that two women died after taking the abortion drug RU 486, also known as mifepristone. Melanie Johnson, a British public health official, admitted that the Committee on Safety of Medicines had received information about two women who died after taking the abortion drug, which was made legal in the UK in 1991. Despite this information, Johnson disputed whether the abortion drug was to blame. "The reporting of a suspected adverse drug reaction does not necessarily mean that the drug was responsible," Johnson told *The Daily Telegraph.* "Many factors, such as the medical condition that is being treated, other pre-existing illnesses or other medications might have contributed." Nuala Scarisbrick was unconvinced. "I hope this tragic news serves as a warning to women about just how dangerous these powerful drugs are. If these women had not taken RU 486 they would probably be alive now—and so would their babies. There is such a conspiracy of silence about the after-effects

---

[11]   I. Kershaw, *Hitler. Nemesis: 1936-1945.* (New York, 2000), p. 257.

of abortion that LIFE is sure that there are other deaths that have not been reported."[12] As of December 2007, the RU 486 drug has killed thirteen women worldwide (in addition to the two in the UK) and injured more than 1,100 women in the United States alone.[13]

Before looking at how LIFE is responding to this conspiracy of silence, it might be helpful to define terms. The British Abortion Act, passed in 1967, differs from the American ruling in Roe v. Wade in that it does not give a woman the right to have an abortion: it protects from prosecution a doctor who performs an abortion if two doctors attest that an abortion should be induced. Grounds for "lawful" abortion include (a) risk to the life of the mother; (b) to prevent grave permanent injury to the physical or mental health of the mother; (c) risk or injury to the physical or mental health of the mother greater than if the pregnancy were terminated; (d) risk of injury to the physical or mental health of existing (i.e. born) children; (e) substantial risk of the child being born seriously handicapped; (f) in an emergency, to save the mother 's life; (g) in an emergency, to prevent grave permanent injury to the physical or mental health of the mother.[14]

If a central claim of the 1967 Act is that "lawful" abortion promotes the health and well-being of pregnant women, Prof. Scarisbrick has been sedulous in calling attention to the various ways in which abortion, far from promoting, threatens the health and well-being of preg-

---

[12] *The Daily Telegraph*, "Revealed: two women die after taking controversial new abortion pill," by M. Day and S. Bisset (17 January 2004) and *Lifenews.com*, "Brit. Gov: Two Women Died After Taking RU 486," Steven Ertelt (19 January 2004).

[13] *LifeNews.com*, "British Physicians Oppose Government Plan for Abortions at Doctors' Offices" (30 December 2007).

[14] LIFE Student Fact Pack.

nant women. In his most recent book, *Let There Be Life* (2007), which gives an excellent overview of the British pro-life movement, Prof. Scarisbrick describes the many studies that have been conducted by academics in Britain and America demonstrating the link between abortion and breast cancer (ABC), a link which Prof. Joel Brind continues to highlight in lectures throughout Britain and the US. Recently, LIFE invited Prof. Brind to their 2007 National Conference, where he showed how 26 of the 32 studies conducted from around the world connected the ABC link. For those who may not know the medical facts surrounding the issue, there are two main points that need to be grasped regarding the ABC link, as Prof. Scarisbrick points out:

> First, it is now widely accepted that a full-term pregnancy, especially if followed by breastfeeding and especially if this is the first pregnancy, provides protection against breast cancer in later years. So, if a woman or girl has her first pregnancy "terminated" she forgoes that protection. Subsequent full-term pregnancy may make good the loss in part, but her defences have been weakened. But that is not all. Studies from around the world suggest that she will have increased the risk of attack, especially if hers is a nulliparous abortion, that is, if she had no full-term pregnancy previously. Since the majority of abortions in Britain are nulliparous, abortion must be playing a part in the alarming and steady increase in the incidence of breast cancer since the late 1970s ... [Secondly], there is a clear biological explanation of the ABC link. In early pregnancy a huge surge in estrogen levels causes the cells of the breast to proliferate. Later in pregnancy these cells differentiate to enable them to produce milk. If this differentiation does not occur the cells become vulnerable to carcinogens. This will happen if the child is born

very prematurely. It does not happen if the abortion
is spontaneous.[15]

Despite this cogent evidence, the Royal College of Obstetricians and Gynecologists (RCOG) continues to argue that
there are no links whatever between abortion and breast
cancer: the evidence is "inconclusive." When LIFE called
attention to the links in 2006, RCOG responded by refusing
even to concede the possibility of such links and argued
instead that rises in the incidence of breast cancer rates were
attributable to obesity, menopause and binge-drinking,
"without," as Prof. Scarisbrick notes, "any statistical evidence" or "biological explanation."[16] The RCOG is equally
dismissive of studies linking abortion and mental illness.

Faced with such continual stonewalling, Prof. Scarisbrick sent off a letter to the president of the College asking
him to say, whether, "in view of the mounting evidence of
the damage which induced abortion can do to women's
minds and bodies, the College continues to believe that a
doctor can still authorize the operation on the ground that
continuance of the pregnancy would involve risk to the
mental health of the woman greater than if the pregnancy
were terminated." This put the president in a well-de-
served dilemma and as yet he has not responded. In a press
release dated November 26, 2007, Prof. Scarisbrick got to
the heart of the matter:

> Ninety-Five percent of abortions are done on the
> ground that they are safer for the mother than going
> to term and having their babies. But there is now
> overwhelming evidence from all over the world that
> induced abortion is a significant risk factor for
> breast cancer, infertility and subsequent premature
> delivery, and that abortion can leave a terrible legacy

---

[15]   J. J. Scarisbrick, *Let There Be Life* (Leamington Spa, 2007), p. 28.
[16]   Ibid., 29.

of guilt, grief, anger, and self-hatred among women. Post-abortion trauma is now a major women's disease. Studies from around the world show that rates of suicide, binge drinking, depression and self-harm are much higher among abortive than non-abortive women. In view of all this, we have asked the president of the RCOG to give a clear ruling on whether a doctor can still confidently authorize or perform one on the ground that it would be better for the mother's physical or mental health than going to term. This is an urgent question. Why will he not answer it?[17]

Why indeed. Such stonewalling is not a British monopoly. In the United States, the Guttmacher Institute, which describes itself as committed to "Advancing sexual and reproductive health worldwide through research, policy analysis and public education," touts the safety of abortion with blithe disregard for the available evidence. Aptly enough, this pseudo-scientific pressure group is the research arm of Planned Parenthood. Indeed the institute was founded by Alan Guttmacher, President of Planned Parenthood from 1962 to 1974 and Vice-President of the American Eugenics Foundation. Readers who go to the institute's website will see that the references attached to the assertions below are uniformly bogus. Women suffering the known ill effects of abortion must read such assertions and seethe.

> Exhaustive reviews by panels convened by the U.S. and British governments have concluded that there is no association between abortion and breast cancer. There is also no indication that abortion is a risk factor for other types of cancer.

---

[17]   LIFE press release (26 November 2007).

> In repeated studies since the early 1980s, leading
> experts have concluded that abortion does not pose
> a hazard to women's mental health.[18]

Prof. Scarisbrick gives an equally telling example of how
British pro-abortionists confront the cause of life. When
David Alton initiated a debate in the House of Lords on the
link between abortion and breast cancer, "he encountered
an angry, almost hysterical refusal even to consider the
question."[19] If the issue at sake were not so vital, there would
be something comical about die-hard lords behaving so
petulantly but alas it is not funny. There is not only something irrational but something *anti-rational* about the
opponents of life. "This, then," as Prof. Scarisbrick observes,
"is abortionism. It cannot engage in reasoned debate. It is
incoherent. It can offer only slogans, assertions, and old
myths. It evades and fudges. It will break with the rules of
scientific research and not hesitate to ignore norms of
academic discourse."[20]

The British government is no more accountable. Rather
than acknowledge that there is considerable evidence that
abortions are harmful to women, it is now suggesting that
nurses be permitted to perform abortions in doctors'
private offices—a plan which the *Daily Telegraph* reported
only fourteen percent of the 2,175 doctors polled support-
ed.[21] The notion that the abortion crisis can be addressed
by making access to abortion easier is an *idée fixe* with the
men and women who rule the British welfare state. Some

---

[18] See the website of the Guttmacher Institute: http://www.guttmacher.org/
pubs/fb_induced_abortion.html.

[19] *Let There Be Life*, p. 29. See also Hansard (Lords) 29 October, cols.
335 ff.

[20] Ibid., p. 29.

[21] *The Daily Telegraph*, "Doctors say no to abortions in their surgeries," Sophie Borland. (29 December 2007).

will always see depravity as the driving force behind official abortionism, but one cannot underestimate the role that incompetence plays in policies of such persistent folly.

Yet, to judge from recent developments, things may be looking up for British pro-lifers. Now that the demographics of the UK are changing—with more and more pro-life immigrants from both Roman Catholic and Islamic traditions recasting the ethnic and religious mix of the country—it is questionable whether the government will be able to continue to make abortionism a centerpiece of the NHS. Some are even suggesting that the UK's surging Catholic population might force the government to jettison the Act of Settlement (1701), which bars Roman Catholics from ascending the throne.[22] Clearly a sea change is taking place in the once squarely Protestant state and this could very well capsize the abortion lobby. The government's latest push to get nurses to perform abortions at a time when more and more doctors refuse to perform them is emblematic of this. Now one in five GPs describe themselves as anti-abortion.[23] As more doctors from Catholic and Muslim backgrounds enter the NHS, that number is likely to increase.

Several years ago, Ann Furedi, now chief executive of the pro-abortion Pregnancy Advisory Service branded the

---

[22] *The Times*, "A Catholic tremor through Westminster," William Rees-Mogg (27 December 2007). Securing a Protestant succession to the throne, according to John Cannon, editor of *The Oxford Companion to British History*, "was done by putting aside more than 50 Catholic claimants and offering the succession to Sophia, electress of Hanover, a granddaughter of James I ... The clauses devoted to the succession [included in the Act of Settlement] took effect in 1714, when Queen Anne was succeeded by Sophia's son George I." See *The Oxford Companion to British History* (Oxford, 1997), p. 854.

[23] *The Daily Telegraph*, "Doctors say no to abortions in their surgeries," Sophie Borland (29 December 2007).

British pro-life movement an unqualified failure: "They've lost the mainstream argument about whether abortion is right or wrong, and they know it." [24] Yet now such gloating seems delusive. To see which side is winning the debate we should look at the arguments made regarding permitting nurses to perform abortions. For the pro-abortion lobby the benefits of involving nurses in the destruction of the unborn are self-evident: Dr Kate Guthrie, a spokesman for the Royal College of Obstetricians and Gynecologists, told *The Daily Telegraph*: "This is logical. As long as standards of care are high and as long as there is adequate training, competent clinical staff should carry out early surgical abortions and it does not matter if it is a doctor or a nurse." Michaela Aston, of LIFE, responded by putting Dr. Guthrie's logic into context: Permitting nurses to perform abortions

> would be a retrograde step and contrary to wide-spread public opinion which believes that we should be finding ways of reducing the number of abortions, not making them more readily available. This is a far cry from what was intended when the Abortion Act was introduced. This would trivialize abortion, trivialize the huge decision that it is for women and trivialize the suffering many women experience after their abortions.

Anthony Ozimic of the Society for the Protection of Unborn Children, made the pro-life case more bluntly still:

> Do nurses really want to perform abortions, the killing of innocent human beings? The pro-abortion lobby claims that so-called safe, legal abortion was necessary to safeguard women's health yet, having achieved legal abortion, it now wants to remove

---

[24] *The Independent*, "New Lease of LIFE the Struggle for Life," Decca Aitkenhead (11 August 1996).

safeguards by getting nurses to do doctors' dirty
work for them.

For years, the pro-abortion lobby has caricatured proponents of life as lunatic. But who is lunatic here: the side that
recommends a policy that will increase the already huge
number of abortions by making them easier or the side that
recognizes that Britain has a serious abortion problem on
its hands, which trivializing abortion will only exacerbate?[25]

Certainly, there is no lack of evidence that the rate and
the incidence of abortion continues to soar. According to
an article in the *Daily Mail*, "The Health Service is spending
around £1million a week providing repeat abortions. Critics
said figures revealed yesterday show thousands of women
are using the procedure as a form of contraception. It is not
unknown for some women to have seven, eight or even nine
terminations in their lifetime. According to the statistics,
single or unmarried women account for five out of every
six repeat terminations. Around a third of all abortions
carried out in England and Wales are repeats. The figures
will fuel the debate on whether abortions, which cost the
NHS up to £1,000 each, are being sanctioned as more of a
lifestyle choice than a medical requirement."[26] How allowing nurses to carry out the grisly business of abortion will
stem this bloody tide is not clear.

What is clear is that by exposing the false logic of the
pro-abortion lobby, Prof. Scarisbrick and LIFE are waking
the British up to the evils of abortion. At the same time, by
offering vital housing, counseling, pro-life education,
hospice care, and other maternity services they provide
practical life-affirming options that truly redound to the

---

[25] *Daily Telegraph*, "Let nurses carry out abortions, experts say," C.
Hall (27 March 2007).

[26] *Daily Mail*, "NHS spends £1m a week on repeat abortions," D.
Martin (13 May 2012).

good health and well-being of mothers-to-be and their newborns. In accomplishing his work with the help of talented American pro-lifers, Prof. Scarisbrick is also renewing the pro-life special relationship, which, *pace* Furedi, mops up the floor with the proponents of the culture of death, who are as muddled as they are unconscionable.

Walker Percy

6

IDENTITY, ABORTION AND
WALKER PERCY

But thou, O Lord,
Aid all this foolish people; let them take
Example, pattern: lead them to thy light.

Alfred Lord Tennyson, "St. Simeon Stylites" (1842)

When a number of books appeared about the American Civil War in the late 1950s, including Bruce Catton's *This Hallowed Ground* and Shelby Foote's *Shiloh!*, the novelist Walker Percy (1916-1990) accounted for the resurgent interest in the long-ago war by surmising that "the whole country, the South included, is just beginning to see the Civil War whole and entire for the first time. The thing was too big and too bloody, too full of suffering and hatred, too closely knit into the fabric of our meaning as a people, to be held off and looked at—until now."[1]

Percy wrote that four years before the publication of his first novel, *The Moviegoer* (1961), which won the National Book Award. Nevertheless, it broached a theme that he would tackle again and again in his six novels: how we understand our identity and claim the inheritance of our fallen nature. In his last novel, *The Thanatos Syndrome* (1987), he returned to this theme by considering what he called "the widespread and ongoing devaluation of human life ... under various sentimental disguises: 'quality of life,'

---

[1] W. Percy, *Signposts in a Strange Land*, ed. P. Samway, SJ (New York, 1991), p. 72.

'pointless suffering,' 'termination of life without meaning,' etc."[2] The form of devaluation with which Percy became most concerned was abortion, though he also decried the related rise of eugenics, euthanasia and pharmacology. Since Western society is still waging its war against unborn children, it is not possible to step back and grasp its full import. Still, Percy recognized that the grounds of that war are, in their way, as inscrutable as the grounds for the Civil War. "Not being a historian, I don't know what the cause of that war was," he admitted in one article, "whether it was fought purely and simply over slavery, or over states' rights, or, as Allen Tate once said, because the South didn't want to be put in Arrow collars."[3] What Percy did know was that the war against unborn children could not be understood simply as a political debate between the pro-life and the pro-abortion—if anything, it was the consequence of an even bigger and bloodier division than the one that pitted Yankees against Confederates. Beginning with Descartes in the seventeenth century, this philosophical division tore body and soul asunder and saddled the Western mind with misconceptions about the nature of human identity that have left it reeling ever since. Percy described the circumstances in which these misconceptions arose with chilling accuracy.

> The old modern age has ended. We live in a post-modern as well as a post-Christian age … It is post-Christian in the sense that people no longer understand themselves, as they understood themselves for some fifteen hundred years, as ensouled creatures under God, born to trouble, and whose salvation depends upon the entrance of God into history as Jesus Christ. It is post-modern because

---

2   *SSL*, p. 394.
3   *SSL*, pp. 79-80.

the Age of Enlightenment with its vision of man as
a rational creature, naturally good and part of the
cosmos, which itself is understandable by natural
science—this also has ended. It ended with the
catastrophes of the twentieth century. The present
age is demented. It is possessed by a sense of
dislocation, a loss of personal identity, an alternat-
ing sentimentality and rage, which, in an individual
patient, could be characterized as dementia. As the
century draws to a close [Percy wrote this in 1990],
it does not have a name, but it can be described. It
is the most scientifically advanced, savage, democratic, inhuman, sentimental, murderous century
in human history ..."[4]

Here was the philosophical context from which abortion
on demand sprang and Percy recognized it with prophetic
clarity. But since no one can read of Percy's life without
seeing that his solicitude for unborn children had deep
roots in his personal history, it is necessary to say something of his life.

Walker Percy was descended from English Protestant
planters who arrived in the South in the eighteenth
century and settled in Birmingham, Alabama. What
distinguished these forbears most, besides their commitment to their families and their neighbors, was their
constitutional melancholy. In 1917, Percy's grandfather
shot himself in the heart with a twelve-gauge shotgun.
Some of his depression might have been attributed to the
loss of two of his children in infancy but what the root
cause was no one could ascertain. Then, in 1929, family
history repeated itself when Percy's father shot himself
with a twenty-gauge shotgun, the coroner later finding
that the bullet had gone clear through the top of his head.
Walker Percy was twelve at the time. Two years later,

---

[4]   *SSL*, p. 309.

Percy's mother died when she drove her car off a bridge, an apparent accident which Percy always suspected had been intentional. At fourteen, Percy, together with his two younger brothers, was an orphan.

However, his life was transformed when his father's brother, William Alexander Percy, adopted him and his two brothers. Uncle Will was a highly regarded lawyer, poet, and autobiographer who introduced Percy not only to a number of living Southern writers but to Shakespeare, Keats, Brahms, and Beethoven—not to mention Richard Wagner, whom Percy always found insufferable, though, as he recalled, he "was dragged every year, to hear Flagstad sing Isolde."[5]

Uncle Will gave Percy more than culture: he gave the gift of himself. "To have lived in Uncle Will's house," Percy later wrote, "was nothing less than to be informed in the deepest sense of the word. What was to be listened to, dwelled on, pondered over for the next thirty years was of course the man himself, the unique human being, and when I say unique I mean it in the most literal sense: he was one of a kind: I never met anyone remotely like him."[6]

The sense of the vulnerability of children, as well the powerful uniqueness of the individual, would profoundly inform Percy's understanding of the abortion issue. The deep understanding of honor that he learned from his uncle would also equip him to see through the tawdry sophistry that paved the way for legalized abortion. Writing in 1973, the year of Roe v. Wade, Percy remarked of his beloved uncle, "Certainly, nothing would surprise him about the collapse of the old moralities; for example, the so-called sexual revolution, which he would more likely define in less polite language as alley-cat morality. I

---

[5]   *SSL*, p. 55.
[6]   *SSL*, p. 55.

can hear him now: 'Fornicating like white trash is one thing, but leave it to this age to call it the new morality.' "[7] Just as importantly, William Percy impressed upon his nephew how vital it was for the individual to understand his true identity. In his brilliant biography of Percy, *Pilgrim in the Ruins*, written two years after Percy's death in 1992, Jay Tolson quoted a passage from William Percy's autobiography, *Lanterns on the Levee* (1941), which goes to the heart of this issue of identity.

> Here among the graves in the twilight I see one thing only, but I see that thing clear. I see the long wall of a rampart somber with sunset, a dusty road at its base. On the tower of the rampart stand the glorious high gods, Death and the rest, insolent and watching. Below on the road stream the tribes of men, tired, bent, hurt, and stumbling, and each man alone. As one comes beneath the tower, the High God descends and faces the wayfarer. He speaks three slow words: "Who are you?" The pilgrim I know should be able to straighten his shoulders, to stand his tallest, and to answer defiantly: "I am your son."[8]

In a moving piece about his Uncle Will's three-story Greek revival house in Greenville, Mississippi, which included an elevator, a huge automatic phonograph known as the Capehart, a rambling garden and a voluminous library, Percy fondly recalled the literary guests who came to visit his uncle, including Carl Sandburg and Langston Hughes, and the unforgettable vitality of the place. Yet he concluded his reminiscence by observing, "It's all gone now, house, garden, Capehart, Beethoven quartets in Victor 78s

---

[7]   *SSL*, p. 58.

[8]   W. A. Percy, *Lanterns on the Levee*, quoted in J. Tolson, *Pilgrim in the Ruins: A Life of Walker Percy* (New York, 1992), p. 17.

... In its place, I think are neat condo-villas of stained board-and-batten siding. Only the garden wall remains. I am not complaining. I have what he left me, and I don't mean things."⁹ Here was proof that the most important lesson that Uncle Will had to impart—the lesson of the inestimable value of the individual before and beyond the graveyard—was not lost on his brilliant nephew.

Percy attended the University of North Carolina at Chapel Hill with his best friend Shelby Foote, the celebrated historian, to whom he was introduced by William Percy in 1930. The correspondence between Percy and Foote records the vital critical support that they gave each other as they mined their respective quarries. When Percy was unsure about whether he was on the right track with regard to *The Thanatos Syndrome*, which caused him more artistic trouble than all his books put together, Shelby offered welcome reassurance. "I say you should write what you want to write about anyone anywhere," he wrote his anxious friend. "That dreadful things can come from do-gooding.... who's going to argue with that?"¹⁰

After graduating from college, Percy trained as a medical doctor at Columbia, where he received his medical degree in 1941. After conducting an autopsy as an intern at Bellevue, he contracted TB. While convalescing at the Trudeau Sanatorium in the Adirondacks, he read Kierkegaard and Dostoevsky, both of whom led him to question whether science could usefully pronounce on the insistent mysteries of life. In 1947, Percy converted to Catholicism and decided to pursue a career in writing rather than medicine. A year earlier, he married Mary Bernice Townsend, a medical technician, with whom he

⁹   *SSL*, p. 66.
¹⁰ *The Correspondence of Shelby Foote and Walker Percy*, ed. J. Tolson (New York, 1997), p. 294.

raised two daughters in Covington, Louisiana, which he once described as lying "in the green heart of green Louisiana, a green jungle of pines, azaleas, camellias, dogwood, grapevines, and billions of blades of grass."[11] So many, in fact, that he once told his wife that if she would allow it, he would prefer finishing his days "in a French cottage on Rue Dauphine [in New Orleans] with a small paved patio and not a single blade of glass." Just short of his 74th birthday, in 1990, Percy died of prostate cancer. He is buried on the grounds of St. Joseph's Abbey in St. Benedict, Louisiana. Although stylistically highly differentiated, all of his novels, *The Moviegoer, The Last Gentleman* (1966), *Love in the Ruins* (1971), *Lancelot* (1977), *The Second Coming* (1980) and *The Thanatos Syndrome* pivot on what for Percy was the all-important question of human identity.

When it came to his own identity, Percy recognized that it was nurtured and sustained by his Catholic faith. Indeed, he was particularly grateful for the dividends his faith paid his art. One hears so much of how faith constrains the artist: it is refreshing to hear Percy reaffirm how it liberated him. "I have the strongest feeling that, whatever else the benefits of the Catholic faith, it is of a particularly felicitous use to the novelist. Indeed, if one had to design a religion for novelists, I can think of no better. What distinguishes Judeo-Christianity in general from other world religions is its emphasis on the value of the individual person, its view of man as a creature in trouble, seeking to get out of it, and accordingly on the move. Add to this ... the sacraments, especially the Eucharist, which, whatever else they do, confer the highest significance upon the ordinary things of this world, bread, wine, water, touch, breath, words, talking, listening—and what do you have?

---

[11] *SSL*, p. 9.

You have a man in a predicament and on the move in a real world of real things, a world which is a sacrament and a mystery: a pilgrim whose life is a searching and finding."[12] One of the reasons why Percy is such a good novelist is that he fully recognizes how well fitted the novel is to explore man's moral pilgrimage.

Percy's faith also reinforced something of the patrician steel in his make-up. In a witty piece called "Why Are You a Catholic?" (1990), he recalled how outré his conversion seemed in a region not known for its fondness for the Church of Rome. When the subject of religion came up in the South, he pointed out, it did so usually as a challenge or a provocation or even an insult.

> It happens once in a while, for example, that one finds oneself in a group of educated persons, one of whom, an educated person of a certain sort, may venture such an offhand remark as: *Of course, the Roman Catholic Church is not only a foreign power but a fascist power.* Or when in a group of less educated persons, perhaps in a small town barbershop, one of whom, let us say an ex-member of the Ku Klux Klan—who are not bad fellows actually, at least hereabouts, except when it comes to blacks, Jews, and Catholics—when one of them comes out with something like *The Catholic Church is a piece of shit* then one feels entitled to a polite rebuttal in both cases, in the one with something like, "Well, hold on, let us examine the terms power, foreign, fascist—" and so on, and in the case of the other, responding in the same tone of casual barbershop bonhomie with, say, "Truthfully, Lester, you're something of a shit yourself, even for white trash—" without in either case disrupting, necessarily, the general amiability.[13]

---

[12]   *SSL*, p. 369.

Such independence of mind would stand Percy in good stead when he went up against the pro-abortion Establishment. But even before the abortion issue arose, he knew that he was not in sync with the consensus of most of his contemporaries, especially those in the medical and academic fields. In a 1987 interview he described what he called the "Holy Office of the Secular Inquisition."

> It is not to be confused with "secular humanism," because ... it is anti-human. Although it drapes itself in the mantle of the scientific method and free scientific inquiry, it is neither free nor scientific. Indeed it relies on certain hidden dogma where dogma has no place. I can think of two holy commandments which the Secular Inquisition lays down for all scientists and believers. The first: In your investigations and theories, thou shalt not find anything unique about the human animal even if the evidence points to such uniqueness. Example: Despite heroic attempts to teach sign language to other animals, the evidence is that even the cleverest chimpanzee has never spontaneously named a single object or uttered a single sentence. Yet dogma requires that, despite traditional belief in the soul or the mind, and the work of more recent workers like Peirce and Langer in man's unique symbolizing capacity, Homo sapiens be declared to be not qualitatively different from other animals. Another dogma: Thou shalt not suggest that there is a unique and fatal flaw in Homo sapiens or indeed any perverse trait that cannot be laid to the influence of Western civilization. Example: An entire generation came under the influence of Margaret Mead's *Coming of Age in Samoa* and its message: that the Samoans were an innocent, happy, and Edenic people until they were corrupted by missionaries

---

[13] *SSL*, pp. 305-306.

and technology. That this turned out not to be true,
that indeed the Samoans appear to have been at
least as neurotic as New Yorkers has not changed
the myth or the mindset.[14]

Here, Percy delineated the baleful outlines of political
correctness, which became liberal orthodoxy in the last
years of the twentieth century. Denying civilized man's
unique symbolizing capacity, while at the same time
inflating the capabilities of savages and chimpanzees,
constituted more than bad anthropology. They were an
assault on the identity of the uniquely human, an assault
which opened the door to the inhumanity of abortion and
euthanasia, eugenics and embryo experimentation. In an
irresponsible science depriving the individual of his true
identity, Percy saw a trend that is still with us; indeed, it
only grows more widespread. "It is easy to criticize the
absurdities of fundamentalist beliefs like 'scientific crea-
tionism,' " he wrote, "but it is also necessary to criticize
other dogmas parading as science and the bad faith of
some scientists who have their own dogmatic agendas to
promote under the guise of 'free scientific inquiry.' Scientific inquiry should, in fact, be free ... If it is not, if it subject
to this or that ideology, then do not be surprised if the
history of the Weimar doctors is repeated. [It was the
leading doctors of Germany's Weimar Republic before the
rise of Hitler and the Nazis who pioneered modern
methods of euthanasia.] Weimar leads to Auschwitz. The
nihilism of some scientists in the name of ideology or
sentimentality and the consequent devaluation of individual human life lead straight to the gas chamber."[15]

For at least some of this point, Percy was clearly
indebted to Flannery O'Connor. In an essay about a young

---

[14]   *SSL*, pp. 395-396.
[15]   *SSL*, pp. 395-396.

girl, a splendid candidate for abortion, who had been born with one eye, the other having been surgically removed, and a most unsightly tumor on the side of her face, O'Connor observed how "One of the tendencies of our age is to use the sufferings of children to discredit the goodness of God ... Ivan Karamazov cannot believe as long as one child is in torment; Camus' hero cannot accept the divinity of Christ, because of the massacre of the innocents. In this popular pity, we mark our gain in sensibility and our loss in vision. If other ages felt less, they saw more, even though they saw with the blind, prophetical, unsentimental eye of acceptance, which is the eye of faith. In the absence of this faith now, we govern by tenderness. It is a tenderness, which, long since cut off from the person of Christ, is wrapped in theory. When tenderness is detached from the source of tenderness, its logical outcome is terror. It ends in forced-labour camps and in the fumes of the gas chamber."[16]

In a letter to a friend in 1973, Percy also deplored this ersatz pity when he related how he "heard Dr. Christiaan Barnard say that what mattered was quality of life and that therefore euthanasia could be defended. Dick Cavett asked him who made the decision about the quality of life. Said Doc Barnard: 'Why the doctors.' Now the time may come when this society does dispose of human life according to pragmatic principles, and come to look upon the 'sacredness of life' as either an empty slogan or an outgrown religious dogma. But if that happens—as in fact it already has—we're in deep trouble ... I think we're much more like the Nazis and Dachau than we imagine ..."[17]

---

[16] F. O'Connor, "A Memoir of Mary Ann" from *Mystery and Manners: Occasional Prose*, ed. Sally and Robert Fitzgerald (New York, 1969), pp. 226-227.

[17] J. Tolson, *Pilgrim in the Ruins: A Life of Walker Percy* (New York,

To some, this might seem needlessly provocative: in making the pro-life case against abortion, many in the pro-life camp argue, we must employ measured arguments. But, as a matter of fact, Weimar did lead to Auschwitz, and the sentimental nihilism that Percy accurately sees as the legacy of Weimar has led in our own time not only to the gas chamber but to the abortion clinic, to destruction and degradation of human life on a scale that the Nazis would have thought scarcely possible. Comparing our own abortion industry, which has killed over 70 million unborn children, to the Nazi death camps and their murder of six million Jews may be provocative but it is accurate, even though it must be remembered that we have been infinitely more successful in doing away with our "life not worth living" than the Nazis were with theirs.

Percy was never afraid to call attention to the link between our ideologically perverted science and our readiness to connive at the killing of unborn children. In an op-ed piece that appeared in *The New York Times* in 1981, Percy noted an irony that the liberal enemies of the Roman Church and unborn children continue to miss. "The con ... perpetrated by some jurists, some editorial writers, and some doctors," he wrote, "is that since there is no agreement about the beginning of human life, it is therefore a private religious or philosophical decision and therefore the state and the courts can do nothing about it ... There is a wonderful irony here. It is this: the onset of individual life is not a dogma of the Church but a fact of science ... Please indulge the novelist if he thinks in novelistic terms. Picture the scene. A Galileo trial in reverse. The Supreme Court is cross-examining a high-school biology teacher and admonishing him that of course it is only his personal opinion that the fertilized

1992), p. 439.

human ovum is an individual human life. He is enjoined not to teach his private beliefs at a public school. Like Galileo he caves in, submits, but in turning away is heard to murmur, *'But, it's still alive!'*[18] After this unanswerable sally, it is perhaps no wonder that the editors of the staunchly pro-abortion *Times* refused even to acknowledge a Letter to the Editor that Percy sent off in 1988 at the behest of J. B. McFadden and the *Human Life Review*.

> Perhaps the most influential book published in German in the first quarter century was entitled *The Justification of the Destruction of Life Devoid of Value*. Its co-authors were the distinguished jurist Karl Binding and the prominent psychiatrist Alfred Hoche. Neither Binding nor Hoche had ever heard of Hitler or the Nazis. Nor, in all likelihood, did Hitler ever read the book. He didn't have to. The point is that the ideas expressed in the book and the policies advocated were not the product of Nazi ideology but rather of the best minds of the pre-Nazi Weimar Republic-physicians, social scientists, jurists and the like who with the best secular intentions wished to improve the lot, socially and genetically of the German people—by getting rid of the unfit and the unwanted. It is hardly necessary to say what use the Nazis made of these ideas. I would not wish to be understood as implying that the respected American institutions I have named are similar to corresponding pre-Nazi institutions. But I do suggest that once the line is crossed, once the principle gains acceptance—juridically, medically, socially—that innocent human life can be destroyed for whatever reason, for the most admirable socio-economic, medical or social reasons—then it does not take a prophet to predict what will happen next, or if not

---

[18] *SSL*, p. 342.

next then sooner or later. At any rate a warning is
in order. Depending on the disposition of the
majority and the opinion polls—now in favor of
allowing women to get rid of unborn and unwanted
babies—it is not difficult to imagine an electorate
or a court ten years, fifty years from now, who
would favor getting rid of useless old people,
retarded children, anti-social blacks, illegal His-
panics, gypsies, Jews ... Why not?—if that is what
is wanted by the majority, the polled opinion, the
polity of the time.[19]

This can be read as something of an abstract of *The
Thanatos Syndrome*, in which Dr. Tom More, a lapsed
Catholic psychologist uncovers a scheme by colleagues
and local Louisiana businessmen to introduce behavior-
altering chemicals into the water supply. "What would you
say, Tom," one of the book's smarmier characters asks,
while listening to a waltz by Strauss, "if I gave you a magic
wand you could wave ... and overnight you could reduce
crime in the streets by eighty percent?"[20] Dr. More recognizes that the sexual behavior of his psychiatric patients
has become arrestingly pongid; their ability to remember
facts has increased exponentially; and their overall deport-
ment has become suspiciously sedate where once it was
impulsive and even violent. The novel's narrative is given
over to Dr. More's discovery of the precise nature of the
scheme, including its effects, which are revealed to be at
once uproariously funny and revoltingly evil. In his crisis
of conscience, Dr. More clearly recalls another More,
though Percy spares his hero the grisly consequences that
befell Henry VIII's Lord Chancellor. In this superbly
satirical novel, which merits a place beside the most

[19] *SSL*, pp. 350-351.
[20] W. Percy, *The Thanatos Syndrome* (New York, 1987), p. 91.

unsettling salvos of Swift and Orwell, Percy takes devastating aim at our arrogant contempt for the laws of God, and in the process skewers pharmacology, euthanasia, eugenics, and abortion. In one representative passage, Dr. More describes the forces of change that have made poor Freud *passé*.

> I am the only poor physician in town, the only one who doesn't drive a Mercedes or a BMW. I still drive the Chevrolet Caprice I owned before I went away. It is a bad time for psychiatrists. Old-fashioned shrinks are out of style and generally out of work. We, who like our mentor Dr. Freud believe there is a psyche, that it is born to trouble as the sparks fly up, that one gets at it, the root of trouble, the soul's own secret, by venturing into the heart of darkness, which is to say, by talking and listening, mostly listening, to another troubled human for months, years—we have been mostly superseded by brain engineers, neuropharmacologists, chemists of the synapses. And why not? If one can prescribe a chemical and overnight turn a haunted soul into a bustling little body, why take on such a quixotic quest as pursing the secret of one's very soul?[21]

The most effective character in the book is the one about whom Percy was most dubious.[22] Father Smith, a Catholic

---

[21]   *TS*, 13.

[22]   *The Correspondence of Shelby Foote and Walker Percy*, ed. Jay Tolson (New York, 1997), p. 297. Percy wrote to his good friend, Shelby Foote, apropos this crucial character, "I deeply appreciate your taking time with that peculiar novel—and pinpointing what's wrong. Well, you're right. Every time Fr. Smith opens his mouth he, I, is in trouble. What I do is cut, cut, cut. Thanks to you, I'll probably cut him again. You can't get away with a Fr. Zossima these days and probably shouldn't." But, as it happened, Percy retained a good portion of the section featuring Father Smith and although many reviewers, including Terrence Rafferty of *The New*

whiskey priest has secluded himself atop a fire tower to protest his society's instruments of death. In modeling Smith after St. Simon Stylites, Percy was calling attention to a form of holy protest which might not be favored by monks today but which is perfectly suitable for what Percy calls our "time of apocalypse." For some sense of what Percy might have had in mind in creating Father Smith, we can revisit what the historian Edward Gibbon had to say about the original St. Simon.

When Gibbon considered the rise of monasticism in the fifth century in his *Decline and Fall of the Roman Empire,* he made a distinction between vulgar and ascetic Christians. The former were easy-going latitudinarians who "reconciled their fervent zeal and implicit faith with the exercise of their profession, the pursuit of their interest, and the indulgence of their passions." But the ascetics were different. "Inspired," as Gibbon says, "by the savage enthusiasm which represents man as criminal .... they seriously renounced the business and pleasures of the age; abjured the use of wine, of flesh, and of marriage; chastised their body, mortified their affections, and embraced a life of misery, as the price of eternal happiness." For Gibbon, the most patently absurd and indeed pernicious of these "wretched votaries" was Simon Stylites, a Syrian shepherd, born about 390, whose "aerial penance" required his residing sixty feet above ground on a pillar six feet in diameter, where he fasted and prayed for over thirty years. "A prince, who should capriciously inflict such tortures would be deemed a tyrant," Gibbon contended. For him,

---

Yorker, had no idea what Percy was up to in creating the Smith character, the decision to retain a good portion of him was artistically sound. For a précis of Rafferty's objections to the novel, see J. Tolson, *Pilgrim in the Ruins: A Life of Walker Percy* (New York, 1992), pp. 469-470.

"This voluntary martyrdom ... gradually destroyed the sensibility both of the mind and body; nor can it be presumed that the fanatics who torment themselves are susceptible of any lively affection for the rest of mankind. A cruel, unfeeling temper has distinguished the monks of every age and country: their stern indifference, which is seldom mollified by personal friendship, is inflamed by religious hatred; and their merciless zeal has strenuously administered the holy office of the Inquisition."[23]

We have already seen what Percy thought of the "Holy Office of the Secular Inquisition." But what is interesting about Gibbon's attack on St. Simon is that he depicted him as "cruel," "unfeeling," and "inflamed by religious hatred"—all the attributes that accurately describe the proponents of abortion, despite the attempts of their publicists to make them appear paragons of niceness. What makes Father Smith such an enjoyable character is that he is the antithesis of nice. And yet while he is by no means a model ascetic, he is anything but cruel or unfeeling. Here Percy draws an important distinction between sentimental and true goodness. Father Smith may be a whiskey priest, he may even have wavered in his faith, but, unlike the advocates of human engineering, he is a compassionate sinner. He cares for the unfortunate; he does not spurn the misbegotten. In one bravura section of the novel, entitled *Father Smith's Confession*, which has a kind of Dostoyevskian boldness, Father Smith abjures the do-gooding sanctimony assumed by so many in the pro-abortion camp without ever compromising his claim to authentic virtue. In one memorable passage, recalling his rocky stint as a parish priest, he admits: "Frankly, I found my fellow men, with few exceptions, either victims

---

[23] E. Gibbon, *The Decline and Fall of the Roman Empire* (Folio Society, 1986), IV, p. 302.

or assholes. I did not exclude myself. The only people I got along with were bums, outcasts, pariahs, family skeletons, and the dying." Here is a St. Simon that wonderfully confounds Gibbon's caricature of sanctity, as well as his Enlightenment contempt for the mysterious, the flawed, the uniquely human. At the end of the novel, when Father Smith makes another impromptu speech, another confession, the sympathetic reader can be excused for listening to him as to a prophet, even though his creator was highly skeptical of novelists making any claim to prophecy.

> Listen to me, dear physicians, dear brothers, dear Qualitarians, abortionists, euthanasists! Do you know why you are going to listen to me? Because every last one of you is a better man than I and you know it! And yet you like me. Every last one of you knows me and what I am, a failed priest, an old drunk, who is only fit to do one thing and to tell one thing. You are good, kind, hardworking doctors, but you like me nevertheless and I know that you will allow me to tell you one thing—no, ask one thing—no, beg, one thing of you. Please do this one favor for me, dear doctors. If you have a patient, young or old, suffering, dying, afflicted, useless, born or unborn, who you for the best of reasons wish to put out of his misery—I beg only one thing of you, dear doctors! Please send him to us. Don't kill them! We'll take them—all of them! Please send them to us! I swear to you, you won't be sorry. We will all be happy about it! I promise you, and I know that you believe me, that we will take care of him, her—we will even call on you to help us take care of them!— and you will not have to make such a decision. God will bless you for it

and you will offend no one except the Great Prince
Satan, who rules the world. That is all.[24]

In a letter to one of his early mentors, the Catholic
Southern novelist, Caroline Gordon, Percy made an
extraordinary admission. "Your letter has the effect of
encouraging me to expectorate a chronic bone-in-the-
throat. It has to do with my main problem as a fiction
writer. Actually, I do not consider myself a novelist but a
moralist ... My spiritual father is Pascal (and/or Kierkegaard). And if I also kneel before the altar of Lawrence and
Joyce and Flaubert, it is not because I wish to do what they
did, even if I could. What I really want to do is to tell
people *what they must do and what they must believe if
they want to live.*"[25]

Some have seen this as proof that Percy confused art
with didacticism and was simply too honest to try to
conceal the fact. But this is not the case. It is true that his
fiction is profoundly moral. It is also true that he wrote to
confront what he regarded as the spiritual desolation of
post-modern man—man after Auschwitz. But that these
moral and spiritual objects somehow vitiated his art is
false. For Percy, fiction, if undertaken honestly, was a kind
of science in its own right, a way of knowing. Of course,
he could be witheringly critical of the presumed reach of
this form of knowing. "The novelist, I have come to
believe," he declared in one essay, "is only good for one or
two things—and they do not include being prophetic or
making broad pronouncements about the decline of the
West, the nature of evil, loneliness, God, and so forth. The
embarrassment of the novelist is that after he masters his
one or two tricks, does his little turn, some readers tend
to ascribe this success to a deeper wisdom—whereas it is

---

[24] *TS*, p. 361.

[25] *Life of Walker Percy*, p. 300.

probably the very condition of his peculiar activity that he doesn't know anything else—which is to say that a person who asks a novelist anything about life and such, how to live, is in a bad way indeed."[26] Yet in the same essay he balanced this grudging assessment with a more generous measure of the practical good that the novelist can accomplish.

> If the novelist's business is, like that of all artists, to tell the truth, even when he is making up a story, he had better tell the truth no matter how odd it is, even if the truth is a kind of upside-downness. And if it is the novelist's business to look and see what is there for everyone to see but is nonetheless not seen, and if the novelist is by his very nature a hopeful man—he has to be hopeful or he would not bother to write at all—then sooner or later he must confront the great paradox of the twentieth century: that no other time has been more life-affirming in its pronouncements, self-fulfilling, creative, autonomous, and so on—and more death-dealing in its actions. It is the century of the love of death.[27]

The Thanatos Syndrome is not flawless. Its satire can be scattershot and its structure wobbly. Nonetheless, what makes it a book that will continue to be read long after its critics have handed in their dinner-pails is that it provides a kind of epidemiology of abortion, an inquest into the roots of the inhumanity of abortion, which one finds nowhere else. Percy does "look and see what is there for everyone to see but is nonetheless not seen." And he locates the cause for this failure of vision in our ignorance of our true identity. In 1974, in an unpublished paper given

---

[26]   *SSL*, p. 155.

[27]   *SSL*, p. 162.

to a group interested in mental health at Louisiana State University, Percy wondered "whether or not we have settled for a view of man which is grossly incoherent by any scientific canon. That is to say, I wonder if through a kind of despair or through sheer weariness we have not given up the attempt to put man back together again, if indeed he was ever whole, or whether man isn't like Humpty Dumpty, who fell off the wall three hundred years ago, or rather was pushed by Descartes, who split man into body and mind ..."[28] Percy was making these speculations a year after Roe v. Wade. Of course, long before, Nazi Germany had already set up the death camps. But forty years after Roe v. Wade, in America, it is clear that Humpty Dumpty's fall has had more than philosophical consequences. An incoherent view of man has resulted in contempt for man, which, in turn, has resulted in the murder of 70 million unborn children. The Nazis justified their destruction of what they called "life not worth living" by appeals to racial purity; we justify ours by appeals to 'reproductive rights,' 'quality of life,' 'family planning,' 'compassion.' Father Smith, the messenger of God, helps Dr. More understand the meaning of these appeals: "You are a member of the first generation of doctors in the history of medicine to turn their backs on the oath of Hippocrates and kill millions of old useless people, unborn children, born malformed children, for the good of man-kind—and to do so without a single murmur from one of you.[29] Not a single letter of protest in the august *New*

---

[28]   *SSL*, p. 115.

[29]   Since the hagiographer John Coulson refers to St. Simon of Stylites as "God's messenger," the same epithet might be fairly accorded his fictional protégé Father Smith. Coulson's portrait of St. Simon is more reliable than Gibbon's. According to Coulson, "Far from being an uncouth fanatic," Simon "showed unruffled patience, gentleness and kindness to all ... He preached daily to crowds. The

England Journal of Medicine..."[30] Scientists could scarcely
diagnose a problem to which they so blindly contributed.
Percy, a scientist who was also a novelist, saw that the
problem was in us: not only in our fallen nature but in our
Pelagian refusal to acknowledge that fallen nature, in our
denial of the Cross. Yet, Percy never counseled despair.
As he has Father Smith assure Dr. More: "if you keep hope
and have a loving heart and do not secretly wish for the
death of others, the Great Prince Satan will not succeed
in destroying the world ... Perhaps the world will end in
fire and the Lord will come—it is not for us to say. But it
is for us to say ... whether hope and faith will come back
into the world."[31]

This is the voice of conscience, the voice of God in our
hearts that also informs Pope John Paul II's brilliant
encyclical, *Evangelium Vitae* (1995), which so much of
Percy's work anticipates. There, Pope John Paul II laid out
not only the satanic assault that is underway against the
sanctity of life but the barriers to the conscience necessary
to defend life against that assault.

> The eclipse of the sense of God and of man inevi-
> tably leads to a practical materialism, which breeds
> individualism, utilitarianism and hedonism. Here
> too we see the permanent validity of the words of
> the Apostle: "And since they did not see fit to

Bedouin from the surrounding deserts flocked to hear him.
Persians, Armenians, and Georgians thronged around him ...
Emperors consulted him and asked his prayers. The Emperor
Marcian visited him incognito. He persuaded the Empress Eudoxia
to abandon the Monophysites. To St. Geneviève, remote in the far
west, he sent greetings and a request for prayers. The Stylite thus
proved himself God's messenger..." See *The Saints: A Concise
Biographical Dictionary,* ed. J. Coulson (New York, 1958), p. 417.

[30]   *TS,* p. 127.

[31]   *TS,* p. 365.

acknowledge God, God gave them up to a base mind and to improper conduct" (Rom 1:28). The values of being are replaced by those of having. The only goal which counts is the pursuit of one's own material well-being. The so-called "quality of life" is interpreted primarily or exclusively as economic efficiency, inordinate consumerism, physical beauty and pleasure, to the neglect of the more profound dimensions-interpersonal, spiritual and religious-of existence.

This is the secular context in all of Percy's work, but John Paul II captures its essence by identifying the peculiar logic of its despair. "In such a context suffering, an inescapable burden of human existence but also a factor of possible personal growth, is 'censored,' rejected as useless, indeed opposed as an evil, always and in every way to be avoided. When it cannot be avoided and the prospect of even some future well-being vanishes, then life appears to have lost all meaning and the temptation grows in man to claim the right to suppress it." And it is in this context, too, that the body's dignity is not only dishonored but rejected, a theme to which Percy gave horrifying expression in *The Thanatos Syndrome,* though John Paul II shows that, in this respect, reality can be just as horrifying as fiction. Here, he itemizes the fruits of our dehumanizing secularism with unsparing precision.

Within this same cultural climate, the body is no longer perceived as a properly personal reality, a sign and place of relations with others, with God and with the world. It is reduced to pure material-ity: it is simply a complex of organs, functions and energies to be used according to the sole criteria of pleasure and efficiency. Consequently, sexuality too is depersonalized and exploited: from being the sign, place and language of love, that is, of the gift of self and acceptance of another, in all the other's richness as a person, it increasingly becomes the occasion and instrument for self-assertion and the selfish satisfaction of personal desires and instincts. Thus the original import of human sexuality is distorted and falsified, and the two meanings, unitive and procreative, inherent in the very nature of the conjugal act, are artificially separated: in this way the marriage union is betrayed and its fruitfulness is subjected to the caprice of the couple. Procreation then becomes the "enemy" to be avoided in sexual activity: if it is welcomed, this is only because it expresses a desire, or indeed the intention, to have a child "at all costs", and not because it signifies the complete acceptance of the other and therefore an openness to the richness of life which the child represents.

Then, again, John Paul II reminded his readers that such evil misapprehensions are not inconsequential. "In the materialistic perspective described so far, interpersonal relations are seriously impoverished. The first to be harmed are women, children, the sick or suffering, and the elderly. The criterion of personal dignity—which demands respect, generosity and service—is replaced by the criterion of efficiency, functionality and usefulness: others are considered not for what they 'are', but for what they 'have, do and produce.' This is the supremacy of the strong over the weak."[32]

It is also the Nietzschean ethos against which Percy makes his defense of the sanctity of life. "Once the line is crossed," he wrote to the *New York Times*, in a letter which that contemptible paper refused to publish, "once the principle gains acceptance—juridically, medically, socially—that innocent human life can be destroyed for what-

---

[32]   Pope John Paul II, *Evangelium Vitae*, 42-43.

ever reason, for the most admirable socio-economic, medical or social reasons—then it does not take a prophet to predict what will happen next, or if not next then sooner or later. At any rate a warning is in order."[33] And for Percy, the form that warning took was an appeal to conscience, about which John Paul II is pellucid.

> It is at the heart of the moral conscience that the eclipse of the sense of God and of man, with all its various and deadly consequences for life, is taking place. It is a question, above all, of the individual conscience, as it stands before God in its singleness and uniqueness. But it is also a question, in a certain sense, of the "moral conscience" of society: in a way it too is responsible, not only because it tolerates or fosters behaviour contrary to life, but also because it encourages the "culture of death", creating and consolidating actual "structures of sin" which go against life. The moral conscience, both individual and social, is today subjected, also as a result of the penetrating influence of the media, to an extremely serious and mortal danger: that of confusion between good and evil, precisely in relation to the fundamental right to life. A large part of contemporary society looks sadly like that humanity which Paul describes in his Letter to the Romans. It is composed "of men who by their wickedness suppress the truth" (1:18): having denied God and believing that they can build the earthly city without him, "they became futile in their thinking" so that "their senseless minds were darkened" (1:21); "claiming to be wise, they became fools" (1:22), carrying out works deserving of death, and "they not only do them but approve those who practise them" (1:32). When conscience, this bright lamp of the soul (cf. Mt 6:22-23), calls "evil good

---

[33] *SSL*, p. 349.

and good evil" (Is 5:20), it is already on the path to the most alarming corruption and the darkest moral blindness.

And yet all the conditioning and efforts to enforce silence fail to stifle the voice of the Lord echoing in the conscience of every individual: it is always from this intimate sanctuary of the conscience that a new journey of love, openness and service to human life can begin.[34]

---

[34]   Pope John Paul II, *Evangelium Vitae*, 42-44.

William Wilberforce

7

WILLIAM WILBERFORCE AND THE FIGHT FOR LIFE

I N THE SPRING of 1797, after devoting ten years of his life to the abolition of the slave trade, William Wilberforce (1759–1833) saw his hopes for abolition once again dashed when the House of Commons voted to refer the issue to the colonial legislatures, which had no interest in even considering the case for abolishing the trade. "In these circumstances," William Hague writes in his brilliant biography of the Great Liberator, "the responsibility resting on Wilberforce's shoulders to sustain the parliamentary battle, develop new lines of attack against wily opponents, and keep the hopes of abolitionists alive at a time when so many had lost heart or abandoned the fight, was immense. Looked at from the standpoint of the twenty-first century, Wilberforce's ultimate victory was inevitable. But looked at from the standpoint in April 1797, after such a string of deeply discouraging defeats, the workings of inevitability would have seemed very hard to discern."[1] In the past, Wilberforce had steadfastly done battle with the economic interests behind the trade, which were considerable, concentrated as they were in England's three wealthiest ports, Liverpool, Bristol and London. But now a new obstacle arose. In the wake of the French Revolution, there was widespread fear that slave rebellions might break out in British-owned colonies in the West

---

[1]   William Hague, *William Wilberforce, The Life of the Great Anti-Slave Trade Campaigner* (New York, 2007), p. 268.

Indies, and the consensus in Parliament and the country was that if abolition were granted these colonies would become ungovernable. So, once again, abolition was scuttled. Yet despite these setbacks, despite the obloquy of contemporaries, Wilberforce and his abolitionists stood their ground. Among his many detractors was no less a figure than Lord Nelson, who spoke for many when he said,

> I was bred in the good old school and taught to appreciate the value of our West Indian posses-sions ... and neither in the field nor the senate shall their just rights be infringed, while I have an arm to fight in their defense or a tongue to launch my voice against the damnable doctrine of Wilberforce and his hypocritical allies.[2]

As it happened, Wilberforce's allies were a good part of what made him so redoubtable. They numbered the Prime Minister William Pitt, who may not have shared his friend's religious convictions but knew that slavery was untenable; John Newton, a former slave trader turned preacher, most of whose youth had been given over to blaspheming and buccaneering; Granville Sharp, a philan-thropist and self-taught scholar, who brought to the abolition campaign the same prodigious determination that he brought to teaching himself Greek and Hebrew; and Thomas Clarkson, the Cambridge-educated pam-phleteer who spent years amassing evidence to document the deep criminality of slavery. In 1787, after putting himself to school to Sharp and Clarkson, Wilberforce was convinced that abolition was a cause that

---

[2]   Nelson, quoted in R. Adkins and L. Adkins, *The War for All the Oceans: From Nelson at the Nile to Napoleon at Waterloo* (London, 2007), pp. 181–182.

> speaks for itself ... As soon as I had arrived thus far
> in my investigation of the slave trade, I confess to
> you, so enormous, so dreadful, so irremediable did
> its wickedness appear that my own mind was
> completely made up for the abolition ... Let the
> consequences be what they would, I, from this time
> determined that I would never rest until I had
> effected its Abolition.[3]

But another reason why Wilberforce prevailed against his opponents was that there was a core of indomitable resilience in the man, which was only reinforced by adversity. The source of this was his strong faith in God, which also left him in no doubt of the eventual triumph of truth. This is why the legacy of William Wilberforce and his campaign to abolish slavery offers such useful encouragement to those committed to protecting life against the scourge of abortion. In long-term campaigns, foot soldiers, no less than commanders need to be reassured that others have prevailed over comparably formidable odds. By revisiting Wilberforce's life and the strategies he pursued, against opposition which must often have seemed insuperable, we can put some of the challenges and setbacks faced by the pro-life movement in some historical perspective.

William Wilberforce was born in the High Street, Hull on the 24th of August 1759, the "year of victories," when the British gained Canada and India for what would become their slave-riddled empire. Wilberforce's paternal grandfather had made the family fortune in the Baltic trade. He was also prominent in local affairs, being mayor of Hull twice and owning landed estates in Yorkshire. His father, Robert Wilberforce, fully expected his son to carry on the family trade. In his wonderfully readable account

---

[3]   Hague, p. 141.

of Wilberforce's life, Hague describes the mercantile hubbub in which Wilberforce grew up. In front of the family's elegant red-brick house, built in the late seventeenth century, carts and wagons were loaded and unloaded with the goods brought back from ships; but

> Such a scene outside the front door of the house was only a hint of what would be happening at the bottom of the garden at the rear; ships were moored to each other as they waited, sometimes for weeks, for customs officers to give permission to unload; when they did so the staithes would groan beneath the weight of imported goods— timber, iron, ore, yarn, hemp, flax and animal hides from Scandinavia, manufactured goods and dyes from Germany and Holland, and, as the century wore on and a growing population took to importing its food, large quantities of wheat, rye, barley, beans, peas, beef, pork and butter, all to be washed down with thousands of gallons of Rheinish Hoch.[4]

Apropos Wilberforce's early life, Hague writes that "Those looking for clues to his later choices in life will not find them in his infant years." And yet, there are clues. The family business impressed on Wilberforce the evil of preventing human beings from exercising their God-given talents. In this, he would have entirely seen Adam Smith's point that slavery was wrong, among other reasons, because "A person who can acquire no property, can have no other interest but to eat as much, and to labour as little as possible. Whatever work he does beyond what is sufficient to purchase his own maintenance can be squeezed out of him by violence only and not be any interest of his own."[5] And Wilberforce's own personal fragility convinced him of the

---

[4] Hague, p. 3.

[5] A. Smith, *The Wealth of Nations* (Penguin, 1999), Bk. III, Ch. II, pp. 488–489.

preciousness of God's gift of life. Later, he was grateful, as he said, "that I was not born in less civilized times, when it would have been thought impossible to rear so delicate a child." So, from an early age, Wilberforce was aware of both the potential and the vulnerability of human life—which he would apply again and again to his campaign to end slavery.

In October, 1776, Wilberforce entered St. John's College, Cambridge, where, as he wrote, "I was introduced on the very first night of my arrival to as licentious a set of men as can well be conceived. They drank hard, and their conversation was even worse than their lives ... often indeed I was horror-struck at their conduct."[6] What Wilberforce encountered at Cambridge was unexceptional: Oxbridge in the eighteenth century was notorious for hard drinking and dissipation. Still, even without these distractions, Wilberforce might still have had a hard time applying himself to his books. His considerable personal fortune, as well as his native generosity—he always had a great Yorkshire pie on offer in his rooms—gave him a prominence in his college that was fatal to diligence. An undergraduate who lived nearby recalled, "By his talents, his wit, his kindness, his social powers, his universal accessibility, and his love of society, he speedily became the centre of attraction to all the clever and the idle of his own college and of other colleges."[7] Despite his social success, he graduated full of regret that he had not lived under a more "strict and wholesome regimen." Nevertheless, in at least one respect, these years foreshadowed his later abolitionist career. However physically unimposing— he was only five foot four and never without his beribboned eyeglass, which was necessary for his poor eyesight—Wilberforce demonstrated at Cambridge the same

---

6   Hague, p. 21.

7   Hague, p. 23.

ability to gather talented companions around him that he would demonstrate in London when he led the campaign against slavery.[8] There was something life-affirming, something infectiously good and giving about the man, and others gravitated to him.

Disinclined to join the family business, Wilberforce chose instead to go into politics and at the age of twenty-one, in September 1780, he became MP for Hull. In the House of Commons, he befriended William Pitt, who often stayed with Wilberforce in his house in what was then still rural Wimbledon, which he inherited from his uncle. Pitt and Wilberforce personified the attraction of opposites. Pitt was shy and haughty, Wilberforce outgoing and ingenuous. There were other complementary differences. As Hague points out, "Pitt had plentiful connections, widespread recognition and a famous name, but no money; Wilberforce had exactly the opposite."

After Wilberforce helped Pitt become prime minister in 1783, at the age of twenty-four, their political alliance was forged, which, with few exceptions, remained intact for the rest of their careers. Nevertheless, Pitt's support for abolition, while helpful, was no more instrumental in securing its political and legal success than Reagan's and Bush's support for the pro-life movement was instrumental in its success. The abolitionists had to establish and maintain widespread, popular support for some sixty years against constant attacks before they could pass abolition in parliament. Winning the debate over slavery in the country as a whole was always more important than

---

[8]   See Sydney Smith to Lord Holland, 21 August 1827 in *The Letters of Sydney Smith,* ed. N. C. Smith (Oxford, 1953), 1, p. 469. "Little Wilberforce is here, and we are great friends. He looks like a little Spirit running about without a body, or in a kind of undress with only half a body."

securing powerful parliamentary connections, useful though those were.

Here pro-lifers can take heart. All the major polls attest that the majority of Americans side with life: 51% of Americans self-identify as pro-life; (Gallup Poll, June 2009); 61% of Americans say abortion is an important issue and 52% think it is too easy to obtain an abortion in America (Rasmussen Survey, June 2009); and 62% of Americans want more limitations placed on abortions, while only 36% believe abortion should be generally available (CBS Poll, June 2009).[9] President Obama and the pro-abortion lobby are working aggressively to roll back protections for the unborn against the will of the majority, which does not bode well for the sustainability of their assault on the innocent.[10]

In 1784 and 1785, in the course of making two continental tours, Wilbeforce underwent a deep conversion experience. As he described it, he was so conscious of his

---

[9]   I am indebted to Phil Lawler for these statistics, a staunch New York pro-lifer.

[10]   According to Lawler (4 August 2009): "The Senate health care bill contains a hidden provision that matches the provisions of the Freedom of Choice Act; it would preempt any state law hindering a woman's access to 'essential health services'—again, a phrase that includes abortion services. Federal health care legislation would overturn the following state laws: 42 states have physician-only laws that limit the practice of abortion; 32 states follow the funding limitations of the federal Hyde Amendment (no taxpayer funding of abortions); 27 states have abortion clinic regulations to protect the health of women; 30 states have informed-consent laws (women receive information about fetal development, fetal pain or the causal link between abortion and breast cancer; or are offered an ultrasound exam); 24 states require a 24-hour waiting period before an abortion; 36 states require some kind of parental involvement: either parental notice (11 states) or parental consent (25 states); and at least 5 states have funded abortion alternatives (pregnancy centers, prenatal assistance, adoption promotion)."

"great sinfulness in having so long neglected the unspeakable mercies of my God and Saviour ... that for months I was in a state of the deepest depression ... nothing which I have ever read in the accounts of others exceeded what I felt." Aware that he had the power to do both great good and great evil, he confided to his Diary in 1785, "I must awake to my dangerous state, and never be at rest till I have made my peace with God." An old school friend suggested that Wilberforce read Philip Doddridge's *The Rise and Progress of Religion in the Soul* (1745), which laid out many of the signal elements of evangelical Christianity. "You will wish to commence a hero in Christ," Doddridge exhorted his reader, "opposing with a vigorous resolution the strongest efforts of the powers of darkness, the inward corruption of your own heart, and all the outward difficulties you may meet with in the way of your duty, while in the cause and in the strength of Christ you go on conquering and to conquer."[11]

Once imbued with his newfound evangelical faith, Wilberforce was unsure whether he should remain in public life. It was Pitt, the least religious of men, who disabused his friend of the notion that public life and faith were somehow incompatible. "You confess that the character of religion is not a gloomy one," Pitt wrote, "and that it is not that of an enthusiast. But why then this preparation of solitude, which can hardly avoid tincturing the mind either with melancholy or superstition? ... Surely the principles as well as the practice of Christianity are simple, and lead not to meditation only but to action."[12]

The next man to whom Wilbeforce went for advice made an even more decisive impression on him. John Newton was a former slave trader from Liverpool turned

---

[11]   Doddridge quoted in Hague, 74.
[12]   Pitt to Wilberforce, quoted in Hague, 86.

preacher whose conversion to evangelical Christianity only gradually opened his eyes to the evils of slavery, but once his eyes were opened he became a fierce anti-slave campaigner, principally from prominent pulpits in the City of London. Newton's autobiography went through ten British and nine American editions before the end of the eighteenth century, and he was at work on a book of hymns with William Cowper before the poet descended into his final madness. He was also the author of such well-known hymns as "How sweet the name of Jesus sounds," "Approach, my soul, the mercy seat," and "Amazing Grace." The advice that Newton gave Wilberforce on whether or not he should remain in public life stayed with him for the rest of his life: "You meet with many things which weary and disgust you," he told the young convert, "which you would avoid in more private life. But then they are inseparably connected with your path of duty. And though you cannot do all the good you wish for, some good is done, and some evil is probably prevented, by your influence and that of a few gentlemen in the House of Commons, like-minded with yourself ... You are not only a Representative for Yorkshire. You have the far greater honour of being a Representative for the Lord, in a place where many know him not, and an opportunity of showing them what are the genuine fruits of that religion which you are known to profess."[13]

Once in receipt of this counsel, from a man who suffered piercing remorse for his own past folly, Wilberforce finally saw his way clear. "My walk is a public one," he wrote; "my business is in the world; and I must mix with the assemblies of men, or quit the post which Providence has assigned me."[14] Were Wilberforce living in our own

---

[13] Newton quoted in Hague, 263.
[14] Wilberforce quoted in Hague, 165.

time, he would have seen something of his own Christian commitment to the fight for life in Father Richard John Neuhaus, who once reminded a gathering of *Human Life Review* supporters: "We are signed on for the duration and the duration is the entirety of the human drama, for the conflict between what John Paul II calls the culture of life and the culture of death is a permanent conflict. It is a conflict built into a wretchedly fallen and terribly ambiguous human condition."[15] There was nothing Pelagian about that prediction.

In 1797, while at Bath, Wilberforce met and married Barbara Ann Spooner, the daughter of a Birmingham banker and his wife, Barbara Gough-Calthorpe, the sister of the first Lord Calthorpe. Scarcely two weeks after Barbara sought Wilberforce out for spiritual advice, he proposed. Their strong, devoted marriage produced seven children, two of whom, Robert Isaac and Henry William, were converted to Roman Catholicism by John Henry Newman. Not surprisingly, Wilberforce delighted in children and was an attentive and playful father, never allowing his political activities to stint his family life.

Wilberforce's long-gestating concern for the plight of slaves took definite shape in 1787, when, under what came to be known as the "Wilberforce oak" in Holwood, Kent, Pitt convinced his good friend to make the anti-slave cause his own. On May 12, 1789 Wilberforce made his formal entry into the parliamentary campaign against slavery by giving a three-and-one-half hour speech detailing the effects of the trade on Africa and the middle passage. Edmund Burke, after hearing the speech, praised it as "most masterly, impressive and eloquent. Principles so admirable, laid down with so much order and force, were

---

[15]   See "Building a Culture of Life" by R. J. Neuhaus, in *Human Life Review* (Winter, 2001).

equal to anything he had ever heard of in modern oratory; and perhaps were not excelled by anything to be met with in Demosthenes."[16] A brief excerpt will bear Burke out:

> Policy ... Sir, is not my principle, and I am not ashamed to say it. There is a principle above everything that is political; and when I reflect on the command which says: "Thou shalt do no murder," believing the authority to be divine, how can I dare to set up any reasonings of my own against it? And, Sir, when we think of eternity and of the future consequences of all human conduct, what is there in this life that should make any man contradict the dictates of conscience, the principles of justice, the laws of religion, and of God? Sir, the nature and all the circumstances of this trade are now laid open to us; we can no longer plead ignorance, we cannot evade it, it is now an object placed before us, we cannot turn aside so as to avoid seeing it; for it is brought now so directly before our eyes that this House must decide, and must justify to all the world, and to their own consciences, the rectitude of the grounds and principles of their decision.[17]

In his biography of Wilberforce, Hague confirms something J. P. McFadden, the founder of the *Human Life Review* knew instinctively: that in any campaign to win hearts and minds "eloquence matters."

Speaking of the eighteenth-century House of Commons, Hague writes how "the readiness of Members of Parliament to switch their votes according to the arguments presented, particularly on an issue such as this

---

[16]   Burke quoted in Hague, p. 184.

[17]   From Wilberforce's speech in the House of Commons (12 May 1789). See *The Folio Book of Historic Speeches*, ed. Ian Pindar (London, 2007), p. 90.

[abolition] where party loyalties did not apply, placed a premium on oratorical ability and persuasiveness which the subsequent rise of disciplined parties would ultimately render almost worthless. The prospect that a speech could make all the difference to the result generally brought out the best in those speaking, just as the disconnection between the quality of the speech and the result obtained would by the twentieth century produce speeches of stultifying morbidity. In the House of Commons of 1789, eloquence mattered." [18] Hague is right and wrong here. He is right about the influential role that good oratory could play in the eighteenth-century House of Commons (though not always—Burke rarely swayed votes); but he is wrong when he claims that "disciplined parties" now render such eloquence "almost worthless." As J. P. McFadden realized, good arguments can always sway votes in and out of legislative assemblies. Hague himself has proven an effective orator as Foreign Secretary. For a good laugh but also a good sense of his adroit debating skills, see Hague's speech (when he was Shadow Foreign Secretary) on Blair's former spin doctor, Peter Mandelson.

It is true that Wilberforce's great speech on slavery did not carry the day when it was first delivered. After Wilberforce urged that abolition would improve the lot of the slaves already in the West Indies and refuted the economic case for continuing the trade, none of the twelve points he introduced in favor of abolition were debated: the interests in support of the trade were so rich and powerful that the question of abolishing it was thought unworthy of debate. On this dispiriting note was joined the fight for life that would consume Wilbeforce for the next fifty years. But it was fitting that he should have started the campaign with such a burst of inspired oratory because when Britain did

---

[18]   Hague, pp. 177–178.

finally abolish the slave trade (1806) and then slavery itself (1833), it was largely as the result of the steady stream of speeches, pamphlets, books and letters that Wilberforce and his abolitionist companions addressed to the moral suffrage of their contemporaries.

One difference between slavery and abortion is that the latter, as a legal practice, is relatively new. Until the late twentieth century, no society had ever imagined that there could be a legal right for women to kill their babies. Slavery's roots, on the other hand, ran deep. From the beginning of recorded time slavery was the inveterate corollary of conquest. After noting the prevalence of this barbarity among Babylonians, Egyptians, Greeks, and Romans, the historian J. M. Roberts had to admit that "The ancient world rested civilization on a great exploitation of man by man; if it was not felt to be very cruel, this is only to say that no other possible way of running things was conceivable."[19] The curious guiltlessness that attached to slave-owning survived well into the nineteenth century. In his classic study, *Southern Honor*, Bertram Wyatt-Brown writes of how "Yankees, most especially the anti-slavery reformers, expected Southern contrition for wrongs of the slaveholding past, but that would have violated Southern honor ..." He quotes Cornelia Spencer, a matron from South Carolina and survivor of the Civil War. "I believe," she wrote at the end of the war, "that the South sinned. Sinned in her pride, her prosperity, her confidence. Sinned in the way she allowed a few fanatical demagogues to precipitate her into the war ... But strongly as I feel all this, so strongly do I feel that, though we have fallen we shall rise again. God chastens whom He loves ... I would rather be the South in her humiliation than the North in her triumph."[20] Such impenitence was an impor-

---

[19]   J. M. Roberts, *History of the World* (Oxford, 1993), p. 49.

tant corollary of slave-owning, and it would make the abolition of slavery doubly difficult. This is why the evidence gathering of Sharp and Clarkson was so crucial: it revealed the full horrors of what the trade was about to people who had no direct experience with it. Agents in our own popular culture work to promote a similar guiltlessness about abortion, by involving the issue in what are now treated as the irresistible "rights of women," but it is dubious whether the attempt will ever entirely succeed. Natural law cannot be indefinitely flouted.

Slavery entered a new and accelerated phase with the emergence of the colonies of the New World, first in the Caribbean and then the American mainland, which were heavily reliant on slave labor. Initially, the Portuguese ruled the trade; then the Dutch; but, beginning in the eighteenth century, the French and English took it over, setting up their own trading posts along Africa's "slave coast." "Altogether," Roberts calculates, "their efforts sent between nine and ten millions of black slaves to the western hemisphere, 80 per cent of them after 1700. The eighteenth century saw the greatest prosperity of the trade; some six million slaves were shipped then. European ports like Bristol and Nantes built a new age of commercial wealth on slaving ... What has disappeared and can now never be measured is the human misery involved, not merely in physical hardship (a black might live only a few years on a West Indian plantation even if he survived the horrible condition of the voyage) but in the psychological and emotional tragedies of this huge migration."[21]

This calls to mind the 50 million plus biographies that should have enriched American history, which legalized

---

[20]   B. Wyatt-Brown, *Southern Honor: Ethics and Behavior in the Old South* (Oxford, 1982), pp. 28–29.

[21]   Roberts, p. 530.

abortion has made impossible. But what is remarkable about this shambles is how many continue to accept it. For an age that battens on self-recrimination—loathing itself for committing every imaginable injustice—it is odd how it never fails to absolve itself of the crime of abortion. When the history of this episode in deliberate moral blindness finds its historian, what a tale will be told of narcissism and heartlessness, bad faith and bad reasoning, guilt and brazen denial of guilt!

Slavery also inspired its fair share of callousness. After approving Sir John Hawkins' slave-trading expeditions, Elizabeth I hoped that no slaves would be taken against their will, for "that would be detestable and call down Heaven upon the undertakers."[22] Here was the deliberate blindness that animated so much collusion in the trade. Even when slave traders had first-hand proof of the misery they were causing, they tended to minimize it. One British captain described how "the men were put in irons and two shackled together, to prevent their mutiny or swimming ashore. The Negroes are so willful and loth to leave their own country that they have often leap'd out of canoes, boat and ship into the sea, and kept under water until they were drowned to avoid being taken up and saved ... they having a more dreadful apprehension of Barbados than we have of hell though, in reality, they live much better there than in their own country; but home is home."[23] Once on board, slaves who refused to eat were force fed or threatened with burning coals; mutinous slaves were flogged "till the poor creatures have not power to groan under their misery;" and female slaves were routinely raped. As John Newton testified, slave ships were "part bedlam and part brothel."[24] And

---

[22]   Hague, p. 116.

[23]   Hague, p. 124.

[24]   Hague p, 124.

yet he himself was living proof that men could feel remorse for conniving at such barbarity and join the good fight to stop it. "Amazing Grace, how sweet the sound/That saved a wretch like me/I once was lost but now am found/Was blind, but now, I see."

Many in the twenty-first century look down their noses at an eighteenth-century social order that could tolerate the inhumanity of slavery. As proof of that inhumanity they cite the Zong Massacre (1781), when Luke Collingwood, captain of the slave ship *Zong* set sail with over 400 slaves from Sao Tome in the Gulf of Guinea en route to Jamaica. After being blown off course, the ship was left without enough water for its enslaved cargo, so Collingwood and his officers proceeded to throw 133 sick and dying slaves overboard to enable the ship's Liverpool owners to avoid paying £30 a head insurance for each dead slave.[25]

The historian James Walvin sums up the massacre thus: "The Zong is an example of how men got away with murder and seems to illustrate the rapacious history of the Western world: an example of the callousness displayed by the dominant and powerful towards the lives of the oppressed and weak."[26] Wikipedia, the popular encyclopedia, corroborates Walvin:

> The term 'Zong Massacre' was not universally used at the time. It was usually called 'The Zong Affair,' the term 'massacre' being used mainly by those considered to be 'dangerous radicals'... At the time, the killing of slaves—individually or *en masse*—was not considered to be murder. In British law, the act was

---

[25] Hague, p. 137.

[26] J. Walvin, *The Zong: A Massacre, the Law and the End of Slavery* (New Haven, 2011), p. 208.

completely legal and could be admitted to the highest
court in the land, without danger of prosecution.

What Captain Collingwood and his officers did in the mid
Atlantic 228 years ago will never cease to horrify the
humane conscience. But it is striking that the legal murder
of abortion inspires no similar outrage. After all, we legally
dispose of unborn children at an infinitely higher rate and
with the same brisk callousness. Perhaps one day, when
the information age has disenthralled itself from the
culture of death, we will see an entry in Wikipedia for "The
Abortion Massacre," one that will read:

> At the time, the killing of unborn children—indi-
> vidually or *en masse*—was not considered to be
> murder. In British and American law, and indeed
> most law around the world, the act was completely
> legal and could be admitted to the highest court in
> the land without danger of prosecution...

Yet this analogy does not entirely hold true because
English law in the eighteenth century did *not* sanction the
murder of slaves or indeed the practice of slavery. Wikipedia, like most ventures involved in political correctness,
falsifies the historical record. In his magisterial history, *A
Polite and Commercial People: England 1727–1783*, Paul
Langford, Professor of Modern History at Lincoln College,
Oxford shows that the eighteenth-century English might
look the other way at the crime of slavery but they would
not degrade their law into sanctioning what they knew was
unsanctionable. Of course, Langford admits that abolitionists had their work cut out for them at a time when slavery
was such an integral part of England's growing empire but
he also shows that abolitionists did make progress,
however incremental.

The most notable victory of the early years was the
verdict of 1772 in the case of James Somerset, a
negro on whose behalf a group of London reformers sought legal redress. [Somerset was an escaped
slave who was recaptured and was being held
aboard a ship in London preliminary to being sold
in Jamaica.] Mansfield was a cautious judge in such
matters and was reluctant to offer a definitive
verdict in a test case of this kind. None the less he
eventually ruled that slavery was "so odious that
nothing can be suffered to support it but positive
law. Whatever inconveniences, therefore, may
follow from this decision, I cannot say this case is
allowed or approved by the law of England; and
therefore the black must be discharged." Though
he hedged his judgement about with qualifications,
it was widely taken to signify that slavery was illegal
in England itself.[27]

Here Lord Mansfield would not apply "positive law" to
repudiate natural law. His reasons for coming down on
the side of Somerset were not dissimilar to those that
impelled Bryon White to come down on the side of the
unborn child in Roe v. Wade, when he wrote in his
splendid dissent: "I find nothing in the language or history
of the Constitution to support the Court's judgment. The
Court simply fashions and announces a new constitutional
right for pregnant mothers [410 U.S. 222] and, with
scarcely any reason or authority for its action, invests that
right with sufficient substance to override most existing
state abortion statutes. The upshot is that the people and
the legislatures of the 50 States are constitutionally dissen-
titled to weigh the relative importance of the continued
existence and development of the fetus, on the one hand,

[27]   P. Langford, *A Polite and Commercial People: England 1727–1783*
(Oxford, 1989), p. 517.

against a spectrum of possible impacts on the mother, on the other hand. As an exercise of raw judicial power, the Court perhaps has authority to do what it does today; but, in my view, its judgment is an improvident and extravagant exercise of the power of judicial review that the Constitution extends to this Court."[28]

In going up against the slave trade, Wilberforce was going up against an entrenched economic interest. This was clear enough when General Tarleton, MP for Liverpool, the former officer of the American War of Independence, notorious for his bloodlust and womanizing, stood up in the House of Commons and announced, "There are in Liverpool alone above 10,000 persons completely engaged in the slave trade, besides countless numbers affected and benefited by it. I have received instructions from my constituents to oppose Mr. Wilberforce's intentions with all my power."[29] As John Ehrman, Pitt's biographer, remarked, slavery was "an integral part of the old Colonial System ... West Indian sugar needed support;

---

[28]   From *Roe v. Wade Supreme Court Decision*, Dissenting Opinion of Justice Byron White, (22 January 1973).

[29]   *History in Hansard 1803–1900: An Anthology of wit, wisdom, non-sense and curious observations to be found in the Debates of Parliament*, ed. S. King-Hall and A. Dewar (London, 1950), p. 9. For a lively portrait of Banastre Tarleton, the Oxford-educated son of a Liverpool merchant, see Christopher Hibbert, *Redcoats and Rebels: The War for America 1770–1781* (Folio Society, 2006), 272. "He was a captain of twenty-three when chosen by Clinton to command the British Legion, a mixed force of cavalry and light infantry. He was almost 'femininely beautiful,' extremely vain, argumentative and none too scrupulous, well deserving many of the unfavourable comments upon his character and activities to be found in the newspapers printed in America in those areas controlled by Congress. He boasted, as Horace Walpole said, 'of having butchered more men and lain with more women than anyone else in the army,' though Sheridan thought 'raped' would have been a more exact description than 'lain.' "

British shipping must retain its strength; and the greatest
British ports—London, Liverpool, and Bristol—had substantial capital tied up in slaves ... Taking a long average,
the number of Africans transported was perhaps 80,000 a
year, of whom probably half were packed into British
ships."[30] In *Slavery and the British Empire*, Kenneth
Morgan breaks this economic interest down into real
numbers. "Slaves together with staple products grown on
plantations (especially tobacco, rice, and sugar) potentially
generated lucrative returns in the early modern British
Atlantic trading world. In 1770 tobacco (worth £906,638)
was the most valuable export commodity from British
North America and rice (worth £340,693) was the fourth
most valuable commodity. In 1772–4 British sugar
imports were worth £2,360,000, making sugar easily the
most valuable commodity imported from anywhere."[31]

The economic interests against which pro-lifers battle
are equally formidable. "The mammoth tax-exempt non-
profit with 122 affiliates nationwide reported revenues ...
of a record $903 million during its 2005–06 fiscal year,"
Charlotte Allen reported of Planned Parenthood in *The
Weekly Standard*, "and it continues to bask in an amazingly
exalted reputation, at least among Democratic politicos,
celebrities, a largely sympathetic and even sycophantic
press and the gigantic family foundations set up by such
tycoons past and present as David Rockefeller, David
Packard, Bill Gates, and the ubiquitous George Soros, all of
whom have donated hundreds of millions of dollars to
Planned Parenthood causes."[32] In April 2008 the annual

---

[30] J. Ehrman, *The Younger Pitt: The Years of Acclaim* (London, 1969),
p. 387.

[31] K. Morgan, *Slavery and the British Empire: From Africa to America*
(Oxford, 2007), p. 34.

[32] C. Allen, "Planned Parenthood's Unseemly Empire: The billion-

report of Planned Parenthood revealed that the abortion provider had a total income of $1.02 billion—with reported profits of nearly $115 million. Taxpayers contribute $336 million to these revenues in the form of government grants and contracts at both the state and federal levels—a third of Planned Parenthood's budget. The 289,650 abortions performed in America in 2006 give some indication of the use to which this funding is being put.

Yet Wilberforce and the abolitionists, like pro-lifers today, were also up against another more insidious foe: the invocation of rights. In the case of the slave trade, this was tantamount to a willful refusal on the part of slave owners to acknowledge the humanity of the enslaved, a refusal justified by the claim that the slave owner had a *right* to such a refusal. "Slavery in its proper sense," Montesquieu wrote in 1748, "is the establishment of a right which makes one man so much the owner of another man that he is the absolute master of his life and of his goods." This was a useful defining of terms. Rights were bandied about in the defense of slavery with the same licentious abandon that they are bandied about today in the defense of abortion. But for Montesquieu the right to slave ownership was indefensible. "It is not good by its nature; it is useful neither to the master nor to the slave: not to the slave, because he can do nothing from virtue; not to the master, because he contracts all sorts of bad habits from [owning slaves], because he imperceptibly grows accustomed to failing in all the moral virtues, because he grows proud, curt, harsh, angry, voluptuous, and cruel." In 1762, Rousseau went further: "The words *slave* and *right* contradict each other, and are mutually

---

dollar 'non-profit' " in *The Weekly Standard* (10/22/2007). See also D. T. Critchlow. *Intended Consequences: Birth Control, Abortion, and the Federal Government in Modern America* (Oxford, 1999).

exclusive." In 1769, the Scottish philosopher Adam Ferguson corroborated Rousseau: "No one is born a slave
because no one, from being a person, can ... become a
thing or subject of property."[33]

Here Montesquieu, Rousseau and Ferguson followed
Burke in insisting that rights had to be judged on their
practical import. Replying to a young Parisian after the
outbreak of the French Revolution, who had asked
whether the French were capable of turning their newfound liberty to responsible account, Burke wrote: "You
have theories enough concerning the rights of men. It may
not be amiss to add a small degree of attention to their
nature and disposition. It is with man in the concrete, it
is with common human life and human Actions you are
to be concerned."[34] What Burke objected to in the French
Revolution was that, in the name of rights, it ran rough-
shod over "common human life." We can see the same
impatience with real life in abortionists and slave drivers.
The proponents of abortion are as little concerned with

[33]   Hague, p. 129. Hague's discussion of the Enlightenment's critique
of slavery is well done. For an amusing sidelight on Ferguson's point
that human beings cannot be treated as property, see P. Langford,
Public Life and the Propertied Englishman 1689–1798 (Oxford,
1991), pp. 7–8. "In the great debate about slavery, it was the
slave-owners who were sometimes driven to abandon the argument
from proprietorship, relying instead on the innate inferiority of
Blacks and the paternalism of the plantation system. Their critics
felt no embarrassment in resorting to propertied rights to justify the
liberation of the slaves, any more than they would in denouncing
the advantages of monopoly companies. There was no contradiction
here. If acquisitiveness is the first, almost the defining characteristic
of human beings as social animals, there could be no greater injustice
than to deprive them of it by making them a form of property. In
this sense, slavery was truly a lost cause."

[34]   Edmund Burke to Monsieur Dupont, October 1789 in *Letters of
Edmund Burke: A Selection,* ed. H. J. Laski (Oxford, 1922), p. 274.

the life of unborn children as the proponents of slavery are with the life of slaves: in both cases an abstract right trumps "man in the concrete."

Seen in this light, the woman who claims a 'right' to end the life of the unborn child exercises the same 'ownership' over that unborn child that the slave owner exercises over the slave. According to this arrogant logic, if the child is an inalienable part of the woman's body and if the woman owns her body, it follows that the woman can do with the child as she likes—even if that means murdering the child. But this right is no more defensible than the right to own slaves. The proponents of abortion, in their solicitude for what they style the 'reproductive rights' of women, like to fancy themselves the heirs of the Enlightenment, but Montesquieu and Rousseau, for all their theoretical vagaries, would have rejected reasoning that claims a right to infanticide. In fact, Rousseau, worried that Europe might become depopulated, pointedly denounced abortion, and argued instead that increasing population was the hallmark of good government.[35]

Wilberforce encountered opposition from yet another quarter: from those who claimed that in seeking to free African slaves, he was neglecting the plight of British laborers. In 1823, William Cobbett took Wilberforce to task for urging that West Indian slaves be put on a footing equal to that of free British labourers. "Your appeal is to the inhabitants of this country," Cobbett wrote in his best polemical vein. "You make your appeal to Piccadilly, London, amongst those who are wallowing in luxuries, proceeding from the labour of the people. You should have gone to the gravel-pits and made your appeal to the wretched creatures with bits of sacks round their shoul-

---

[35] See T. E. Cook, "Rousseau: Education and Politics" in *The Journal of Politics*, Vol. 37, No. 1 (Feb. 1975), pp. 108–128.

ders, and haybands round their legs: you should have gone to the roadside, and made your appeal to the emaciated, half-dead things who are there cracking stones to make roads as level as a die for the tax-eaters to ride on. What an insult it is, and what an unfeeling, what a cold-blooded hypocrite he must be that can send it forth; what an insult to call upon people under the name of free British labourers; to appeal to them in behalf of Black slaves, when these British labourers, these poor, mocked, degraded wretches would be happy to lick the dishes and bowls out of which the Black slaves have breakfasted, dined or supped."[36] After reading this, one can appreciate G. M. Young's observation in *Portrait of an Age*: "At the sight of Wilberforce, Cobbett put his head down and charged."[37]

Pro-lifers are often attacked for concentrating their efforts on the plight of the unborn at the expense of the born, agitating against abortion, so this reasoning goes, when they ought to be remedying the poverty that leaves so many children without health care or sufficient food, clothing and shelter. In such invidious criticism Wilberforce would have recognized a familiar ploy. A good example of this was reported in *The Wall Street Journal* apropos the debate regarding health care and abortion:

> Federal law currently prohibits tax funding of abortion except in the rare cases of rape, incest or threat to the woman's life. Many private insurance plans offered by employers also exclude abortion coverage. That could change, though. Most congressional proposals would set up a federal oversight panel, which could require some plans to cover abortion.

---

[36] *Cobbett's England: A Selection from the Writings of William Cobbett,* ed. J. Derry (London, 1968), p. 98.

[37] G. M. Young, *Victorian England: Portrait of an Age,* Second Edition (Oxford, 1953), p. 44.

Given that possibility, Judie Brown, president of the
American Life League, a Catholic anti-abortion
group, says she finds it "diabolical" that some Catholics are pressing for congressional action. But other
Catholic groups say the abortion issue distracts
from pressing needs. The lack of good care, they
argue, is in itself immoral, and so Catholics must
make an overwhelming push to get Congress to act
on behalf of the tens of millions of uninsured.
"That's the real pro-life message," says Victoria
Kovari, who runs Catholics in Alliance for the
Common Good, a left-leaning advocacy group.[38]

The Zong Massacre points up another parallel between
Wilberforce's campaign against slavery and the pro-life
campaign against abortion. The horrors of the middle
passage, thanks to the evidence gathered by Sharp and
Clarkson, were increasingly put before the British public,
as were the torments that awaited slaves once they were
delivered to market. In Rio de Janeiro, for example, they
were herded together in shops, offered for sale stark naked,
and bought like cattle. Yet in British politics it was thought
axiomatic that abolishing the slave trade was unthinkable.
And indeed there were many who argued before parliament that the trade actually benefited slaves. As Hague
points out, slaver traders "sought to persuade the Privy
Council that the slave trade maintained high standards of
care and that the slaves themselves were often happy with
their lot ... Such assertions may seem ridiculous, but there
were certainly people sitting in London disposed to believe
them and in a world with no photographic or recording
devices it was difficult to prove to universal satisfaction
that they were false."[39] Here we have a striking precursor

---

[38] "Health-Care Overhaul Creates Dilemma for Some Catholics" by
S. Simon, *Wall Street Journal* (8 May 2009).

[39] Hague, p. 172.

to the Orwellian logic of Planned Parenthood, which never ceases to present its brutal assaults against the unborn as the ministrations of benevolence, though, with the emergence of sonograms and other recording devices, we have no excuse for continuing to credit the monstrous falsehoods of this unscrupulous organization.

The hurdles that faced Wilberforce when he launched his anti-slavery campaign in parliament are not at all dissimilar from the hurdles faced by pro-lifers, who are told again and again that what has become the now deeply entrenched institution of abortion is similarly irresistible. Pro-lifers must continue to follow Wilberforce in taking the case for life to the country at large. A public opinion thoroughly acquainted with the evils of abortion will force the political establishment to repudiate those pressure groups that try to suggest that abortion is a species of healthcare or has the support of the majority of Americans.

Of course, in the case of abolition, it took British public opinion centuries to come round to the recognition that slavery was unacceptable. In the late eighteenth and early nineteenth centuries, there was always the temptation for a people consumed with many other concerns—revolution, war, bad harvests, economic depression, the dislocations of industrialization—to postpone abolition. Then, again, there was a reluctance to consider abolition because of the practical difficulties it would introduce. If abolition were granted, what would become of the slaves? Would they be able to be integrated into the society of free men? Or simply appropriated by Britain's enemies? Yet, despite these difficulties, the education of public opinion undertaken first by Sharp, Clarkson and Wilberforce and then by members of the Clapham Sect, including Thomas Babington Macaulay's father Zachary and Sir James Stephen, the grandfather of Virginia Woolf, bore fruit.

Once public opinion was shown the facts of the matter, conscience undertook an importunate campaign of its own—a campaign which did not stop with the passing of the Slave Trade Abolition Act in 1807 or the Abolition of Slavery Bill in 1833, which outlawed slavery throughout the British Empire.

In 1840, in response to stirrings of his own conscience, Turner painted "The Slave Ship," which he based on the Zong Massacre and described as "Slavers throwing overboard the dead and dying—typhoon coming on." The artist in Thackeray marveled at the terrible vividness with which Turner recreated this vision of horror. "The sun glares down upon a horrible sea of emerald and purple, into which chocolate-coloured slaves are plunged, and chains that will not sink; and round these are floundering such a race of fishes as never was seen since the saeculum of Pyrrhae ..."[40] Ruskin thought the painting contained "the noblest sea that Turner has ever painted," and confessed that "if I were reduced to rest Turner's immortality upon any single work, I should choose this."[41] Ruskin's

---

[40] Thackeray quoted in A. J. Finberg, *The Life of J.M.W. Turner* (Oxford, 1961), 378. In the phrase "saeculum of Pyrrhae," Thackeray alludes to the Deluge. "Pyrrha, daughter of Epimetheus and Pandora was the wife of Deucalion, the Noah of Greek mythology. Many people believed that the earth would one day be overwhelmed in a second flood, and the dreadful prodigy of Jove hurling his bolts at his own temple was to the superstitious a warning that the time was at hand." See C. L. Smith, *The Odes and Epodes of Horace* (Boston, 1903), p. 7.

[41] J. Ruskin, *Modern Painters,* ed. David Barrie (New York, 1987), pp. 158–160. Ruskin thought so highly of "The Slave Ship" because, as he said, "Its daring conception, ideal in the highest sense of the word, is based on the purest truth, and wrought out with the concentrated knowledge of life ..." For him, "the whole picture" was "dedicated to the most sublime of subjects ... the power, majesty, and deathfulness of the open, deep, illimitable sea." See

142

Culture and Abortion

father, after reading his son's rapt description of the picture in *Modern Painters*, bought it for him. Yet once the old man died, Ruskin got rid of it: the subject was too painful for him. That it hangs now in the Museum of Fine Arts in Boston is a macabre irony. Once a city fiercely opposed to slavery—William Lloyd Garrison personified its passion for abolition for decades in the nineteenth century—Boston is now a byword for abortionism.

Turner's painting captures the despair of a man who looked out onto the world and saw only a sea of predators and "chains that will not sink." Even Ruskin had to admit that Turner "was without hope."[42] Similar despair always threatens the pro-life movement. This is why Wilberforce is such a salutary figure. He is a constant reminder of the power of hope, which is inseparable from the power of truth. "Accustom yourself to look first to the dreadful consequences of failure," he urged his fellow abolitionists, "and then fix your eye on the glorious prize which is before you; and when your strength begins to fail, and your spirits are well nigh exhausted, let the animating view rekindle your resolution, and call forth in renewed vigour the fainting energies of your soul."[43] This was the hope that animated Wilberforce in his fight against slavery, one rooted in courage. Of course, he urged his fellow abolitionists to show their opposition magnanimity and forbearance. "Let true Christians ... strive in all things to recommend their profession ...," he wrote. "Let them be active, useful, and generous towards others; manifestly moderate and self-denying in themselves ... Let them countenance men of real piety wherever they are found; and encourage in

Modern Painters, 160.

[42] Ruskin quoted in "The Artist Grows Old" in K. Clark, *Moments of Vision* (London, 1981), 164.

[43] Hague, p. 276.

others every attempt to repress the progress of vice, and to revive and diffuse the influence of Religion and Virtue … Let them pray continually for their country in this season of national difficulty."[44] But he also recognized that there was a time for taking off the gloves, and this is the Wilberforce who speaks most compellingly to us today. In a letter to a friend he complained of opponents in high places. "It was truly humiliating to see, in the House of Lords, four of the Royal Family come down to vote against the poor, helpless, friendless Slaves. I sometimes think the Almighty can scarcely suffer us to be rid of such a load of wickedness, to which we cling so fondly … It is often the way of Heaven to let the error bring its own punishment along with it. Well, my friend, it will one day be consoling that you and I exerted ourselves to clear the ship of this stinking cargo."[45]

We too must clear our ship of stinking cargo, especially that perfidious cargo that would usurp our liberties by making abortion a mandatory component of healthcare. This is the most pressing battle in our own fight for life and the heroic assiduity of William Wilberforce and his abolitionist movement can help us win it.

---

[44] Hague, p. 275.
[45] Hague, pp. 318–319.

Nathaniel Hawthorne

(Mother Mary Alphonsa, OSD)
1851-1926

Rose Hawthorne

8

ROSE HAWTHORNE AND THE COMMUNION OF SAINTS

For Elsie Karwowski

ONE FINE AUTUMNAL evening, Father Aquinas Guilbeau, a young Dominican priest, with whom I had been reading the Church Fathers, asked if I knew anything about Nathaniel Hawthorne's daughter, Rose. I had a vague memory of reading something about her many years before but I could not place her. Who was she? Why was he asking? Well, he replied, she was an extraordinary convert, and after visiting with the Order of Sisters she founded—the Dominican Sisters of Hawthorne—in a place called Hawthorne in Westchester County, New York, and seeing the work they do on behalf of incurable cancer patients, he was convinced that there was a good deal about her and her Order that should be better known, especially at a time when the majority party in Washington was moving aggressively to bring health care under state control. Rose also happened to be a candidate for sainthood. Would I be interested in writing about her and her Order? If I was, he would arrange a meeting with the Mother Superior and drive me up himself to their Rosary Hill Home.

Here was Dominican preaching at its practical best and I readily took Father Guilbeau up on his kind, intriguing offer.

The next morning we met in the high-ceilinged old Priory of St. Vincent Ferrer on Lexington Avenue and set out in the parish automobile for Hawthorne. Once on the road, we were treated to brilliant foliage. It was one of those October days tailor-made for New York: The air was brisk and pungent; the light was of a radiant sharpness; the leaves were in their autumn beauty: crimson and jasper, saffron and sienna. On fall days like this, no one thinks of the death of summer but only of the extravagant preciousness of being alive. Later, Mother Mary Francis of Rosary Hill Home (founded by Rose Hawthorne in 1901) likened her cancer patients to fall leaves, which reminded me of those lovely lines from John Donne: "No spring nor summer beauty hath such grace / As I have seen in one autumnal face." Later still, when I met with some of the residents, I found myself confirming the accuracy of this observation.

Mother Mary Francis, a petite dynamo of a woman, whose smile radiates good sense and good fun, greeted us in Chapel, where she was praying with thirty or so other Sisters of varying ages from very young to very old. Father Guilbeau told me that whenever he visits the Sisters, it is always here that he finds them. When we sit down in a cozy old parlor, we are joined by Sister Mary Joseph and Sister de Paul, one an astute, gentle Southerner from Georgia and the other the Order's knowledgeable archivist from Philadelphia. To understand the work of the Dominican Sisters of Hawthorne, they stress, it is necessary to know something of their founder, Rose Hawthorne, because she personified the love of Christ and the love of Christ's poor that animates all they do.[1]

---

[1]   For my own understanding of Rose Hawthorne and her work I am heavily indebted to the following books: Sister M. Joseph, OP, *Out of Many Hearts* (New York, 1965); Theodore Maynard, *A Fire Was Lighted: The Life of Rose Hawthorne Lathrop* (New York, 1948); K. Burton, *Sorrow Built a Bridge: A Daughter of Hawthorne* (New York, 1937); and *Rose Hawthorne Lathrop: Selected Writings*, ed. D.

In her introduction to *A Memoir of Mary Ann* (1961), Flannery O'Connor described how Nathaniel Hawthorne's encounter with a rheumy child in a Liverpool workhouse changed his daughter's life forever. In his notebooks, Hawthorne had confided how "a child about six years old, but I know not whether girl or boy immediately took the strangest fancy for me. It was a wretched, pale, half-torpid little thing, with a humor in its eye which the Governor said was the scurvy." In responding to the child, Hawthorne was responding to something at once in and beyond himself.

> I never saw ... a child that I should feel less inclined to fondle. But this sickly, humor-eaten fright prowled round me, taking hold of my skirts, following at my heels, smiled in my face, and standing directly before me, insisted on my taking it up ... It was as if God had promised the child this favor on my behalf, and that I must fulfill the contract. I held my undesirable burden a little while, and after setting the child down, it still followed me, holding two of my fingers and playing with them, just as if it were a child of my own. It was a foundling, and out of all human kind it chose me to be its father! We went upstairs into another ward; and on coming down again there was this same child waiting for me, with a sickly smile around its defaced mouth ... I should never have forgiven myself if I had repelled its advances.[2]

Culbertson (New York, 1993). I should also like to thank Mother Mary Francis and the Dominican Sisters of Hawthorne for their generous assistance, as well as Father Aquinas Guilbeau, OP. Lastly, I should like to thank Sister de Paul, the archivist of the Dominican Sisters of Hawthorne for her special, generous guidance.

[2] F. O'Connor, *Mystery and Manners: Occasional Prose*, selected by Sally and Robert Fitzgerald (New York, 1969), pp. 218–219.

Later, in *Our Old Home* (1863), his account of his English
sojourn, Hawthorne attributed this experience to a name-
less gentleman, "burdened with more than an Englishman's customary reserve, shy of actual contact with
human beings, afflicted with a peculiar distaste for whatever was ugly, and ... accustomed to that habit of observation from an insulated standpoint which is said (but I hope
erroneously) to have the tendency of putting ice in the
blood. So I watched the struggle in his mind with a good
deal of interest, and am seriously of the opinion that he
did a heroic act and effected more than he dreamed of
towards his final salvation when he took up the loathsome
child and caressed it as tenderly as if he had been its father."[3]

It was characteristic of the storyteller in Hawthorne to
attribute this to an imaginary figure rather than himself.
Modesty played some part in this, but also a kind of awe.
Responding to that wretched child's yearning to be held,
he told his wife, brought him closer to God than he had
ever been before. After revealing that the man referred to
in the passage was Hawthorne himself, Rose judged it "the
greatest passage my father ever wrote."[4] In Hawthorne's
"small act of Christlikeness," as O'Connor characterized
it, Rose had seen something of the sanctity of life that
transformed her own life.[5]

Born in Lenox, Massachusetts, Rose Hawthorne (1851–
1926) was the third and youngest child of Hawthorne and
Sophia Peabody. She spent most of her happy childhood
in England, where her father was appointed American

3   *Hawthorne in England: Selections from "Our Old Home" and "The
    English Note-books,"* ed. C. Strout (Ithaca, 1965), pp. 224–225.

4   R. Hawthorne quoted in "A Legacy from Hawthorne," a review by
    M. Francis Egan, *New York Times Book Review and Magazine* (16
    April 1922), p. 6.

5   *Mystery and Manners*, p. 228.

consul by his good friend President Franklin Pierce. When Hawthorne resigned his post, the family traveled to Italy. In Florence, they resided in Bellosguardo, about which Hawthorne reported to a friend, "The house stands on a hill, overlooking Florence, and is big enough to quarter a regiment... At one end of the house there was a moss-grown tower, haunted by owls and by the ghost of a monk who was burnt at the stake in the principal square of Florence. I hire the villa, tower and all, at twenty-eight dollars a month."[6] The monk was Girolamo Savonarola (1452–98), whose "bonfires of the vanities" sent him to his own bonfire in Palazzo Vecchio. That he happened to be a Dominican friar was an amusing harbinger of Rose's later vocation.

Before returning to America, the family stayed for another year in England in Leamington Spa in Warwick-shire, where, coincidentally enough, Jack and Nuala Scaris-brick established the headquarters of their pro-life charity forty years ago. Recently, I visited with them and one morning we walked down the Parade to Lansdowne Circus where the Hawthorne family lived and where, on the unassuming white Regency house, a plaque has been mounted commemorating their happy residence. In *Our Old Home*, Hawthorne admitted that one reason he enjoyed the place so much was that "the ordinary stream of life does not run through this little, quiet pool, and few or none of the inhabitants seem to be troubled with any business or outside activities. I used to set them down as half-pay officers, dowagers of narrow income, elderly maiden ladies, and other people of respectability, but small account, such as hang on the world's skirts rather than actually belong to it."[7] In several visits to Rosary Hill Home, I saw how the

---

6   H. James, *Hawthorne* (Trent Editions, 1999), p. 127.
7   From "Leamington Spa" in *Hawthorne in England*, p. 40.

residents there also seemed to "hang on the world's skirts," without actually belonging to it, though, in the eyes of the Hawthorne Sisters, this only entitles them to more loving kindness and care.

It has to be said that such a view is not widespread in England, where assisted suicide is debated from the standpoint of whether it should be regulated, not banned. Unaware that life is a gift from God, many of the English are convinced that they can dispose of it as they please. But this could change. In mounting their Hawthorne plaque, the good people of Leamington are commemorating more than the father of American literature; they are commemorating the father of a saint—as yet uncanonized but a saint nonetheless. When Rose Hawthorne is canonized, she will be an enormously influential witness to the inviolability of life, and it is not only the English who will benefit from that. Many in America also need to be disabused of the notion that killing the inconveniently elderly and infirm is somehow merciful.

Although Rose was educated by private tutors and governesses, it was from her parents that she received the special tutelage and love that helped sustain her throughout her difficult adulthood. She was deeply attached to her father and when he died in 1864, just shy of her thirteenth birthday, she was heartbroken. In her wonderful *Memories of Hawthorne* (1897) she recalled how "Hawthorne worked hard and nobly. Not even the mechanic who toils for his family all day, all week-days of the year ... toils more nobly than this sensitive, warm-hearted, brave, recluse, much-seeing man. He teaches the spiritual greatness of the smallest fidelity, and the spiritual destruction in the most familiar temptations."[8]

---

[8]   R. Hawthorne Lathrop, *Memories of Hawthorne* (New York, 1897), p. 450.

Hawthorne has never been without sympathetic critics. Henry James spoke of him as one who "had lived primarily in his domestic affections, which were of the tenderest kind; and then—without eagerness, without pretension, but with a great deal of quiet devotion—in his charming art."[9] James also recognized that "man's conscience was his theme."[10] Yet his daughter Rose captured aspects of the man and the artist that James overlooked. "Every touch of inner meaning that he gives speaks of his affection, his desire to bring us accounts of what he has learned of God's benevolence, in his long walks on the thoroughfares and in the byways, and over the uncontaminated open country, of human hope. Poverty, trouble, sin, fraudulent begging, stupidity, conceit—nothing forced him absolutely to turn away his observation of all these usual rebuffs to sympathy, if his inconvenience could be made another's gain."[11] Here, again, one can see how her father's work inspired Rose to undertake her own. But her mother also played a formative role in her choice of vocation.

Sophia Peabody, to judge from her letters, was a vivacious, cultivated, discriminating woman. She was also free of the pantheism that muddled so many of the Unitarians among whom she and her husband moved. When Sophia spoke of God, she meant God, not what Ralph Waldo Emerson called the "Over-Soul." Moreover, she was not impressed with the practical issue of New England's armchair philosophy: "I hate transcendentalism," she once exclaimed, "because it is full of immoderate dicta which would disorganize society."[12] A painter and sculptor, Sophia understood the immersed detachment that made

---

[9]   H. James, *Hawthorne* (Trent Editions, 1999), p. 142.

[10]   Ibid.

[11]   *Memories of Hawthorne*, pp. 450–451.

[12]   Ibid., p. 358.

her husband an artist. "Never upon the face of any mortal
was there such a divine expression of sweetness and
kindliness," she wrote to Hawthorne when they were
courting. "Yet it was also the expression of a witness and
hearer."[13] James also recognized this same quality in
Hawthorne: "He is outside of everything, and an alien
everywhere. He is an aesthetic solitary."[14]

Later, after the couple married, Sophia reveled in her
husband's companionable intelligence. "There is something so penetrating and clear in Mr. Hawthorne's intellect," she wrote. "When he reads to me, it is the acutest
criticism. Such a voice, too—such sweet thunder!"[15] Surrounded by her family, Sophia exulted in her matriarchy.
"As for me, you know I am composed of Hope and Faith,
and while I have my husband and the children [Una, Julian
and Rose] I feel as if Montezuma's diamonds and emeralds
were spiritually my possession."[16] In Sophia's delightful
letters it is clear that, of all her children, it was the
youngest who inherited her zest for life. "Rose raised all
the echoes of the country by screaming with joy over her
blooming crocuses," Sophia wrote in one letter. "The
spring intoxicates her with 'remembering wine.' "[17]

---

[13] Ibid., p. 46.

[14] See "Nathaniel Hawthorne" (1897) in *The House of Fiction: Essays
on The Novel by Henry James*, ed. L. Edel (London, 1957), p. 186.

[15] *Memories of Hawthorne*, pp. 54–55.

[16] Ibid., p. 94.

[17] Ibid., p. 426. Here, Sophia was quoting from Ralph Waldo Emer-
son's poem "Bacchus" (1847), which ends with these lively lines.
Pour, Bacchus! the remembering wine;
Retrieve the loss of men and mine!
Vine for vine be antidote,
And the grape requite the lote!
Haste to cure the old despair,
Reason in Nature's lotus drenched,

The family was not without its trials—Hawthorne was often hard up in a literary world where editors paid poorly and piracy was the norm—but it was always close-knit. Something of this happy cohesiveness may have been attributable to Hawthorne's honesty. "In love-quarrels," he wrote in one notebook entry, "a man goes off on stilts, and comes back on his knees."[18] But it was Sophia who was the family's true center. The love she lavished on her family home would be replicated by Rose in her home, where, as Mother Alphonsa, she insisted that residents be treated as honored family guests. What Sophia said of her mother, Rose might have said of hers: "Such a mother seldom falls to the lot of mortals. She was the angel of my life. Her looks and tones and her acts of high-bred womanhood were the light and music and model of my childhood."[19]

After Hawthorne's death, Sophia moved the family to Germany so Rose could study art. In Dresden, she met George Lathrop, who would become associate editor of *The Atlantic Monthly* under James' good friend, the novelist William Dean Howells. It was apparently in his early days as a journalist that George first took up the excessive drinking that would later escalate into full-blown

---

The memory of ages quenched;
Give them again to shine;
A dazzling memory revive;
Refresh the faded tints,
Recut the aged prints,
And write my old adventures with the pen
Which on the first day drew,
Upon the tablets blue,
The dancing Pleiads and eternal men.

[18] Hawthorne quoted in J. Mellow, *Nathaniel Hawthorne and His Times* (New York, 1980), p. 119.

[19] *Memories of Hawthorne*, p. 479.

alcoholism, albeit behind closed doors. In 1871, shortly
after Rose's mother died, the couple returned to New York,
after marrying in London at the same church, St. Luke's
in Chelsea, where Dickens was married. In 1876, the
Lathrops were blessed with a son, Francis, who inherited
not only his mother's ebullience but her red-gold hair. To
help support her budding family, Rose wrote for various
papers, including *The Atlantic Monthly*, the *Boston Cou-
rier*, and the *Ladies' Home Journal*. When Rose and George
bought the old Hawthorne home in Concord, "Wayside,"
where Rose had such vivid memories of listening to her
father read by the fireside, they looked forward to a happy
future.

Then, in 1881, Francis suddenly died of diphtheria;
George's alcoholism deteriorated; and the Lathrop marriage began to disintegrate. To find solace in her bereave-
ment and to try to salvage her marriage Rose turned more
and more to her Christian faith. Apropos her faith, it is
worth pointing out that it was George who first introduced
her to Catholicism by sharing with her James Cardinal
Gibbons' *The Faith of Our Fathers* (1876), a catechetical
primer still in print. If George could not bring himself to
desist from tippling, he was clear enough about the
reasonableness of the Roman faith. To one correspondent
who suggested that his conversion had been perfunctory,
George responded with admirable clarity of purpose:

> The attempt to inform myself about the Church
> began with the same impartiality, the same candor
> and receptiveness that I should use towards any
> other subject upon which I honestly desired to form
> a just conclusion. Notwithstanding that my educa-
> tion had surrounded me with prejudice, my mind
> was convinced as to the truth, the validity and
> supremacy of the Roman Catholic Church, by the
> clear and comprehensive reasoning upon which it

> is based. And while the reasoning of other religious organizations continually shifts and wavers, leaving their adherents—as we now see almost every day—to fall into rationalism and agnostic denial, the reasoning of the Church, I found, led directly into sublime and inspiring faith.[20]

Diana Culbertson, OP, who has edited the various writings of Rose Hawthorne, points out that what particularly appealed to George about the Church was its recognition of the Communion of Saints: "The present, active, and incessant spirituality of the Church does not stop with this life or end in that pagan acceptance of death as an impassable barrier, which one meets with in Protestant denominations," he wrote. "It links together the religious souls of all periods, whether now on earth or in the world beyond."[21] That George should have played his own pivotal part in the Communion of Saints must have pleased Rose.

After reading various works of Catholic apologetics on their own, including Cardinal Wiseman's *Lectures on Doctrines of the Church* (1836), which had some modest bearing on John Henry Newman's conversion, Rose and George befriended Alfred Chappell, a prominent convert from New London, Connecticut, who gave them the run of his extensive theological library. In 1891, Rose and George were received into the Church by Father Alfred Young, CSP, an English convert and learned advocate of Gregorian chant, who was then attached to the Church of St. Paul the Apostle in New York. Nevertheless, George's furtive drinking worsened and finally Rose had no alternative but to separate from him. Once embarked on her new life, Rose dedicated herself to caring for the cancerous

---

[20] G. Lathrop quoted in *Rose Hawthorne Lathrop: Selected Writings*, ed. D. Culbertson (New York, 1993), pp. 32–33.

[21] Ibid., p. 33.

poor, who, at the time, were barred from the city's hospitals and left to rot on Blackwell's Island. After the death of her husband, over whose deathbed she prayed, she founded the Dominican Sisters of Hawthorne to advance her sacramental work with the help of Father Clement Thuente, OP, pastor of St. Vincent Ferrer Church. At her profession she took the name of Alphonsa in honor of Saint Alphonsus Liguori, the eighteenth-century Neapolitan whose chance visit to a hospital for incurables convinced him of the reality of his vocation, after which he abandoned his lucrative law career and founded the Redemptorist Order of priests.[22]

In the conduct of her vocation, Rose was influenced by a number of more contemporary figures. Rose's friend Emma Lazarus, wrote lines which adorn the Statue of Liberty:

> Give me your tired, your poor
> Your huddled masses yearning to breathe free...

Emma herself died of cancer at the age of 38, and introduced Rose to the needs of New York's poor by sharing with her the work she was doing on behalf of indigent Jews on the Lower East Side. After reading a news story about pogroms in Russia, Lazarus told Rose: "I forgot Emerson. I forgot everything except that my people were in need of help." Here was a woman after Rose's own heart. Yet, later, when Josephine Lazarus, Emma's sister, wrote Rose and told her that what she was trying to do what "could not be done"—she had attempted to set up a similar charity in memory of Emma and it had failed—Rose was undiscouraged.[23]

---

[22] K. Burton, *Sorrow Built a Bridge: A Daughter of Hawthorne* (New York, 1937), p. 185.

[23] *Rose Hawthorne Lathrop: Selected Writings*, ed. Diana Culbertson

When Rose bought her first home on Cherry Street on the Lower East Side she must have thought of her father's diplomatic offices. In *Our Old Home*, Hawthorne described the consulate in Liverpool as situated in what was "by no means a polite or elegant portion of England's great commercial city."

> The staircase and passageway were often thronged, of a morning, with a set of beggarly and piratical-looking scoundrels ... shipwrecked crews in quest of bed, board, and clothing; invalids asking permits for the hospital; bruised and bloody wretches complaining of ill-treatment by their officers; drunkards, desperadoes, vagabonds, and cheats, perplexingly intermingled with an uncertain proportion of reasonably honest men.[24]

The immigrant poor among whom Rose worked were an equally unregenerate lot. To fund the homes she set up for her patients first in Manhattan and, later, in Hawthorne, Rose published appeals in the *New York Times*, one of which ran: "Let the poor, the patient, the destitute and the hopeless receive from our compassion what we would give to our own families, if we were really generous to them."[25]

Of all the many responses she received, one stood out. "If there is an unassailably good cause in the world, it is this one undertaken by the Dominican Sisters, of housing, nourishing and nursing the most pathetically unfortunate of all the afflicted among us—men and women sentenced to a painful and lingering death by incurable disease ... I am glad in the prosperous issue of your work, and glad to

---

(New York, 1993), p. 235.

[24] *Hawthorne in England: Selections from "Our Old Home" and "The English Note-books,"* pp. 5–6.

[25] *Rose Hawthorne Lathrop: Selected Writings*, p. 54.

know that this prosperity will continue, and be permanent—a thing which I do know, for that endowment is banked where it cannot fail until pity fails in the hearts of men, and that will never be."[26] Throughout his life, Mark Twain was one of Rose's staunchest supporters.

Today, Mother Mary Francis tells me, the Sisters continue to receive funding from individuals and private foundations. After visiting Rosary Hill Home on several occasions and talking with the Sisters and residents, I can see why. There is a joyousness about the place that is as extraordinary as it is unexpected. Although the Sisters are fully trained nurses, they bring more to their residents than palliative care: They bring the love of Christ. For Mother Alphonsa, serving the poor as Christ served the poor was an exacting charge: "Christ may have placed it first in the series of His commands because we could immediately understand it, and because it abases pride at a stroke... All else in the spiritual life develops from this act, or it never really develops at all. Piety without humble works is that subtle monstrosity, self-righteousness."[27]

One of the residents, a charming German woman who grew up in the Bronx, the daughter of a man who owned a string of ice-cream parlors, tells me that the serenity that suffuses the 72-bed Rosary Hill Home stems directly from the commitment the Sisters show to their Founder's Rule: "They do everything for love of Jesus." Later, when I ask this good Lutheran woman if she joins the Sisters in Chapel, she looks at me with a terrible plaintiveness and says, "I did once but I could not go back. There was too much love in that chapel: I wanted to cry." I have been to many nursing homes over the years but I do not remember

---

[26]   Mark Twain quoted in "A Legacy from Hawthorne," a review by Maurice Francis Egan, p. 13.

[27]   *Rose Hawthorne Lathrop: Selected Writings*, p. 197.

encountering conversation of this sort in any of them. Later, this same woman tells me that what makes the Sisters truly special is that they do not treat the residents as "throwaways." "Everyone else wants to treat us as throwaways," she says. "For the Sisters, we are keepers."

Another resident is an affable Virginian who has spent most of his adult life working in New York, first as a short-order cook with the Automats of Horn & Hardart and then stripping and refinishing hardwood floors— skilled labor of which he is justly proud. When I share with him a postcard of a painting in the Musée d'Orsay of workers stripping hardwood floors in nineteenth-century Paris—"Les raboteurs de parquet" (1875) by Gustave Caillebotte—he studies it with a connoisseur's intensity.

Afterwards, when I remark to Sister Mary Joseph about what strikes me as his high intelligence, she confirms my impression, telling me that, though only a graduate of the fourth grade, our mutual friend is fascinated by all things related to the Royal Navy. Indeed, he also devours books on Lord Nelson. And yet, before coming to Rosary Hill Home, this gentle, dignified, talented man, who, in clement weather, spends most of his time in the garden, was so desperately wracked with pain related to his cancer that he actually tried to kill himself by jumping onto the subway tracks at 23rd Street. After being rescued, he was transferred to the care of the Hawthorne Sisters and ever since he has accounted these unstintingly attentive women his angels of mercy.

That the Sisters ask for no money for what they do from residents or their families—or from state, local, or federal government, or from private insurance companies—only underscores the integrity of their charitable mission. As they point out on their website: "In accordance with their

Rule, the Sisters place their trust in the loving providence of God. That trust has never failed."

One of the older Hawthorne Sisters with whom I speak insists that there is nothing saintly about the Sisters or their work: They are only doing their job. She is indeed so insistent on this point that she tells me that if I call her saintly in print, she will hunt me down and see that I regret it. Another nun, a younger one from the Philippines (from a town called St. Augustine) tells me that the real work of the Sisters is "to give birth to souls—to act as midwives to eternity." If there is a way of speaking of this without mentioning the saintly I am not aware of it.

Father Guilbeau was right: There is a story that needs telling about Rose Hawthorne and her Hawthorne Sisters and it is the story of how they embody the love of Christ. At a time when unscrupulous politicians are moving to bureaucratize health care, for no other reason than to aggrandize the State, the Hawthorne Sisters remind us of the personal, loving, sacramental character of true health care. At a time when life is under attack, not only the life of the elderly and the infirm but also that of the disabled and the unborn, they reaffirm the sanctity of life. For their compassionate vision of health care, the Dominican Sisters of Hawthorne can site the authority of Benedict XVI, who wrote in his first encyclical:

> Love—*caritas*—will always prove necessary, even in the most just society. There is no ordering of the State so just that it can eliminate the need for a service of love. Whoever wants to eliminate love is preparing to eliminate man as such. There will always be suffering which cries out for consolation and help. There will always be loneliness. There will always be situations of material need where help in the form of concrete love of neighbor is indispensable. The State which would provide

everything, absorbing everything into itself, would ultimately become a mere bureaucracy incapable of guaranteeing the very thing which the suffering person—every person—needs: namely, loving personal concern.[28]

Flannery O'Connor got at the very essence of the mission of the Dominican Hawthorne Sisters when she observed how "the action by which charity grows invisibly among us, entwining the living and the dead, is called by the Church the Communion of Saints. It is a communion created upon imperfection, created from what we make of our grotesque state."[29]

Once again, the rheumy child who made such an appeal to Hawthorne appeals to us. And his appeal is a reminder of what Saint Paul teaches, that

> none of us liveth to himself, and no man dieth to himself. For whether we live, we live unto the Lord, and whether we die, we die unto the Lord: whether we live therefore, or die, we are the Lord's. For to this end, Christ both died, and rose, and revived, that he might be Lord both of the dead and living.[30]

This is the story of Rose Hawthorne and the Dominican Sisters of Hawthorne and it is one that includes us all.

---

[28] Pope Benedict XVI, *Deus Caritas Est.*
[29] *Mystery and Manners*, p. 228.
[30] Romans 14:7–10.

Pope Paul VI

9

TEENAGE DAUGHTERS AND THE GREAT WORK

I knew Seraphina; Nature gave her hue,
Glance, sympathy, note, like one from Eden,
I saw her smile warp, heard her lyric deaden;
She turned to harlotry;— this I took to be new.

Edmund Blunden, "Report on Experience"

T HE DAY-TO-DAY FIGHT against abortion can be so all-consuming that we can forget that if we are against the taking away of innocent life in the womb, we must also be for reaffirming the sanctity of life beyond the womb, a sanctity which our general culture does not begin to understand, much less honor. Many of my readers might have seen the piece in *The Wall Street Journal* by Jennifer Moses, in which she asked: "Why do so many of us not only permit our teenage daughters to dress like ... prostitutes ... but pay for them to do it with our AmEx cards?"[1] That Moses hit a very sensitive nerve in posing this question is borne out by the tremendous response that the article received—a response only equaled by that to another *Journal* article about child rearing by a woman convinced that Asians have some edge in this always vexing enterprise. Yet if Moses addresses an issue that is on the minds of many readers, her understanding of it is deeply ambivalent.

---

[1] J. Moses, "Why Do We Let Them Dress Like That?" in *Wall Street Journal* (March 19, 2011).

For example, she posits the theory that mothers today acquiesce in the degradation of their daughters because they were degraded themselves when they were young. "It has to do with how conflicted my own generation of women is about our own past," she writes, "when many of us behaved in ways that we now regret. A woman I know, with two mature daughters, said, 'If I could do it again, I wouldn't even have slept with my own husband before marriage. Sex is the most powerful thing there is, and our generation, what did we know?' " This theory sounds plausible enough: the sins of mothers do have a way of being visited upon daughters. Readers who need fresh evidence for this can consult Mary Karr, Wendy Burden and Ivana Lowell, all of whose memoirs richly document how the bad behaviour of mothers can leave lifelong scars on vulnerable daughters.[2]

But what is striking about Moses is that she offers no explanation as to why she and her friend should regard sex as "the most powerful thing there is." Why do they think that? What do they mean by "powerful"? And why do they now wonder if this is something that a woman should only share with her husband after marriage? Perhaps they miss in our own culture that deep appreciation for the dignity of marriage, to which George Crabbe gave such moving expression.

> The ring so worn as you behold,
> So thin, so pale, is yet of gold:
> The passion such it was to prove;
> Worn with life's cares, love yet was love.[3]

---

[2]   See M. Karr, *Lit* (New York, 2009); W. Burden, *Dead Gene Pool* (New York 2010); and I. Lowell, *Why Not Say What Happened?* (New York, 2010).

[3]   George Crabbe, (1754–1832) wrote of the country poor in such faithfully realistic poems as *The Village* (1783), *The Parish Register*

Moses does not say why she now recognizes the importance of marriage, though many, after reading her article,
will be reminded of the opening words of *Humanae Vitae*,
Pope Paul VI's historic encyclical, in which he wrote of
how "The transmission of human life is a most serious role
in which married people collaborate freely and responsibly
with God the Creator."[4] Here is the marvel of marriage,
with which promiscuity wars. Who would now speak of
the love of marriage with the unapologetic devotion of
Anne Bradstreet?

> If ever two were one, then surely we.
> If ever man were loved by wife, then thee;
> If ever wife was happy in a man,
> Compare with me ye women if you can.
> I prize thy love more than whole mines of gold,
> Or all the riches that the East doth hold.
> My love is such that rivers cannot quench,
> Nor ought but love from thee, give recompence.
> Thy love is such I can no way repay,
> The heavens reward thee manifold I pray.
> Then while we live, in love let's so persever,
> That when we live no more, we may live ever.[5]

Ford Madox Ford captured the wondrous finality of the
thing from a different perspective when he wrote of how:
"For every man there comes at last a time of life when the
women who then sets her seal upon his imagination has
set her seal for good. He will travel over no more horizons;
he will never again set the knapsack over his shoulders; he

(1807) and *The Borough* (1810). Edmund Burke, Samuel Johnson,
John Henry Newman and James Joyce were some of his more
notable admirers.

[4]   Pope Paul VI, *Humanae Vitae*, 1.

[5]   Anne Bradstreet, "To My Dear and Loving Husband" (1678).

will retire from those scenes. He will have gone out of business."[6]

It is coincidental that Ford should once have been a neighbor of Henry James in Rye because James, too, in his complicated way, understood the momentous no-turning-back that heralds marriage. In *The Wings of the Dove*, he describes such an encounter between his heroine Kate Croy and her indolent beau, Merton Densher:

> They had found themselves looking at each other straight, and for a longer time on end than was usual even at parties in galleries; but that, after all, would have been a small affair, if there hadn't been something else with it. It wasn't, in a word, simply that their eyes had met; other conscious organs, faculties, feelers had met as well, and when Kate afterwards imaged to herself the sharp, deep fact she saw it, in the oddest way, as a particular performance. She had observed a ladder against a garden wall, and had trusted herself so to climb it as to be able to see over into the probable garden on the other side. On reaching the top she had found herself face to face with a gentleman engaged in a like calculation at the same moment, and the two inquirers had remained confronted on their ladders. The great point was that for the rest of that evening they had been perched—they had not climbed down; and indeed, during the time that followed, Kate at least had had the perched feeling—it was as if she were there aloft without a retreat.[7]

Moses may be vague when it comes to marriage, and entirely mum on that now superannuated thing, courtship,

---

F. M. Ford, *The Good Soldier* (London, 1915), p. 136.

[7]   H. James, *The Wings of the Dove* (London, 1902), p. 60.

but she is revelatory about how she sees her place within the scheme of generational history.

> We are the first moms in history to have grown up with widely available birth control, the first who didn't have to worry about getting knocked up. We were also the first not only to be free of old-fashioned fears about our reputations but actually pressured by our peers and the wider culture to find our true womanhood in the bedroom. Not all of us are former good-time girls now drowning in regret—I know women of my generation who waited until marriage—but that's certainly the norm among my peers.

> So here we are, the feminist and postfeminist and postpill generation. We somehow survived our own teen and college years (except for those who didn't), and now, with the exception of some Mormons, evangelicals and Orthodox Jews, scads of us don't know how to teach our own sons and daughters not to give away their bodies so readily. We're embarrassed, and we don't want to be, God forbid, hypocrites.

There is a good deal that is tell-tale about this. First of all, the author does not seem to realize how hornswoggled she and so many of her other peers have been by the false promises of feminism, which have not served the interests of either single or married women. Moreover, while the damage feminism has done to the social fabric as a whole might be incalculable, it has certainly played a very culpable part in the shattering of the family and the neglect of children. Yet Moses continues to pay homage to the myth of feminist liberation: "We are the first moms in history to have grown up with widely available birth control, the first who didn't have to worry about getting knocked up."

What a sorry boast this is! And how pitiably misguided for any mother to say that she cannot dissuade her daughter from repeating her own follies because it would make her a hypocrite! If that logic were followed, few mothers could instruct their young in any of the virtues.

Then, again, although she seems vaguely aware that contraception might have had something to do with the promiscuity that coarsened her generation, she does not question whether this was a good or a bad thing. Pope Paul VI, after affirming the Church's adherence to the moral law on the issue of contraception, gave prescient expression to what he recognized would be the pernicious results of breaking that law, "how easily this course of action could open wide the way for marital infidelity and a general lowering of moral standards." Indeed, for the pope, whose familiarity with the confessional would have left him in no doubt about such matters

> Not much experience is needed to be fully aware of human weakness and to understand that human beings—and especially the young, who are so exposed to temptation—need incentives to keep the moral law, and it is an evil thing to make it easy for them to break that law.[8]

What is also remarkable about Moses is how she does not seem to grasp what a continuing role the breaking of this law plays in the even more rampant promiscuity that obtains among her daughter's contemporaries. She wishes to suggest that there is something comparable about her own generation's attitudes toward sex and that of her daughter's but clearly this is not the case, especially when we consult the picture she provides herself of what constitutes "the current social norm," which includes "'sexting'

---

[8]   Pope Paul VI, *Humanae Vitae*, 8.

among preteens, 'hooking up' among teens and college students, and a constant stream of semi-pornography from just about every media outlet." Here is the real harvest of contraception, which turns human sexuality into a diversion and blinds men and women to the procreative sanctity of that sexuality.

Another thing it does is rob the young of the discoveries of courtship, to which Shakespeare and the Elizabethans were so exquisitely alive.

> Love's feeling is more soft and sensitive
> Than are the tender horns of cockled snails ...[9]

No one could ever enter into that precious aperçu that treated his sexuality as simply a means of brute gratification.

In light of the remorseless debasement of the young, which now has the support of both the popular culture and the public authorities, Moses, speaking for herself and her friends, admits that "the desire to push back is strong." Indeed, she goes further and concedes that she does not know one of her friends "who doesn't have feelings of lingering discomfort regarding her own sexual past." In fact, none "wishes she'd 'experimented' more."

Here, at least, is proof of the importunity of conscience. Yet Moses also shows how false reason can muddle conscience. In an attempt to enter into the psychology of teenage girls, for example, she asks: "What teenage girl doesn't want to be attractive, sought-after and popular?"— as if the mere existence of such wishes justified their indulgence.

Of course, teenage girls desire the acceptance of their peers, but they should be encouraged to seek such acceptance on their own terms—because of their virtues, their

---

[9]   *Love's Labours Lost*, 4.3.

talents, their intelligence, their charm—not because they are willing to do the bidding of the popular culture. That culture has now convinced a good many teenage girls that the only way to be "attractive, sought-after and popular" is by dressing up and behaving like trollops. Should a responsible mother accede to such exploitation? Or sit her daughter down and explain that there will be many times when she will have to do the unpopular thing in order to do the right thing?

Moses never asks these questions because she assumes that most mothers will simply join her in succumbing to what might be called "daughter pressure." But then she makes an admission that stops one in one's tracks.

> In my own case, when I see my daughter in drop-dead gorgeous mode, I experience something akin to a thrill—especially since I myself am somewhat past the age to turn heads.

When a mother can admit such a thing, and do so with the air of someone who fully expects her readers to agree with what she is saying, we know we have arrived at a pretty pass. What Moses is saying, in effect, is that she and her friends not only connive in the debauching of their daughters but actually enjoy it. This makes the force of her conclusion all the more compelling because she does not spare herself.

> I wouldn't want us to return to the age of the corset or even of the double standard, because a double standard that lets the promiscuous male off the hook while condemning his female counterpart is both stupid and destructive ... But it's easy for parents to slip into denial. We wouldn't dream of dropping our daughters off at college and saying: "Study hard and floss every night, honey—and for heaven's sake, get laid!" But that's essentially what

we're saying by allowing them to dress the way they
do while they're still living under our own roofs.

The value of Moses' piece is not that it calls attention to
the lamentable corruption of our teen-age girls. Anyone
who walks our streets can see that. No, its real value is that
it proves that we cannot simply combat the culture of
death by combating abortion: we also have to promote the
culture of life, and this requires pro-lifers to be willing to
exhibit what Paul VI called "signs of contradiction" to a
society intent on deriding virtue and applauding vice.

Perhaps one initial thing that we can do to recover
something of what we have lost with respect to understanding and nurturing the innocence of girlhood is to
remind ourselves that the current debasement of girls is
of no long vintage. For centuries and centuries girls went
about the business of being girls without feeling obliged
to emulate the dress and mien of strumpets. I am sure at
least some of my readers recall that delightful passage in
Our Village (1824–1832), where the memoirist Mary
Russell Mitford describes the progress of girls unspoiled
by the accelerated vice that characterizes our own culture.[10]

> I pique myself on knowing by sight, and by name,
> almost every man and boy in our parish, from eight
> years old to eighty—I cannot say quite so much for
> the women. They—the elder of them at least—are
> more within doors, more hidden. One does not
> meet them in the fields and highways; their duties
> are close housekeepers, and live under cover. The
> girls, to be sure, are often enough in sight, "true

---

[10]　My Irish readers will be amused to know that when she was a girl
of ten and living in Reading, Mary picked the winning number of
the Irish Lottery Office and won £20,000—a huge sum at the
time—so she knew what she was talking about when she described
girlish glee. See Ronald Blythe's introduction to the Folio edition
of *Our Village*.

creatures of the element," basking in the sun, racing in the wind, rolling in the dust, dabbling in the water,— hardier, dirtier, noisier, more sturdy defiers of heat, and cold, and wet, than boys themselves. One sees them quite often enough to know them; but then the little elves alter so much at every step of their approach to womanhood, that recognition becomes difficult, if not impossible. It is not merely growing,— boys grow;— it is positive, perplexing, and perpetual change: a butterfly hath not undergone more transmogrifications in its progress through this life, than a village belle in her arrival at the age of seventeen.

The first appearance of the little lass is something after the manner of a caterpillar, crawling and creeping upon the grass, set down to roll by some tired little nurse of an elder sister, or mother with her hands full. There it lies—a fat, boneless, rosy piece of health, aspiring to the accomplishments of walking and talking; stretching its chubby limbs; scrambling and sprawling; laughing and roaring; there it sits, in all the dignity of the baby, adorned in a pink-checked frock, a blue spotted pinafore, and a little white cap, tolerably clean, and quite whole. One is forced to ask if it be boy or girl; for these hardy country rogues are all alike, open-eyed, and weather-stained, and nothing fearing. There is no more mark of sex in the countenance than in the dress.

In the next stage, dirt-incrusted enough to pass for the chrysalis, if it were not so very unquiet, the gender remains equally uncertain. It is a fine, stout, curly-pated creature of three or four, playing and rolling about, amongst grass or mud, all daylong; shouting, jumping, screeching—the happiest compound of noise and idleness, rags and rebellion, that ever trod the earth.

Then comes a sun-burnt gipsy of six, beginning to grow tall and thin, and to find the cares of the world gathering about her; with a pitcher in one hand, a mop in the other, an old straw bonnet of ambiguous shape, half hiding her tangled hair; a tattered stuff petticoat, once green, hanging below an equally tattered cotton frock, once purple; her longing eyes fixed on a game of baseball at the corner of the green, till she reaches the cottage door, flings down the mop and pitcher, and darts off to her companions, quite regardless of the storm of scolding with which the mother follows her run-away steps.

So the world wags till ten; then the little damsel gets admission to the charity school, and trips mincingly thither every morning, dressed in the old-fashioned blue gown, and white cap, and tippet, and bib and apron of that primitive institution, looking as demure as a Nun, and as tidy; her thoughts fixed on button-holes and spelling-books—those ensigns of promotion; despising dirt and baseballs, and all their joys.

Then at twelve the little lass comes home again, uncapped, untippeted, unschooled; brown as a berry, wild as a colt, busy as a bee—working in the fields, digging in the garden, frying rashers, boiling potatoes, shelling beans, darning stockings, nursing children, feeding pigs;— all these employments varied by occasional fits of romping and flirting, and idle play, according as the nascent coquetry, or the lurking love of sport, happens to preponderate; merry, and pretty, and good with all her little faults. It would be well if a country girl could stand at thirteen. Then she is charming. But the clock will move forward, and at fourteen she gets a service in a neighbouring town; and her next appearance is in the perfection of the butterfly

> state, fluttering, glittering, inconstant, vain,— the gayest and gaudiest insect that ever skimmed over a village green. And this is the true progress of a rustic beauty, the average lot of our country girls— so they spring up, flourish, change, and disappear.[11]

For Mitford, girls grow stage by stage. Forcing them to become young women prematurely—and very debauched young women—betrays the glory of girlhood, the innocence of girlhood, which the culture of knowledge is always ready to despoil.

In light of this remorseless sullying of our young, pro-lifers must be prepared, as the pope urged, "to create an atmosphere favorable to the growth of chastity so that true liberty may prevail over license and the norms of the moral law may be fully safeguarded." This requires our denouncing the sexualization not only of our teenage girls but of our teenage boys as well, too many of whom are encouraged to see sexuality in terms of the travesties of pornography, the very essence of which is to mock chastity. That pornography disables young men from entering into the obligations of sexuality by confusing it with onanism goes without saying, but what our culture is in peril of forgetting is that without chastity love is impossible. And without chastity there can be no welcoming respect for the gift of new life. Pope John Paul II clearly acknowledged this in his encyclical *Evangelium Vitae* (1995), when he observed how

> The trivialization of sexuality is among the principal factors which have led to contempt for new life. Only a true love is able to protect life. There can be no avoiding the duty to offer, especially to adolescents and young adults, an authentic education in sexuality and in love, an education which

---

[11] M. R. Mitford, *Our Village* (Folio Society, 1997), pp. 165–167.

involves training in chastity as a virtue which fosters personal maturity and makes one capable of respecting the "spousal" meaning of the body.[12]

It was to foster the "growth of chastity" that Pope Paul VI urged those united in Christian marriage to personify the norms of the moral law in their very unions. "Let Christian husbands and wives be mindful of their vocation to the Christian life," he exhorted the faithful, "a vocation which, deriving from their Baptism, has been confirmed anew

> and made more explicit by the Sacrament of Matrimony. For by this sacrament they are strengthened and, one might almost say, consecrated to the faithful fulfillment of their duties. Thus will they realize to the full their calling and bear witness as becomes them, to Christ before the world. For the Lord has entrusted to them the task of making visible to men and women the holiness and joy of the law which united inseparably their love for one another and the cooperation they give to God's love, God who is the Author of human life.[13]

By embodying these truths in their own lives, married couples can share them with other married couples, since, as the pope observes, "Among the fruits that ripen if the law of God be resolutely obeyed, the most precious is certainly this, that married couples themselves will often desire to communicate their own experience to others.

> Thus it comes about that in the fullness of the lay vocation will be included a novel and outstanding form of the apostolate by which, like ministering to like, married couples themselves by the leadership they offer will become apostles to other

---

[12] Pope John Paul II, *Evangelium Vitae*, 152.

[13] Pope Paul VI, *Humanae Vitae*, 12.

married couples. And surely among all the forms
of the Christian apostolate it is hard to think of one
more opportune for the present time.[14]

Pope Paul VI wrote that in 1968, before contraception had
begun to wreak its havoc. Now that we find ourselves
surrounded by that havoc, we must rededicate ourselves
to what the pope called the "great work" of reaffirming the
sacred obligations inherent in sex and marriage, procreation and child rearing, which are the wellsprings of the
culture of life and love. "For," as the pope so prophetically
warned the world over four decades ago, "man cannot
attain that true happiness for which he yearns with all the
strength of his spirit, unless he keeps the laws which the
Most High God has engraved in his very nature."

---

[14] Ibid., 14–15.

Charles Dickens

10

CHARLES DICKENS AND
THE CRY OF LIFE

I N *DOMBEY AND Son* there is a brilliant scene in which the hero, Paul Dombey, a City merchant who has lost his beloved heir, is approached on a railway platform by Mr. Toodle, a stoker, whose wife was the wet-nurse of Dombey's son. After telling Dombey that he will "have the honor of stokin' you down," Toodle shares with him that he and his wife have lost a baby of their own," which, instead of inspiring commiseration in the aggrieved merchant, returns him to his proud, inconsolable grief.

> To think of this presumptuous raker among coals and ashes going on before there, with his sign of mourning! To think that he dared to enter, even by a common show like that, into the trial and disappointment of a proud gentleman's secret heart! To think that this lost child, who was to have divided with him his riches, and his power, and allied with whom he was to have shut out all the world as with a double door of gold, should have let in such a herd to insult him with their knowledge of his defeated hopes, and their boasts of claiming community of feeling with himself, so far removed: if not of having crept into the place wherein he would have lorded it, alone![1]

Dombey then boards his train but rather than enjoying the "rich and varied country" passing outside his window, he can only brood on "a wilderness of blighted plans and

---

[1]   C. Dickens, *Dombey and Son* (Oxford, 1953), p. 280.

gnawing jealousies." His child's death has rendered him incapable of enjoying life. Still, he is sentient enough to recognize that the train embodies his distress. Indeed, for Dombey, the "very speed at which the train was whirled along mocked the swift course of the young life that had been borne away so steadily and so inexorably to its foredoomed end. The power that forced itself upon its iron way... defiant of all paths and roads, piercing through the heart of every obstacle, and dragging living creatures of all classes, ages, and degrees behind it, was a type of the triumphant monster, Death."[2]

Dickens himself suffered the loss of a child and told a correspondent who was grieving for the loss of his own child, "It is nearly two years ago since I lost in one short night a young and lovely creature whom—I can say to you now—I loved with the warmest affection that our nature is capable of, and in whom I had the fondest father's pride. The first burst of anguish over, I have never thought of her with pain—never. I have never connected her ... with the grave in which she lies ... I have long since learned to separate her from all this litter of dust and ashes, and to picture her to myself with every well-remembered grace and beauty heightened by the light of Heaven and the power of that Merciful Being who never try our earthly affections so severely but to make their objects happy, and lead our thoughts to follow them."[3]

Death, of course, was a Victorian obsession, the inexpellable incubus of an entire age. Queen Victoria exhibited something of Dombey's egomaniacal grief when she used Prince Albert's death as a pretext for keeping aloof from her subjects, dodging dull duties, and spending an inordi-

---

[2]   Ibid., p. 280.
[3]   Dickens to J. Forster (3 March 1839) in *Selected Letters of Charles Dickens,* ed. Jenny Hartley (Oxford, 2012), pp. 1–2.

nate amount of time with her bibulous highland servant, John Brown. The son of her Private Secretary, Henry Ponsonby, elaborated on this in his biography of his father.

> The Queen's strict retirement was primarily based on her over-indulgence in what may be called the luxury of woe. Balmoral reminded her more than any other place of the Prince Consort. She cherished his memory, had an annual service at his tomb at Frogmore, collected relics of him, never altered her attire of deep mourning and her characteristic widow's cap, and even retained over half an inch of black edge on her notepaper till the end. Deaths and anniversaries of deaths drew from her repeated expressions of grief sometimes in rather exaggerated terms as if to make up for not having paid much attention to the deceased when they were alive. Mixed with her genuine sorrow one cannot help detecting on occasions a note of resentment if not anger at the loss, so that one almost expects to find some direction in her best style of political indignation instructing her Private Secretary to address some remonstrance to the Almighty.[4]

Cardinal Newman gave death his due when he spoke of it in "The Dream of Gerontius" (1865) as "that shapeless, scopeless, blank abyss/That utter nothingness, of which I came." Tennyson, too, one of Queen Victoria's favorite poets, never left off ruminating on death. He might have insisted that "Maud" (1855) was a dramatic monologue, not a first-person avowal, but no one familiar with the poet

---

[4]   A. Ponsonby, *Henry Ponsonby: Queen Victoria's Private Secretary: His Life in Letters* (New York, 1943), pp. 79–80. Ponsonby took it upon himself to destroy the memoir that the Queen wrote in 1883 recounting what amounted to her infatuation with Brown, as well as Brown's diaries. See ODNB.

or his work would mistake lines like these for the effusions
of fiction.

> Dead, long dead,
> Long dead!
> And my heart is a handful of dust,
> And the wheels go over my head,
> And my bones are shaken with pain,
> For into a shallow grave they are thrust,
> Only a yard beneath the street,
> And the hoofs of the horses beat, beat,
> The hoofs of the horses beat,
> Beat into my scalp and my brain,
> With never an end to the stream of passing feet,
> Driving, hurrying, marrying, burying,
> Clamour and rumble, and ringing and clatter,
> And here beneath it is all as bad,
> For I thought the dead had peace, but it is not so;
> To have no peace in the grave, is that not sad?
> But up and down and to and fro,
> Ever about me the dead men go;
> And then to hear a dead man chatter
> Is enough to drive one mad.

In *Dombey and Son*, Dickens contrived to see the train
bearing Dombey as a kind of messenger of death since "its
way ... like the way of Death is strewn with ashes ...
Everything around is blackened. There are dark pools of
water, muddy lanes, and miserable habitations far below.
There are jagged walls and falling houses close at hand,
and through the battered roofs and broken windows
wretched rooms are seen, where want and fever hide
themselves in many wretched shapes, while smoke and
crowded gables, and distorted chimneys, and deformity of
brick and mortar penning up deformity of mind and body,
choke the murky distance."[5] Yet, even though Dickens has

---

[5]   *Dombey and Son*, p. 281.

Mr. Dombey regard this analogy as emblematic of "the end of everything; it was so ruinous and dreary," he nevertheless differs from his contemporaries in seeing death as suggestive not so much of the unknown or the terrible but of its opposite: death-defying, irrepressible life.[6]

One can see this in the wonderful opening scenes of *Oliver Twist*, where the champion of life in Dickens is at his finest.

> Although I am not disposed to maintain that the being born in a workhouse is in itself the most fortunate and enviable circumstance that can possibly befall a human being, I do mean to say that in this particular instance, it was the best thing for Oliver Twist that could by possibility have occurred. The fact is, that there was considerable difficulty in inducing Oliver to take upon himself the office of respiration,— a troublesome practice, but one which custom has rendered necessary to our easy existence; and for some time he lay gasping on a little flock mattress, rather unequally poised between this world and the next: the balance being decidedly in favour of the latter. Now, if, during this brief period, Oliver had been surrounded by careful grandmothers, anxious aunts, experienced nurses, and doctors of profound wisdom, he would most inevitably and indubitably have been killed in no time. There being nobody by, however, but a pauper old woman, who was rendered rather misty by an unwonted allowance of beer; and a parish surgeon who did such matters by contract; Oliver and Nature fought out the point between them. The result was, that, after a few struggles, Oliver breathed, sneezed, and proceeded

---

6   Ibid., p. 282.

> to advertise to the inmates of the workhouse the
> fact of a new burden having been imposed upon
> the parish, by setting up as loud a cry as could
> reasonably have been expected from a male infant
> who had not been possessed of that very useful
> appendage, a voice, for a much longer space of time
> than three minutes and a quarter.[7]

Like Dombey, Oliver's mother shows a love for her child
that is nothing less than fierce, though unlike Dombey she
does so in a way that is altogether unselfish. In trying to
make her way to the workhouse, where her child can be
born, Oliver's mother subordinates her own life to that of
her child, a deeply maternal instinct, which no amount of
dreary propaganda from the abortion lobby will ever
eradicate. In this moving instance of self-sacrifice, Dickens
confounds the pseudo-compassion of the abortionists,
which would spare the unwed mother the difficulty of
bringing an inexpedient child into the world by relieving
her of the child altogether. Indeed, abortionists reading
this brilliant first chapter of *Oliver Twist* must marvel at
how benighted Dickens and his characters are to insist on
such an ill-advised birth, when it could have been so easily
averted. Pro-lifers, on the other hand, reading the same
chapter will be reacquainted with that indomitable
primacy of life, even in the most woebegone of circumstances, which they have pledged their lives to protect.
What makes Dickens's approach to Oliver and his suffering mother so compelling is his refusal to see them in
anything but the most concrete terms of life and death.

> As Oliver gave this first proof of the free and proper
> action of his lungs, the patchwork coverlet which was
> carelessly flung over the iron bedstead, rustled; the pale
> face of a young woman was raised feebly from the pillow;

---

[7]   C. Dickens, *Oliver Twist* (Oxford, 1953), pp. 1–2.

and a faint voice imperfectly articulated the words, "Let me see the child, and die."

The surgeon had been sitting with his face turned towards the fire: giving the palms of his hands a warm and a rub alternately. As the young woman spoke, he rose, and advancing to the bed's head, said, with more kindness than might have been expected of him:

"Oh, you must not talk about dying, yet."

"Lor bless her dear heart, no!" interposed the nurse, hastily depositing in her pocket a green glass bottle, the contents of which she had been tasting in a corner with evident satisfaction. "Lor bless her dear heart, when she has lived as long as I have, sir, and had thirteen children of her own, and all on 'em dead except two, and them in the wurkus with me, she'll know better than to take on in that way, bless her dear heart! Think what it is to be a mother, there's a dear young lamb, do."

Apparently this consolatory perspective of a mother's prospects failed in producing its due effect. The patient shook her head, and stretched out her hand towards the child.

The surgeon deposited it in her arms. She imprinted her cold white lips passionately on its forehead; passed her hands over her face; gazed wildly round; shuddered; fell back—and died. They chafed her breast, hands, and temples; but the blood had stopped forever. They talked of hope and comfort. They had been strangers too long.

"It's all over, Mrs. Thingummy!" said the surgeon at last.

"Ah, poor dear, so it is!" said the nurse, picking up the cork of the green bottle, which had fallen out on the pillow, as she stooped to take up the child. "Poor dear!"

"You needn't mind sending up to me, if the child cries, nurse," said the surgeon, putting on his gloves with great deliberation. "It's very likely it *will* be troublesome. Give it a little gruel if it is." He put on his hat, and, pausing by the bed-side on his way to the door, added, "She was a good looking girl, too; where did she come from?"

"She was brought here last night," replied the old woman, "by the overseer's order. She was found lying in the street. She had walked some distance, for her shoes were worn to pieces; but where she came from, or where she was going to, nobody knows."

The surgeon leaned over the body, and raised the left hand. "The old story," he said, shaking his head: "no wedding-ring, I see. Ah! Good-night!"[8]

Another striking thing about these opening passages is how Dickens gives the lie to the abortionists' claim that respect for life somehow breeds indifference to the injustices of life. Those who insist on protecting life within the womb, abortionists never tire of asserting, will have no interest in addressing the needs of the child outside the womb. But here Dickens shows how respect for life sharpens the sense of such injustice. "What an excellent example of the power of dress young Oliver Twist was! Wrapped in the blanket which had hitherto formed his only covering, he might have been the child of a nobleman or a beggar; it would have been hard for the haughtiest stranger to have assigned him his proper station in society. But now that he was enveloped in the old calico robes which had grown yellow in the same service, he was badged and ticketed, and fell into his place at once—a parish child—the orphan of a workhouse—the humble, half starved drudge—to be cuffed and buffeted through the world—despised by all, and pitied by none."[9]

If the inequities that accompany us from the cradle were not lost on Dickens, he never sought to remove them with the sort of Draconian measures of which the abor-

---

[8]   Ibid., pp. 2–3.

[9]   Ibid., p. 3.

tionists approve. Instead, he met the problems of life with the cry of life. "Oliver cried lustily," Dickens has his narrator tell his readers, only adding that "If he could have known that he was an orphan, left to the tender mercies of churchwardens and overseers, perhaps he would have cried the louder." Throughout Dickens' work—whether in *David Copperfield* or *The Old Curiosity Shop* or *David Copperfield* or *Little Dorrit*—new life, the resiliency and bravery and exuberance of new life is always shown at odds with old injustice.

This perennial contest between good and evil is at the heart of *Oliver Twist*. One can see it not only in Oliver and Fagin but in Nancy and Fagin. Nancy may have been brought up by Fagin to take her place in the criminal underworld alongside the remorselessly brutal Bill Sykes but she is also conscientious enough to see that Oliver can be saved from this underworld by her courage and this selfless solicitude for the good of another is what impels her to betray the man who otherwise has such undue power over her. These are the aspects of the book that make it so applicable to the contest between good and evil with regard to abortion. The cynical selfishness at the root of abortion, for example, is completely in line with Fagin's philosophy of life.

> "Every man's his own friend, my dear," replied Fagin, with his most insinuating grin. "He hasn't as good a one as himself anywhere."
> "Except sometimes," replied Morris Bolter, assuming the air of a man of the world. "Some people are nobody's enemies but their own, yer know."
> "Don't believe that," said the Jew. "When a man's his own enemy, it's only because he's too much his own friend; not because he's careful for everybody but himself. Pooh! pooh! There ain't such a thing in nature."

"There oughtn't to be, if there is," replied Mr. Bolter. "That stands to reason," said the Jew. "Some conjurers say that number three is the magic number, and some say number seven. It's neither, my friend, neither. It's number one."

"Ha! ha!" cried Mr. Bolter. "Number one forever."

"In a little community like ours, my dear," said the Jew, who felt it necessary to qualify this position, "we have a general number one; that is, you can't consider yourself as number one, without considering me too as the same, and all the other young people."

"Oh, the devil!" exclaimed Mr. Bolter. "You see," pursued the Jew, affecting to disregard this interruption, "we are so mixed up together, and identified in our interests, that it must be so. For instance, it's your object to take care of number one—meaning yourself."

"Certainly," replied Mr. Bolter. "Yer about right there." "Well! You can't take care of yourself, number one, without taking care of me, number one."

"Number two, you mean," said Mr. Bolter, who was largely endowed with the quality of selfishness.

"No, I don't!" retorted the Jew. "I'm of the same importance to you, as you are to yourself."

"I say," interrupted Mr. Bolter, "yer a very nice man, and I'm very fond of yer; but we ain't quite so thick together, as all that comes to."

"Only think," said the Jew, shrugging his shoulders, and stretching out his hands; "only consider. You've done what's a very pretty thing, and what I love you for doing; but what at the same time would put the cravat round your throat that's so very easily tied and so very difficult to unloose—in plain English, the halter!"

Mr. Bolter put his hand to his neckerchief, as if he felt it inconveniently tight; and murmured an assent, qualified in tone but not in substance.

"The gallows," continued Fagin, "the gallows, my dear, is an ugly finger-post, which points out a very short and sharp turning that has stopped many a bold fellow's career on the broad highway. To keep in the easy road, and keep it at a distance, is object number one with you."

"Of course it is," replied Mr. Bolter. "What do yer talk about such things for?"

"Only to show you my meaning clearly," said the Jew, raising his eyebrows. "To be able to do that, you depend upon me. To keep my little business all snug, I depend upon you. The first is your number one, the second my number one. The more you value your number one, the more careful you must be of mine; so we come at last to what I told you at first—that a regard for number one holds us all together, and must do so, unless we would all go to pieces in company."

"That's true," rejoined Mr. Bolter, thoughtfully. "Oh! yer a cunning old codger!"[10]

Here, Dickens was satirizing the Benthamite calculus of the New Poor Law, which the Whigs passed in 1834 in an attempt to make up for the loss of the centuries-old almshouses that the Eighth Harry destroyed when he dissolved the monasteries. But what is most remarkable about this passage for our purposes is how clearly Fagin anticipates the predatory sway that the Servile State has come to exercise over its dependent citizenry. In return for votes, in return for the grant of legislative powers that now extends even to the definition of marriage (God help us all) the Servile State furnishes the subsidies that perpetuate dependency, and among these none are more loudly touted than the State-approved means of contraception and abortion, which the advocates of abortion have misled the public into equating with healthcare. If Fagin offers his dependants room and board and at least the promise of protection from the hangman's noose in return for an ample cut of their collective swag, the Servile State offers

---

[10] Ibid., pp. 327–328.

its dependants nearly everything they could possibly require in sublunary benefits in return for their liberty, indeed their very conscience.

In his cell, before he is brought out to be hanged, Fagin is described trying to cajole Oliver into somehow saving him. "Say I've gone to sleep—they'll believe *you*," he says. "You can get me out …" Oliver, instead of scorning his erstwhile captor, prays for him. "Oh! God forgive this wretched man!" Still, there will be no reprieve for Fagin and Dickens describes his end with moving fellow feeling—an empathy entirely denied the condemned unborn. "The men laid hands upon him, and disengaging Oliver from his grasp, held him back. He struggled with the power of desperation, for an instant; and, then sent up cry upon cry that penetrated even those massive walls, and rang in their ears until they reached the open yard." For Dickens, so elemental is the cry of life that even the hard-hearted Fagin succumbs to it, faced as he is with "the black stage, the cross-beam, the rope, and all the hideous apparatus of death."[11]

---

[11]   Ibid., pp. 410–411.

G. K. Chesterton

11

DICKENS, CHESTERTON AND THE PRO-LIFE GENIUS OF *LITTLE DORRIT*

I N HIS INTRODUCTION to *Little Dorrit* Chesterton wrote of Dickens' eleventh novel as "very interesting, sincere, and fascinating" but "for all that, his one collapse." Indeed, for Chesterton the novel stood "chiefly as a signal of how far [Dickens] went down the road of realism, of sadness, and of what is called modernity." Moreover, if Chesterton saw excessive darkness in the book, he also saw insufficient ebullience. While noting how the leisurely, *ad hoc*, meandering quality of the book was reminiscent of *The Pickwick Papers* and *David Copperfield*, he still felt that it failed to achieve anything like the effervescent life of those earlier books. "Even in assuming his old liberty, he cannot resume his old hilarity," Chesterton complained. "He can recreate the anarchy, but not the revelry."[1]

These were ironic reservations because elsewhere, in commentary that had nothing specifically to do with *Little Dorrit*, Chesterton provided an indispensable key to the genuine merits of the novel. In this chapter, I shall demonstrate how this commentary can help us to appreciate the pro-life genius of the book, as well as the nature of the pro-life fight that we continue to wage with those who insist that killing babies in the womb is somehow benefi-

---

[1]   G. K. Chesterton, *Collected Works: Volume XV: Chesterton on Dickens* (San Francisco, 1989), p. 365.

cial to women. Before revisiting that commentary, however, I shall give a brief overview of the plot and some of
the more prominent themes of the novel.

Little Dorrit, the novelist's eleventh novel, ran in twenty
monthly parts from December 1855 to June 1857.
Although full of Dickens' characteristically involved plot-
ting, the main story of *Little Dorrit* is straightforward. The
book opens with William Dorrit imprisoned in the Marshalsea for debt, which he regards as an affront to his
rightful social standing. His youngest child, Amy whose
nickname is Little Dorrit, is actually born in the Marshalsea and much of the story is told from her perspective—in
the same way that *Oliver Twist* is told from the perspective
of Oliver. Amy is in love with Arthur Clennam, the
frustrated son of Mrs. Clennam, an embittered old Calvin-
ist cripple, whom Arthur mistakenly imagines the cause
of Dorrit's unjust imprisonment. After years of presenting
himself to his fellow debtors and those beyond the prison
gates as the very personification of distressed gentility,
Dorrit has an unsuspected fortune settled on him, after
which he takes his family abroad, where they live in
itinerant splendor. However, no sooner do they become
familiar with the ways of society than they see that the
world beyond the Marshalsea constitutes a prison of its
own. Little Dorrit discovers this most arrestingly amidst
the cosmopolitan flotsam and jetsam of Venice.

> It appeared on the whole ... that this same society
> in which they lived, greatly resembled a superior
> sort of Marshalsea. Numbers of people seemed to
> come abroad, pretty much as people had come into
> the prison; through debt, through idleness, relation-
> ship, curiosity, and general unfitness for getting on
> at home. They were brought into these foreign
> towns in the custody of couriers and local followers,
> just as the debtors had been brought into the

prison. They prowled about the churches and picture-galleries, much in the old, dreary, prison-yard manner. They were usually going away again to-morrow or next week, and rarely knew their own minds, and seldom did what they said they would do, or went where they said they would go: in all this again, very like the prison debtors. They paid high for poor accommodation, and disparaged a place while they pretended to like it: which was exactly the Marshalsea custom. They were envied when they went away, by people left behind feigning not to want to go: and that again was the Marshal-sea habit invariably. A certain set of words and phrases, as much belonging to tourists as the College and the Snuggery belonged to the jail, was always in their mouths. They had precisely the same incapacity for settling down to anything, as the prisoners used to have; they rather deteriorated one another, as the prisoners used to do; and they wore untidy dresses, and fell into a slouching way of life: still, always like the people in the Marshalsea.[2]

Indeed, imprisonment gives the book its unifying meta-phor. If Dorrit is imprisoned by delusions of gentility, other characters are imprisoned by delusions of power and prestige. Bernard Shaw famously claimed that the novel converted him to socialism. "*Little Dorrit* is a more seditious book than *Das Kapital*," the playwright declared. "All over Europe men and women are in prison for pamphlets and speeches which are to *Little Dorrit* as red pepper to dynamite."[3] In the exposure of the financer, Merdle, who commits suicide when he is shown to be a forger and thief, Shaw saw the exposure of the inherent

---

[2]   C. Dickens, *Little Dorrit* (Oxford: 1953), p. 478.

[3]   *Bernard Shaw's Non-dramatic Criticism,* ed. S. Weintraub (London, 1972), p. xxii.

evils of capitalism.[4] The ruin of the idol of Lombard Street, "that illustrious man and great national ornament," as Dickens dubs him, would forever confirm Shaw in his Fabian prejudices.[5] Yet since its primary target is not the alleged sins of capitalism but the sins of selfishness and the unreality to which selfishness gives rise, the book is much more revolutionary than Shaw realized. If Merdle is imprisoned by delusions of wealth, Mrs. Merdle is imprisoned by the society into which that wealth has given her entrée, which she knows, or thinks she knows, is "hollow and conventional and worldly and very shocking" but which nevertheless, she insists, must be consulted, "unless we are Savages in the Tropical seas ..."[6]

Amy alone is free of such imprisoning delusions by being free of selfishness. "It is enough that she was inspired to be something which was not what the rest were," the narrator observes, "and to be something different and laborious, for the sake of the rest. Inspired? Yes. Shall we speak of the inspiration of a poet or a priest, and not of the heart impelled by love and self-devotion to the lowliest work in the lowliest way of life?"[7]

While much of the novel is given over to the pretensions of Dorrit and those by whom he wishes to be accepted, an equal share is given over to Amy's good-heartedness and the way in which her love overcomes her father's and the world's failings. As Lionel Trilling wrote

---

[4]   "Mr. Merdle's complaint," Dickens told his first biographer, John Forster, "which you find in the end to be fraud and forgery, came into my mind as the last drop in the silver cream-jug on Hempstead Heath." *Selected Letters of Charles Dickens,* ed. Jenny Hartley (Oxford, 2012), p. 304.

[5]   LD, p. 710.

[6]   LD, p. 239.

[7]   LD, p. 71.

in an influential introduction to the Oxford Illustrated Dickens edition of the novel, Amy is the "Beatrice of the Comedy, the Paraclete in female form. Even the physical littleness of this grown woman, an attribute which is insisted on and which seems so likely to repel us, does not do so, for we perceive it to be the sign that she not only is the Child of the Marshalsea, as she is called, but also the Child of the Parable, the negation of the social will."[8] Accordingly, as Dickens remarks, "it may often be observed in life, that spirits like Little Dorrit do not appear to reason half as carefully as the folks who get the better of them."[9] Of course, some have complained that she is too good or good in a way that is somehow incredible. Yet V. S. Pritchett is surely right when he says that "Dickens was not the first or the last novelist to find virtue more difficult to portray than the wish for it."[10] Moreover, the very fact that such a good and loving creature should be born in a debtors' prison is itself a negation of that social will's worldly calculations. The same, of course, can be said for Oliver's being born in a workhouse. For our purposes, it is also a negation of the established view among pro-abortion elites in Britain and America and around the world that certain children must be killed in the womb in order to save them from ending up in modern-day debtors' prisons and workhouses. For Dickens, on the contrary, it is because children are born in such places that the goodness of life is reaffirmed.

In *Little Dorrit, Oliver Twist, David Copperfield, Great Expectations* and so many of his other books, the uncertainty and vulnerability of his young heroes is central to Dickens' appreciation of the precious value of life and in

---

[8]   LD, p. xvi.

[9]   LD, p. 503.

[10]   V. S. Pritchett, *Complete Collected Essays* (London, 1991), p. 516.

this he affirms Pope John Paul II's great insight into the
Gospel of Life.

> In Jesus' own life, from beginning to end, we find
> a singular "dialectic" between the experience of the
> uncertainty of human life and the affirmation of its
> value. Jesus' life is marked by uncertainty from the
> very moment of his birth. He is certainly accepted
> by the righteous, who echo Mary's immediate and
> joyful "yes" (cf. Lk 1:38). But there is also, from the
> start, rejection on the part of a world which grows
> hostile and looks for the child in order "to destroy
> him" (Mt 2:13); a world which remains indifferent
> and unconcerned about the fulfilment of the
> mystery of this life entering the world: "there was
> no place for them in the inn" (Lk 2:7). In this
> contrast between threats and insecurity on the one
> hand and the power of God's gift on the other,
> there shines forth all the more clearly the glory
> which radiates from the house at Nazareth and
> from the manger at Bethlehem: this life which is
> born is salvation for all humanity (cf. Lk 2:11).

The obligations that follow from the reality of God's gift
are unambiguous: *"the task of accepting and serving life
involves everyone; and this task must be fulfilled above all
towards life when it is at its weakest.* It is Christ himself
who reminds us of this when he asks to be loved and served
in his brothers and sisters who are suffering in any way,
the hungry, the thirsty, the foreigner, the naked, the sick,
the imprisoned … Whatever is done to each of them is
done to Christ himself (cf. Mt 25:31–46)".[11]

A scene in *Little Dorrit* dramatizes this which, again,
has deep pro-life undertones. Dorrit is in the Marshalsea
prison in "his black velvet cap and old grey gown," and he
has been giving vent to his accustomed self-pity, to which

---

[11] Pope John Paul II, *Evangelium Vitae*, 72–77.

his daughter responds with her accustomed forbearance: "Dear Father, loved father, darling of my heart ..."[12] If Dorrit remains locked in self pity, this only prompts his daughter to show him more forbearing love. "While he smoked out his cigar in peace, [Amy] made his bed, and put the small room in order for his repose. Being weary then, owing to the advanced hour and his emotions, he came out of his chair to bless her and wish her Good Night. All this time he had never once thought of *her* dress, her shoes, her need of anything. No other person upon earth, save herself, could have been so unmindful of her wants."[13] Here is the sacrifice of self so absent from the indulgence of self at the root of abortion.

It is also absent from the aggrieved self of Miss Wade, the tortured lesbian, whose house Dickens describes as "a dead sort of house, with a dead wall over the way and a dead gateway at the side, where a pendant bell-handle produced two dead tinkles, and a knocker produced a dead, flat surface-tapping, that seemed not to have depth enough in it to penetrate even the cracked door. However, the door jarred open on a dead sort of spring; and he closed it behind him as he entered a dull yard, soon brought to a close at the back of another dead wall, where an attempt had been made to train some creeping shrubs, which were dead ..."[14] The inordinate length of Dickens' novels often left his muse frazzled but, even so, passages like these prove that he could coax a very droll humour from rhetorical fatigue.

There is nothing dead in the generosity and good heartedness of Little Dorrit. In addition to her poor wreck of a father, she shows unflagging love to her vain, petulant,

---

[12] LD, p. 228.

[13] LD, pp. 229–230.

[14] LD, p. 654.

scheming sister Fanny as well as to her even less admirable
brother Edward, an impudent flâneur, who spends most
of his days drinking and gambling. She is also unstintingly
charitable to a character named Maggy, a poor waif of a
woman who calls Little Dorrit "Mother"—a touching
nickname for the maternal heroine who has lost her own
mother. In one vivid scene, the two are locked out of the
Marshalsea and spend the night walking the streets of
London. "Three o'clock, and half-past three, and they had
passed over London Bridge. They had heard the rush of
the tide against obstacles; had looked down, awed, through
the dark vapor on the river; had seen little spots of lighted
water, where the bridge lamps were reflected, shining like
demon eyes, with a terrible fascination in them for guilt
and misery. They had shrunk past homeless people, lying
coiled up in nooks. They had run from drunkards. They
had started from slinking men, whistling and signing to
one another at by-corners, or running away at full speed."[15]

Then, too, Little Dorrit is solicitude itself to her uncle
Frederick, an aloof, distrait, hapless man, a clarinetist in a
music hall, about whom "the carpenters had a joke to the
effect that he was dead without being aware of it."[16] Uncle
Frederick is not unlike another character, Old Nandy, of
whom Amy is also fond, though her sister considers him
"an old pauper," an equally dilapidated castaway who "said
nothing about its being his birthday, or [his neighbors]
might have kept him in; for such old men should not be
born." [17]

As these instances of her charity demonstrate, Amy
stands out among Dickens' vast array of characters precisely because she is willing to engage and help people

[15] LD, p. 174.
[16] LD, p. 236.
[17] LD, p. 366.

despite their failings, the inconvenience they cause, their bother. "For," as V. S. Pritchett noticed, with typical insight, "the convivial and gregarious extravagance and picaresque disorder which are supposedly Dickensian are not Dickens' special contribution to the English novel. They are inheritances from Sterne, Smollet and the sentimental side of Richardson, an inheritance which may be traced back to the comedy of Jonson ..." For Pritchett, "the distinguishing quality of Dickens' people is that they are solitaries. They are people caught living in a world of their own. They soliloquize in it. They do not talk to one another; they talk to themselves."[18] This is true of Dorrit, Fanny, Edward, Merdle, Mrs. Gowan, Mrs. General, Miss Wade, Blandois, Casby, the quintessentially extortionate landlord, and many other characters of *Little Dorrit* but it is not true of Amy. She lives through and for and with people, and never more so than when they are vulnerable or weak, and here, again, we can see her pro-life significance.

What is also extraordinary about Amy and the love that she shows her less than lovable family is how much she reminds one of what Chesterton has to say about the family. Here, Chesterton illuminates the true virtues of the book, about which elsewhere he is so unaccountably mum. "Falling in love has been often regarded as the supreme adventure, the supreme romantic accident," Chesterton writes in an essay entitled "On Certain Modern Writers and the Institution of the Family" from his collection *Heretics* (1905).

> In so much as there is in it something outside ourselves, something of a sort of merry fatalism, this is very true. Love does take us and transfigure

---

[18] V. S. Pritchett, *Complete Collected Essays* (London, 1991), pp. 208–209.

and torture us. It does break our hearts with an
unbearable beauty, like the unbearable beauty of
music. But in so far as we have certainly something
to do with the matter; in so far as we are in some
sense prepared to fall in love and in some sense
jump into it; in so far as we do to some extent
choose and to some extent even judge—in all this
falling in love is not truly romantic, is not truly
adventurous at all. In this degree the supreme
adventure is not falling in love. The supreme
adventure is being born. There we do walk suddenly into a splendid and startling trap. There we
do see something of which we have not dreamed
before. Our father and mother do lie in wait for us
and leap out on us, like brigands from a bush. Our
uncle is a surprise. Our aunt is, in the beautiful
common expression, a bolt from the blue. When
we step into the family, by the act of being born,
we do step into a world which is incalculable, into
a world which has its own strange laws, into a
world which could do without us, into a world that
we have not made. In other words, when we step
into the family we step into a fairy-tale.[19]

In reading *Little Dorrit*, we encounter precisely the sort of
fairy-tale that Chesterton describes, one in which Amy
may not have any control over her incorrigible family but
loves them nevertheless. And despite Dickens' profound
disenchantment with the world of the novel, with its crass
calculations, its "surface and varnish and show without
substance," he never entirely gives up on it. In this sense,
he is like his hero, Arthur Clennam, whom he describes
as "a dreamer ... because he was a man who had, deep-
rooted in his nature, a belief in all the gentle and good

---

[19]   G. K. Chesterton, *Collected Works: Volume I: Orthodoxy, Heretics,
       Blatchford Controversies* (San Francisco, 1986), p. 143.

things his life had been without. Bred in meanness and hard dealing, this had rescued him to be a man of honourable mind and open hand. Bred in coldness and severity, this had rescued him to have a warm and sympathetic heart. Bred in a creed too darkly audacious to pursue, through its process of reversing the making of man in the image of an erring man, this had rescued him to judge not, and, in humility, to be merciful and have hope and charity."[20] And, again, Chesterton acknowledges the animating power of this hope and charity in his commentary on the family.

> This colour as of a fantastic narrative ought to cling to the family and to our relations with it throughout life. Romance is the deepest thing in life; romance is deeper even than reality. For even if reality could be proved to be misleading, it still could not be proved to be unimportant or unimpressive. Even if the facts are false, they are still very strange. And this strangeness of life, this unexpected and even perverse element of things as they fall out, remains incurably interesting. The circumstances we can regulate may become tame or pessimistic; but the "circumstances over which we have no control" remain god-like to those who, like Mr. Micawber, an improvident but lovable character in Dickens' *David Copperfield*, who eventually becomes a colonial magistrate, can call on them and renew their strength. People wonder why the novel is the most popular form of literature; people wonder why it is read more than books of science or books of metaphysics. The reason is very simple; it is merely that the novel is more true than they are. Life may sometimes legitimately appear as a book of science. Life may sometimes

---

[20]   LD, p. 165.

appear, and with a much greater legitimacy, as a book of metaphysics. But life is always a novel. Our existence may cease to be a song; it may cease even to be a beautiful lament. Our existence may not be an intelligible justice, or even a recognizable wrong. But our existence is still a story. In the fiery alphabet of every sunset is written, "to be continued in our next." If we have sufficient intellect, we can finish a philosophical and exact deduction, and be certain that we are finishing it right. With the adequate brain-power we could finish any scientific discovery, and be certain that we were finishing it right. But not with the most gigantic intellect could we finish the simplest or silliest story, and be certain that we were finishing it right. That is because a story has behind it, not merely intellect which is partly mechanical, but will, which is in its essence divine. The narrative writer can send his hero to the gallows if he likes in the last chapter but one. He can do it by the same divine caprice whereby he, the author, can go to the gallows himself, and to hell afterwards if he chooses. And the same civilization, the chivalric European civilization which asserted freewill in the thirteenth century, produced the thing called "fiction" in the eighteenth. When Thomas Aquinas asserted the spiritual liberty of man, he created all the bad novels in the circulating libraries.[21]

Here Chesterton shows how deeply wrongheaded it is for the individual to try to treat life as though it were something that he can control to his own selfish satisfaction. He also shows how it is in delineating the futility of that yearning for control that the novelist discovers the real treasures of his chosen form—an insight which the author of *Little Dorrit* would doubtless have appreciated. Indeed,

---

[21]   CW, I, pp. 143–144.

one can readily imagine Dickens assenting to nearly every line of this most Chestertonian of essays, especially where the great champion of the family remarks how "in order that life should be a story or romance to us, it is necessary that a great part of it, at any rate, should be settled for us without our permission. If we wish life to be a system, this may be a nuisance; but if we wish it to be a drama, it is an essential. It may often happen, no doubt, that a drama may be written by somebody else which we like very little. But we should like it still less if the author came before the curtain every hour or so, and forced on us the whole trouble of inventing the next act. A man has control over many things in his life; he has control over enough things to be the hero of a novel. But if he had control over everything, there would be so much hero that there would be no novel."[22]

Dickens then proceeds to make another observation that throws light on *Little Dorrit*: "the reason why the lives of the rich are at bottom so tame and uneventful is simply that they can choose the events. They are dull because they are omnipotent. They fail to feel adventures because they can make the adventures."[23] When imprisoned in the Marshalsea, Dorrit spends most of his time sustaining the illusion that he is the grand seigneur of the place by extracting monetary testimonials and even cigars from his obliging fellow prisoners; but once rich enough to join what passes for the great world beyond the prison gates he discovers the desolation of the unregenerate self's materialized desires. This is what gives the wonderful scene, where Dorrit forgets himself and his surroundings and harangues a Roman dinner party as though he is still in the Marshalsea, its pathetic poetry. After he stuns his

---

[22]   CW, I, p. 144.
[23]   CW, I, p. 144.

fellow dinner guests, he is put to bed. "And from that hour
his poor maimed spirit, only remembering the place where
it had broken its wings, cancelled the dream through
which it had groped, and knew of nothing beyond the
Marshalsea."[24] That Dorrit is partly based on Dickens' own
father gives this great poignancy. The very writing of the
novel was an act of profound filial love on the part of the
novelist. Amy's creator had something of Amy herself in
his deeply empathetic imagination.

At the same time, we can see something of the groping
Christian in Dickens in his fascination with Dorrit's failure
to realize his dreams of genteel enjoyment. As Chesterton
once remarked, "The great psychological discovery of
Paganism, which turned it into Christianity, can be
expressed with some accuracy in one phrase. The pagan
set out, with admirable sense, to enjoy himself. By the end
of his civilization he had discovered that a man cannot
enjoy himself and continue to enjoy anything else."[25]
Again, for Chesterton, as for Dickens, the real adventure
of life can only be enjoyed when the pernicious dream of
selfish enjoyment is renounced—an ancient truth that our
abortionists and their toadying historians refuse to
acknowledge.

> The thing which keeps life romantic and full of
> fiery possibilities is the existence of these great
> plain limitations which force all of us to meet the
> things we do not like or do not expect. It is vain for
> the supercilious moderns to talk of being in uncon-
> genial surroundings. To be in a romance is to be
> in uncongenial surroundings. To be born into this
> earth is to be born into uncongenial surroundings,
> hence to be born into a romance. Of all these great

---

[24] LD, p. 649.

[25] CW, I, p. 127.

limitations and frameworks which fashion and
create the poetry and variety of life, the family is
the most definite and important. Hence it is mis-
understood by the moderns, who imagine that
romance would exist most perfectly in a complete
state of what they call liberty. They think that if a
man makes a gesture it would be a startling and
romantic matter that the sun should fall from the
sky. But the startling and romantic thing about the
sun is that it does not fall from the sky. They are
seeking under every shape and form a world where
there are no limitations—that is, a world where
there are no outlines; that is, a world where there
are no shapes. There is nothing baser that that
infinity. They say they wish to be as strong as the
universe, but they really wish the whole universe
as weak as themselves.[26]

"A world where there are no limitations ... a world where
there are no outlines:" this is the world of the abortionist,
who makes what amounts to complete license the govern-
ing principle of his moral life and insists that children only
be born in circumstances congenial to that license. The
description of Little Dorrit's birth in the Marshalsea is one
of the great pro-life passages in all of literature precisely
because it so richly confutes the abortionists' claim that
birth is something that we are not only authorized but
obliged to control, whether on the grounds of expedience
or what the world accounts self-fulfillment. As if to drive
home the immense evil of this claim, the artist in Dickens
saw to it that Little Dorrit should have her birth not only
in the most unpropitious of circumstances but in those
most redolent of our inalienable fallenness.

---

[26] CW, I, p. 145.

The doctor was amazingly shabby, in a torn and darned roughweather sea-jacket, out at elbows, and eminently short of buttons (he had been in his time the experienced surgeon carried by a passenger ship), the dirtiest white trousers conceivable by mortal man, carpet slippers, and no visible linen. "Childbed?" said the doctor. "I'm the boy!" With that the doctor took a comb from the chimney-piece, and stuck his hair upright—which appeared to be his way of washing himself—produced a professional chest or case, of most abject appearance, from the cupboard where his cup and saucer and coals were, settled his chin in the frowzy wrapper round his neck, and became a ghastly medical scarecrow.

In addition to this marvelous, ramshackle doctor, flies attend the unlikely birth. "The flies trouble you, don't they, my dear?" says the charwoman of the Marshalsea, Mrs. Bangham to the expectant mother. "But p'raps they'll take your mind off it, and do you good. What between the buryin'-ground, the grocers, the waggon-stables, and the paunch trade, the Marshalsea flies gets very large. P'raps they're sent as a consolation, if we only knowed it. How are you now, my dear? No better? No, my dear, it ain't to be expected; you'll be worse before you're better, and you know it, don't you? Yes. That's right!" But then the philosophical Mrs. Bangham encourages her pregnant charge to keep her spirits up by remembering the great imminent blessing that is about to arrive. "And to think of a sweet little cherub being born inside the lock! Now ain't it pretty, ain't that something to carry you through it pleasant? Why, we ain't had such a thing happen here, my dear, not for I couldn't name the time when." To which the doctor gamely responds: "We are as right as we can be, Mrs. Bangham, and we shall come out of this like a house afire;" before instructing the good woman to go out and fetch some brandy.

> Mrs. Bangham submitted, and the doctor, having administered her potion, took his own. He repeated the treatment every hour, being very determined with Mrs. Bangham. Three or four hours passed; the flies fell into the traps by hundreds; and at length one little life, hardly stronger than theirs, appeared among the multitudes of lesser deaths.
>
> "A very nice little girl indeed," said the doctor; "little, but well-formed. Halloa, Mrs. Bangham! You're looking queer! You be off, ma'am, this minute, and fetch a little more brandy, or we shall have you in hysterics."

This is Dickens' brilliant paean to birth in the real world, not the dystopia of the abortionists. Here there is poverty and debt and sickness and want but there is also God-given life. And, again, for Dickens to have set his scene in the Marshalsea was a masterstroke, for the world of the natural man is a prison into which every child brings the promise of the Christ child. "That a child would be born to you in a place like this?" said the doctor. "Bah, bah, sir, what does it signify? A little more elbow-room is all we want here..."[27]

The religious implications of this wonderful scene are unmistakable. We are not gods; we are not masters of the universe; we are fallen creatures born into a fallen world in desperate need of God's salvation. Many have questioned whether Dickens had any real religious sense. For Graham Greene, "The world of Dickens is a world without God; and as a substitute for the power and the glory of the omnipotent and omniscient are a few sentimental references to heaven, angels, the sweet faces of the dead and Oliver saying, 'Heaven is a long way off, and they are too happy there to come down to the bedside of a poor boy!'"[28] Hilaire Belloc was convinced that Dickens had "one great

---

[27] LD, pp. 61–63.

[28] G. Greene, *Collected Essays* (London, 1970), p. 85.

area of weakness" and that was that "He lapses into that worst of heresies, the Gospel of Kindliness."

> He cannot be blamed; it was of his time. He lived in that generation when the old transcendental faith of Englishmen was beginning to break down (it has long ago disappeared), and he clung to such fragments of it as could still appeal to the heart. In truth, this Gospel of Kindliness is an abomination before the Lord. This gospel of easy charity and nothing else mattering is the very essence of topsy-turvydom in moral values; for it refuses to inquire why a good deed is good or what it is which makes it a good deed; and it reduces all judgment in such things to the basest of tests, a sort of comfortable warmth. At bottom all those morals are the morals of confusion.[29]

This may be true of some aspects of Dickens' work but the wonderful scene of the birth of Amy Dorrit surely shows that he was alive to the world-confounding glory of the Incarnation. Then, too, in Amy he embodies the redemptive power of self-sacrifice, even if in no overtly Christian way. Dickens, after all, was enough of a realist to appreciate that it would have been false to the pagan setting of Victorian London to make his heroine more pointedly Christian. A memorable passage early on in the novel drives home the character of this pagan setting, without which the Christian impulses of Amy and Arthur would lose half their significance.

> It was a Sunday evening in London, gloomy, close and stale. Maddening church bells of all degrees of dissonance, sharp and flat, cracked and clear, fast and slow, made the brick-and-mortar echoes hideous. Melancholy streets in a penitential garb of

---

[29]   H. Belloc, *A Conversation with An Angel* (London, 1928), p. 45.

soot, steeped the souls of the people who were condemned to look at them out of windows, in dire despondency. In every thoroughfare, up almost every alley, and down almost every turning, some doleful bell was throbbing, jerking, tolling, as if the Plague were in the city and the dead-carts were going round. Everything was bolted and barred that could by possibility furnish relief to an over-worked people. No pictures, no unfamiliar animals, no rare plants or flowers, no natural or artificial wonders of the ancient world—all *taboo* with that enlightened strictness, that the ugly South Sea gods in the British Museum might have supposed them-selves at home again. Nothing to see but streets, streets, streets. Nothing to breathe but streets, streets, streets. Nothing to change the brooding mind, or raise it up. Nothing for the spent toiler to do, but to compare the monotony of his seventh day with the monotony of his six days, think what a weary life he led, and make the best of it—or the worst, according to the probabilities.[30]

This captures the extent to which religion was absent from the streets of Victorian London—the London Mayhew documented—where Sunday was seen not as a day of Christian thanksgiving or worship but grinding, oppres-sive ennui. "The costers have no religion at all," a coster-monger told Mayhew, "and very little notion, or none at all, of what religion or a future state is. Of all things they hate tracts. They hate them because the people leaving them never give them anything, and they can't read the tract—not one in forty—they're vexed to be bothered with it"— a reality that doubtless disconcerted the Anglican Newman and his tract-writing friends.[31] Instead of the

---

[30] LD, p. 28.

[31] H. Mayhew, *London Labour and the London Poor,* ed. Christopher

festivity of faith, Dickens encounters only the dreary evils
of absentee landlords.

> Fifty thousand lairs surrounded him where people
> lived so unwholesomely, that fair water put into
> their crowded rooms on Saturday night, would be
> corrupt on Sunday morning; albeit my lord, their
> county member, was amazed that they failed to
> sleep in company with their butcher's meat. Miles
> of close wells and pits of houses, where the inhab-
> itants gasped for air, stretched far away towards
> every point of the compass. Through the heart of
> the town a deadly sewer ebbed and flowed, in the
> place of a fine fresh river.

And it is here, in the form of city church bells, that Dickens
presents the appeal of Christianity, an appeal that the
Victorian English can scarcely tolerate.

> Mr. Arthur Clennam sat in the window of the
> coffee-house on Ludgate Hill, counting one of the
> neighbouring bells, making sentences and burdens
> of songs out of it in spite of himself, and wondering
> how many sick people it might be the death of in
> the course of the year. As the hour approached, its
> changes of measure made it more and more exas-
> perating. At the quarter, it went off into a condition
> of deadly-lively importunity, urging the populace
> in a voluble manner to Come to church, Come to
> church, Come to church! At the ten minutes, it
> became aware that the congregation would be
> scanty, and slowly hammered out in low spirits,
> They won't come, they won't come, they won't
> come! At the five minutes, it abandoned hope, and
> shook every house in the neighbourhood for three
> hundred seconds, with one dismal swing per
> second, as a groan of despair.[32]

Hibbert (Folio Society, 1996), p. 18.

Ian Ker gives a good example of the way Chesterton saw
Dickens' treatment of despair in his superb critical life of
the great journalist and poet, where he concedes that "Like
all writers with a very distinctive, idiosyncratic style,
Chesterton hovers constantly on the verge of self-parody,
always liable to abuse or overuse of paradox ..." Yet Ker
also reminds his readers that Chesterton can make his
paradoxes "brilliantly illuminating," and for instance he
quotes the passage where Chesterton encapsulates the
optimism of Dickens by inverting the words that Dante
inscribed over the gates of hell: "abandon hopelessness, all
ye who enter here."[33] This is the summons to courage that
animates so much of Dickens' greatest work and no one
articulates it better than Chesterton.

> If optimism means a general approval, it is certainly
> true that the more a man becomes an optimist the
> more he becomes a melancholy man. If he manages
> to praise everything, his praise will develop an
> alarming resemblance to a polite boredom. He will
> say that the marsh is as good as the garden; he will
> mean that the garden is as dull as the marsh. He
> may force himself to say that emptiness is good,
> but he will hardly prevent himself from asking what
> is the good of such good. This optimism does
> exist—this optimism which is more hopeless than
> pessimism—this optimism which is the very heart
> of hell. Against such an aching vacuum of joyless

---

[32] LD, p. 29. Here it might be amusing to note that Virginia Woolf
detested the sound of church bells, which she found "sullen" and
"didactic." Indeed, the effect of these bells on her precarious
mental state might have contributed to her last fatal bout of
madness. As Hermione Lee points out, "she disliked them as much
for what they represented as for their insistence." See H. Lee,
Virginia Woolf (London, 1997), p. 421.

[33] I. Ker, *G. K. Chesterton: A Biography* (Oxford, 2011), p. 166.

approval there is only one antidote—a sudden and
pugnacious belief in positive evil. This world can
be made beautiful again by beholding it as a battle-
field. When we have defined and isolated the evil
thing, the colours come back into everything else.
When evil things have become evil, good things, in
a blazing apocalypse, become good. There are
some men who are dreary because they do not
believe in God; but there are many others who are
dreary because they do not believe in the devil. The
grass grows green again when we believe in the
devil, the roses grow red again when we believe in
the devil.[34]

Having defined his terms, Chesterton proceeds to
expound the moral character of Dickens' optimism. "No
man was more filled with the sense of this bellicose basis
of all cheerfulness than Dickens. He knew very well the
essential truth, that the true optimist can only continue
an optimist so long as he is discontented. For the full value
of this life can only be got by fighting; the violent take it
by storm. And if we have accepted everything, we have
missed something—war. This life of ours is a very enjoyable fight, but a very miserable truce."[35] And in order to
give his characters the ability to do jubilant battle with evil,
Dickens was never hesitant to draw his villains in bold and
lurid colors, a fact which caused Chesterton to observe
how "strange" it is that "so few critics of Dickens or of
other romantic writers have noticed this philosophical
meaning in the undiluted villain. The villain is not in the
story to be a character; he is there to be a danger—a
ceaseless, ruthless, and uncompromising menace, like that
of wild beasts or the sea. For the full satisfaction of the

---

[34] CW, XV, pp. 201–202.

[35] CW, XV, p. 202.

sense of combat, which everywhere and always involves a sense of equality, it is necessary to make the evil thing a man; but it is not always necessary, it is not even always artistic, to make him a mixed and probable man. In any tale, the tone of which is at all symbolic, he may quite legitimately be made an aboriginal and infernal energy. He must be a man only in the sense that he must have a wit and will to be matched with the wit and will of the man chiefly fighting. The evil may be inhuman, but it must not be impersonal, which is almost exactly the position occupied by Satan in the theological scheme."[36]

These are useful discriminations when it comes to *Little Dorrit* because the villain of the book is not so much Blandois but the world personified by Blandois, the bounder who yearns to be thought a gentleman, the scoundrel who tries to convince others that he is really a Good Samaritan. And it is characteristic of Dickens to personify the villainy of the world with other characters as well, most of whom would pass for eminently respectable people in nineteenth-century or any London: Pancks, the indefatigable rent collector, whose philosophy is "Take all you can get, and keep back all you can't be forced to give up;"[37] Mr. Barnacle, the high official in the Circumlocution Office, who "wound and wound folds and folds of white cravat round his neck, as he wound and wound folds of tape and paper round the country" and "seemed to have been sitting for his portrait to Sir Thomas Lawrence all the days of his life;"[38] Mr. Gowan, the cynical society artist, about whom the narrator observes, "he has sauntered into the Arts at a leisurely Pall Mall pace and I doubt if they care to be taken quite so coolly;"[39] and Mrs. General, the

---

[36]   CW, XV, p. 202.
[37]   LD, p. 278.
[38]   LD, p. 111.

great arbitress of what is and what is not fit, "always on her coach-box keeping the proprieties well together."[40]

> Mrs. General had no opinions. Her way of forming a mind was to prevent it from forming opinions. She had a little circular set of mental grooves or rails on which she started little trains of other people's opinions, which never overtook one another, and never got anywhere. Even her propriety could not dispute that there was impropriety in the world; but Mrs. General's way of getting rid of it was to put it out of sight, and make believe that there was no such thing. This was another of her ways of forming a mind—to cram all articles of difficulty into cupboards, lock them up, and say they had no existence. It was the easiest way, and, beyond all comparison, the properest.[41]

Besides being an ardent proponent of that unreality for which the characters of *Little Dorrit* exhibit such an insatiable appetite, Mrs. General is a magnificent avatar of the political correctness that now gags our own twittering world.

Again, all of this might seem to confirm what Chesterton regarded as the insufferable pessimism of the book, a pessimism that might please George Gissing but bore Dickensians. For Chesterton, there was something "a little modern and a little sad" about the book, something "out of tune with the main trend of Dickens's moral feeling…" And he identified that difference in what appeared to be a failure of hope. "It is but a faint fleck of shadow. But the illimitable white light of human hopefulness … is ebbing away… and the night of necessitarianism cometh when no

---

[39]   LD, p. 206.

[40]   LD, p. 503.

[41]   LD, pp. 450–451.

man can work."[42] This was how he described the book in his introduction to the Everyman edition. Yet, as we have seen, we can get a far more accurate sense of the book's real character from Chesterton's brilliant insight into the optimism of the novelist, which did not abandon the author of *Little Dorrit.*

> ... when all is said, as I have remarked before, the chief fountain in Dickens of what I have called cheerfulness, and some prefer to call optimism, is something deeper than a verbal philosophy. It is, after all, an incomparable hunger and pleasure for the vitality and the variety, for the infinite eccentricity of existence. And this word "eccentricity" brings us, perhaps, nearer to the matter than any other. It is, perhaps, the strongest mark of the divinity of man that he talks of this world as "a strange world," though he has seen no other. We feel that all there is is eccentric, though we do not know what is the centre. This sentiment of the grotesqueness of the universe ran through Dickens's brain and body like the mad blood of the elves. He saw all his streets in fantastic perspectives, he saw all his cockney villas as top heavy and wild, he saw every man's nose twice as big as it was, and every man's eyes like saucers. And this was the basis of his gaiety—the only real basis of any philosophical gaiety. This world is not to be justified as it is justified by the mechanical optimists; it is not to be justified as the best of all possible worlds. Its merit is not that it is orderly and explicable; its merit is that it is wild and utterly unexplained. Its merit is precisely that none of us could have conceived such a thing, that we should have rejected the bare idea of it as miracle and unreason. It is the best of all impossible worlds.[43]

---

[42] CW, XV, p. 170.

Little Dorrit, as Chesterton helps us to see, is only partially
about the disenchantments of the world: what it is most
interested in is how the family transcends those disenchantments. In the end when Amy and Arthur marry,
Dickens describes their future in a way that shows this
transcendence in all of its quotidian, familial joy.

> And they were married, with the sun shining on them
> through the painted figure of Our Saviour on the
> window. And they went into the very room where
> Little Dorrit had slumbered after her party, to sign the
> Marriage Register ... They all gave place when the
> signing was done, and Little Dorrit and her husband
> walked out of the church alone. They paused for a
> moment on the steps of the portico, looking at the
> fresh perspective of the street in the autumn morning
> sun's bright rays, and then went down.
>
> Went down into a modest life of usefulness and
> happiness. Went down to give a mother's care, in
> the fulness of time, to Fanny's neglected children
> no less than to their own, and to leave that lady
> going into Society for ever and a day. Went down
> to give a tender nurse and friend to Tip [Edward
> Dorrit] for some few years, who was never vexed
> by the great exactions he made of her, in return for
> the riches he might have given her if he had ever
> had them, and who lovingly closed his eyes upon
> the Marshalsea and all its blighted fruits. They
> went quietly down into the roaring streets, insep-
> arable and blessed; and as they passed along in
> sunshine and in shade, the noisy and the eager, and
> the arrogant and the froward and the vain, fretted,
> and chafed, and made their usual uproar.[44]

⁴³ CW, XV, p. 203.

⁴⁴ LD, p. 826.

That Dickens should describe the happy newlyweds of his pro-life comedy as "inseparable" and "blessed" is apt. In their love for each other and for their future children they will partake as one flesh of what John Paul II rightly sees as the great gift of procreation—a "certain sharing by man in God's lordship," which "is evident in the specific responsibility which he is given for human life as such." And for Chesterton, as for Dickens, this

> is a responsibility which reaches its highest point in the giving of life through procreation by man and woman in marriage. As the Second Vatican Council teaches: "God himself, who said 'It is not good for man to be alone' (Gen 2:18) and made man from the beginning male and female" (Mt 19:4), wished to share with man a certain special participation in his own creative work. Thus he blessed male and female saying: "Increase and multiply" (Gen 1:28).[45]

Of course, these are realities that Chesterton's society was already beginning to dispute. In one piece of his decrying contraception he looked into a crystal ball of sorts and compared England and Prussia with respect to what might be their future appetite for State-mandated contraception and worse.

> Suppose ... Compulsory Sterilisation or Compulsory Contraception really stalks through the modern State, leading the march of human progress through abortion to infanticide. If the heathens in North Germany received it, they would accept it with howls of barbaric joy, as one of the sacred commands of the Race Religion; the proceedings very probably terminating (by that time) with a little human sacrifice. If the English received

---

[45]   Pope John Paul II, *Evangelium Vitae*, 71.

it, they would accept it as law-abiding citizens; that
is, as something between well-trained servants and
bewildered children.[46]

Well, as we all know, the entire world is now on this
ghastly "march of human progress" but the English will
not accept such a wicked thing, nor will the Germans, nor
will any people of good faith, if they "discover anew," as
Pope John Paul II recommends, in a passage which makes
good use of Dickens' prison metaphor, "the humility and
the courage to *pray and fast* so that power from on high
will break down the walls of lies and deceit: the walls which
conceal from the sight of so many of our brothers and
sisters the evil of practices and laws which are hostile to
life. May this same power turn their hearts to resolutions
and goals inspired by the civilization of life and love."[47]

---

[46] G. K. Chesterton, *Collected Works: Volume III, The Catholic
Church and Conversion and others* (San Francisco, 1990), p. 530.

[47] Pope John Paul II, *Evangelium Vitae*, 158.

Blessed Pope John Paul II

12

Abortion and the Historians

N O ONE CAN read the social history of certain well-regarded British and American historians without being struck by their partiality towards abortion. Partiality is not necessarily a bad thing in a good historian. John Lingard was partial to the Catholics in his history; Anthony Froude was partial to the Protestants. Macaulay described the Duke of Marlborough in terms that were warmly partial.

> His stature was commanding, his face handsome, his address singularly winning, yet of such dignity that the most impertinent fops never ventured to take any liberty with him; his temper, even in the most vexatious and irritating circumstances, always under perfect command. His education had been so much neglected that he could not spell the most common words of his own language; but his acute and vigorous understanding amply supplied the place of book learning. He was not talkative; but when he was forced to speak in public, his natural eloquence moved the envy of practiced rhetoricians. His courage was singularly cool and imperturbable. During many years of anxiety and peril, he never, in any emergency, lost, even for a moment, the perfect use of his admirable judgement.[1]

Macaulay was partial to Marlborough for good reasons: the duke was willing to support the cause of William of

---

[1] T. B. Macaulay, *The History of England From the Accession of James II* (Folio Society, 2009), p. 349.

Orange, he was a rich and varied figure on whose career the stylist in Macaulay could train his sprightly rhetoric, and he was a magnificent soldier.[2] Yet why our own historians should be so partial to abortionists cannot be answered so easily. Queen Victoria once told her daughter Vicky that while she did not hate babies, she did "hate the inordinate worship of them and the disgusting details of their animal existence, which," as she said, she tried "to ignore;" but there is no indication in any of her voluminous correspondence that she was in favor of killing babies in the womb.[3] Where our historians obtained their partiality to abortion is a complicated tale and in this chapter I shall revisit some of their histories to try to understand the character of that partiality and to determine what these narratives say about the relation between abortion and the writing of history in our contemporary milieu. I shall also take a look at the work of the many non-professional historians—the honest chroniclers—who record what so many of the historians in our midst refuse to record.

Kenneth O. Morgan, in his highly popular survey of the history of Britain, for which he wrote the sections on the twentieth and the twenty-first centuries, attempts to place the gradual acceptance of abortion in some historical context by linking it to the newly permissive attitudes to homosexuality that arose in Britain in the 1960s. Specifi-

---

[2]   Hilaire Belloc was not an unqualified fan of Macaulay's style: "It is to the glory of this facile rhetorician, that after an active lifetime since a last reading, and more than a lifetime from his first writing, it is still as clear and clean and fresh as reasonably good water out of a large tap in the public wash-house of an industrial town." See H. Belloc, *A Conversation with an Angel* (London, 1928), p. 197.

[3]   Queen Victoria to Vicky, Empress of Germany (22 February 1865), *Letters to Vicky: The Correspondence between Queen Victoria and her daughter Victoria, Empress of Germany, 1858–1901,* ed. Andrew Roberts (Folio Society, 2011), p. 206.

cally, he observes how, "Here was a permissiveness which drew less on the new youth culture, and more on ideas of a liberal society developed by John Stuart Mill in the 1850s, with his distinction between public and private life. The campaign to have abortion legalized made similar progress, and David Steel passed a bill to this effect in 1967, despite pressure from Roman Catholic and other religious lobbies. Henceforth, the terrors of backstreet abortions and other non-professional ways of terminating pregnancies could be avoided."[4] Whether tracing the rationale for abortion back to Mill's ideas does that rationale any favors Morgan does not say, though his very silence on the matter suggests that this is a descent that he imagines most of his readers will find favorable to abortion.

In his two surveys completing the *New Oxford History of England*, Brian Harrison also cites this concern regarding illegal abortion, remarking how "Within a secularizing society a pragmatic preoccupation with health gained over the older and principled restrictive morality. In 1958, in one of his many boldly humane assertions, Glanville Williams noted that 'the chief evil of an abortion is no longer thought to be the loss of the unborn child, but the injury done to the mother by the unskilled abortionist.' "[5]

The doyen of progressive historians, Ross McKibbin takes issue with this by pointing out that although there "was a contemporary view that the slums of England teemed with back-street abortionists, to whom working-class women regularly had recourse," it seems likelier that "most women who successfully aborted a pregnancy did so by self-induced miscarriage, usually by the consumption of

---

[4]   K. O. Morgan, *The People's Peace: British History 1945–1989* (Oxford, 1990), p. 260.

[5]   B. Harrison, *In Search of a Role: The United Kingdom 1951–1970* (Oxford, 2009), p. 248.

powerful emetics or purgatives ... whose genteel names, like 'Penny Royal' or 'Bitter Apples' deceived no one ..."[6]

Nevertheless, McKibbin is entirely sympathetic to the movement that eventually led to the 1967 Abortion Bill and beyond. In his introduction to Marie Stopes' paean to birth control, *Married Love* (1918), he writes of one of the heroines of the English abortion movement how "It had become clear by the end of 1918 that Stopes' interests were moving from the middle to the working classes. Some did not like this. Bernard Shaw told her that she really was 'a matrimonial expert, which is something much wider and more needed than a specialist in contraception. You should make it clear that you are a doctor, not a Malthusian nor a trader in sterilizing devices.' " But Stopes would not limit herself to matrimonial advice. In 1922, while sitting beneath a yew tree at Norbury Park, her manor house in Dorking, she claimed to have received a directive from God Himself telling her that she must inform the bishops assembled for the Lambeth Conference that the primary purpose of marital intercourse was not the procreation of children. To this startling communication the bishops made no reply. Undeterred, Stopes sent out questionnaires asking their views on family planning. She was no more successful in endearing herself to the Society for Constructive Birth Control, who found her egotistical and imperious, even though she was their founding president. Then, again, she rowed with her son when he became engaged to a woman who wore spectacles because the eugenicist in her could not bear the thought of having a woman in the family with defective eyesight.[7] Still, McKibbin stands by Stopes, insisting that, her less admi-

---

6   R. McKibbin, *Classes and Cultures: England 1918–1951* (Oxford, 1998), pp. 307–308.

7   *Oxford Dictionary of National Biography.*

rable traits notwithstanding, "It took courage to write
Married Love … It took courage to argue the case for birth
control as she did. It took courage to take on such formidable opponents as the Roman Catholic Church and polite
opinion. And she had a sense of the way society was
evolving; how futile it was to resist social evolution."[8]

That contraception and abortion must be counte-
nanced because they are part of an irresistible "social
evolution" is a logic that can also be found in those calling
for a revival of eugenics. Nathan Cohen, associate professor of the history of medicine at the Johns Hopkins
University, and author of *The Science of Human Perfection:
How Genes Became the Heart of American Medicine* (2012)
is a good case in point. Arguing that it is shortsighted to
stigmatize eugenics by associating it with the Nazis, Cohen
is convinced that we should seek instead to rehabilitate it
by stressing the great benefits that lie in store for a new
and improved eugenics.

> The eugenic impulse drives us to eliminate disease,
> to live longer and healthier, with greater intelligence
> and a better adjustment to the conditions of society.
> It arises whenever the humanitarian desire for
> happiness and social betterment combines with an
> emphasis on heredity as the essence of human
> nature. It is the aim of control, the denial of fatalism,
> the rejection of chance. The dream of engineering
> ourselves, of reducing suffering now and forever.
>
> The question is not one of whether there ought to
> be such an impulse, whether it should be called
> eugenics, or even whether biomedicine ought to
> focus so much on genetics. These things just are.
> And besides, the health benefits, the intellectual

---

[8]　R. McKibbin, "Introduction" to Marie Stopes, *Married Love*
(Oxford World Classics, 2008), p. 1i.

thrill, and the profits of genetic biomedicine are too great for us to do otherwise. Resistance would be ill-advised and futile.[9]

The notion that "resistance" to "social evolution" is "ill-advised" and "futile" is not new. J. B. Bury, Gibbon's editor, traces it back to Herbert Spencer's idea of progress.

> Progress then is not an accident, but a necessity. Civilization is a part of nature, being a development of man's latent capabilities under the action of favourable circumstances which were certain at some time or other to occur. Here Spencer's argument assumes a final cause. The ultimate purpose of creation, he asserts, is to produce the greatest amount of happiness, and to fulfill this aim it is necessary that each member of the race should possess faculties enabling him to experience the highest enjoyment of life, yet in such a way as not to diminish the power of others to receive like satisfaction. Beings thus constituted cannot multiply in a world tenanted by inferior creatures these, therefore, must be dispossessed to make room and to dispossess them aboriginal man must have an inferior constitution to begin with; he must be predatory, he must have the desire to kill. In general, given an unsubdued earth, and the human being 'appointed' to overspread and occupy it, then, the laws of life being what they are, no other series of changes than that which has actually occurred could have occurred.[10]

If this "queer religion of destiny," as Chesterton put it, was music to Hitler's ears when he set out to help himself to

[9]   N. Cohen, "The Eugenic Impulse" in *The Chronicle of Higher Education* (12 November 2012).

[10] J. B. Bury, *The Idea of Progress* (Cambridge, 1926), p. 185.

Lebensraum, it continues to animate those who clamor
for 'reproductive rights.'[11]

The readiness of such social engineers as Spencer and
Cohen to gloss over the concrete human consequences of
their eugenicist enterprises can be found among those
sympathetic to abortion as well. With regard to the
unintended consequences of David Steel's bill, for
instance, Harrison makes a show of evenhandedness when
he remarks how if illegal abortions consistently declined,
the number of legal abortions rose dramatically: by 1979
there were 100,000 being carried out annually in Britain
alone. Moreover, as Harrison notes, "The proportion of
abortions to live births rose fairly steadily in the 1970s and
by 1983 had reached one in five ..." Harrison also concedes
that "David Steel ... pointed out in 1981 that 'abortion is,
I am afraid, being used as a contraceptive.' " Yet even
Harrison cannot evade the clear conclusion that "By
extending doctor's discretion and allowing social reasons
to justify abortion, the Act in practice advanced beyond
its author's intentions."[12]

The historian Paul Addison also makes this point,
arguing how "The Abortion Law Reform Association, a
women's group of feminist outlook, had called initially for
'abortion on demand'— that is, for women to have the
right to an abortion. Such a proposal would have been too
radical for acceptance by the House of Commons. In order
to lend more respectability to the process Steel agreed that
the decision to terminate should be an exclusively medical
one, for which the approval of two doctors would be

[11] *The Collected Works of G. K. Chesterton, Vol. III: The Catholic
Church and Conversion; Where All Roads Lead; The Well and the
Shallows; and others* (San Francisco, 1990), p. 421.

[12] B. Harrison, *Finding a Role? The United Kingdom 1970–1990*
(Oxford, 2010), pp. 212–213.

required. One of the main arguments put forward by the supporters of the bill was that it would reduce the number of dangerous back-street abortions ... In the event the 'safeguard' of medical control proved to be little more than a formality and abortion on demand was in effect conceded. The number of recorded abortions rose from 35,000 per year in 1968 to 141,000 in 1975."[13]

However, no sooner does Harrison concede the rise of abortion on demand than he sets about putting as positive a spin on it as possible. In the permissive England that followed the passing of the Abortion Act in 1967 abortion might have become nothing more than a kind of insouciant contraceptive but Harrison reminds his readers that contraception played an indispensable role in achieving key social aspects of the progressive agenda. "Self-consciously progressive people," he argues, "had long viewed birth control's divorce between sexuality and procreation as integral to completing a woman's emancipation. On such a view, the nineteenth-century feminist attempt to raise male standards of sexual abstinence to female was a mere feminist staging-post before reliable birth-control could sexually emancipate both sexes."[14]

Another well-known progressive historian, Arthur Marwick in his survey of Britain since the Second World War is equally upbeat about the salutary impact of abortionism. "From the middle seventies, contraceptives became free through the National Health Service, though the problem remained that too few people availed themselves

---

[13] P. Addison, *No Turning Back: The Peacetime Revolutions of Post-War Britain* (Oxford, 2010), pp. 207–208. It dismays me to have to number Addison among the pro-abortion historians because he has written some good books, particularly a wonderfully succinct, incisive one about Churchill published by Oxford.

[14] B. Harrison, *Finding a Role? The United Kingdom 1970–1990* (Oxford, 2010), p. 215.

of this facility. In the opinion of most experts the reformed abortion law of the sixties was now working humanely under effective supervision and was much in the interests of the health and well-being of women in general."[15]

The air of whiggish triumphalism here is unmistakable. One reason why Harrison is disinclined to take a dim view of contraception and abortion is because, in his estimation, they helped to bring about a better order of things, one which he takes every opportunity to applaud, though it is striking how much the sexual mores of this new order resemble those that Captain Cook encountered in 1769 on his first voyage to Tahiti. After observing the sexual licentiousness of the Tahitians, and their ruthlessness with respect to unwanted children, Cook, who was neither an ill-informed nor prudish man had no hesitation in regarding both as truly exceptional. "There is a scale in dissolute sensuality which these people have ascended, wholly unknown to every other nation whose manners have been recorded from the beginning of the world to the present hour," he wrote, "and which no imagination would possibly conceive." [16] And yet what Cook's most recent biographer Frank McLynn nicely calls a "general tourbillion of sexuality" is now the norm in Britain and America, where millions have adopted the promiscuity that so shocked not only the Quaker but the man of the world in Cook.[17]

> A very considerable number of the principal people
> of Otaheite, of both sexes, have formed themselves
> into a society in which every woman is common to
> every man, thus securing a perpetual variety as

[15] A. Marwick, *British Society Since 1945* (London, 2003), p. 193.

[16] *Captain Cook's Voyages 1768–1779*: Selected and edited by G. Williams (Folio Society, 1997), p. 56.

[17] F. McLynn, *Captain Cook: Master of the Seas* (New Haven, 2011), p. 113.

often as their inclination prompts them to seek it
... These societies are distinguished by the name
of *arreoy* and the members have meetings, at which
no one is present, where the men amuse themselves by wrestling and the women, notwithstanding their occasional connection with different men,
dance the *timoradoee* in all its latitude, as an
incitement to desires, which it is said are frequently
gratified upon the spot. This, however, is compar-
atively nothing. If any of the women happen to be
with child, which in this manner of life happens
less frequently than if they were to cohabit only
with one man, the poor infant is smothered the
moment it is born, that it may be no encumbrance
to the father, nor interrupt the mother in the
pleasures of her diabolical prostitution. It sometimes indeed happens that the passion which
prompts a woman to enter into this society is
surmounted when she becomes a mother by that
instinctive affection which Nature has given to all
creatures for the preservation of their offspring;
but even in this case, she is not permitted to spare
the life of her infant, except she can find a man who
will patronize it as his child. If this can be done, the
murder is prevented, but both the man and the
woman, being deemed by this act to have appropriated each other, are ejected from the community and forfeit all claim to the privileges of *arreoy*
for the future; the woman from that time being
distinguished by the term *whannownow*, 'bearer of
children,' which is here a term of reproach, though
none can be more honourable in the estimation of
wisdom and humanity, of right reason, and every
passion that distinguishes the man from the
brute.[18]

---

[18]   *Captain Cook's Voyages*, pp. 56–57.

Here is the face of primitive selfishness in all of its heartlessness, and it is instructive how little it differs from the selfishness that informs the sexual irresponsibility that progressives have done so much to foment.[19]

Apropos this emancipation, Theodore Dalrymple, who worked for many years as a prison doctor, has been a voice of consistent, excoriating dissent. Writing of the "sexual chaos" that now obtains throughout England, and its ruinous effects on the family, Dalrymple observes how "It might be argued ... that such obviously wrongful behavior has occurred always: for when it comes to sexual misdemeanor there is nothing new under the sun, and history shows plentiful examples of almost any perversion or dishonorable conduct. But this is the first time in history there has been mass denial that sexual relations are a proper subject of moral reflection or need to be governed by moral restrictions. The result of this denial, not surprisingly, has been soaring divorce rates and mass illegitimacy ... The sexual revolution has been above all a change in moral sensibility," with the result that there has been "a thorough coarsening of feeling, thought, and behavior."[20] And to illustrate his point, Dalrymple describes viewing a film in a cinema from the 1950s in which an indignant father of an unmarried pregnant daughter demanded that the young father marry her. Dalrymple notes how this caused the audience to laugh, as though the father's demand were somehow self-evidently ridiculous, which

---

[19] In his superb biography of Cook, McLynn points out how, "The esoterica of religious ceremonies aside, at the basic level Europeans and Polynesians understood each other well enough; the only thing that seriously puzzled the islanders was that the strangers had no women with them." See McLynn, p. 415.

[20] T. Dalrymple, *Our Culture, What's Left of It* (New York, 2005), p. 236.

prompts him to look more closely at the selfishness at the heart of the progressive view of sexuality.

> Who, one might ask, had the deeper and subtler moral understanding of human relations: the audience of the mid-1950s or that of today? To the 1950s audience, it would have been unnecessary to point out that, once a child had been conceived, the father owed a duty not only to the child but to the mother; that his own wishes in the matter were not paramount, let alone all-important, and that he was not simply an individual but a member of a society whose expectations he had to meet if he were to retain its respect; and that a sense of moral obligations toward a woman was not inimical to a satisfying relationship with her but a precondition of it. To the present-day audience, by contrast, the only considerations in such a situation would be the individual inclinations of the parties involved, floating free of all moral or social constraints. In the modern view, unbridled personal freedom is the only good to be pursued; any obstacle to it is a problem to be overcome.

And elsewhere Dalrymple shows how it was the widespread adoption of the views of Margaret Mead's anthropological study, *Coming of Age in Samoa* (1927), in which she held up the allegedly jolly promiscuity of Samoan adolescents as a model for the repressive West that accelerated this disastrously "anything goes" approach to sexual morality.[21] As we have seen, Captain Cook, not Mead, was the more accurate judge of whether island paradises had anything to teach us about the ethics of coition.

Still, even in the carefully expurgated accounts of progressive historians, it is striking how frequently the tiresome facts keep interjecting themselves. For example,

---

[21] Ibid., pp. 240–242.

after hailing contraception as the great grail of the sexually emancipated, Harrison is constrained to admit that "By the mid-1980s the UK was at the top of the illegitimacy league in Europe outside Scandinavia, with about one child in five born out of wedlock," though, at the same time, he refuses to admit that these numbers might in any way be detrimental to the children born out of wedlock. "If traditional attitudes to legitimacy had persisted, these changes would have been disastrous for the children, but in reality they reflected a change in attitudes to marriage ..."[22] In other words, in Harrison's view, if a society takes it into its head to regard illegitimacy as acceptable, the adverse consequences of illegitimacy simply go away. He and his fellow progressives respond similarly to the adverse effects of abortion—whether to the breast cancer, obesity or post-traumatic stress it causes, let alone the destruction of an innocent, defenseless life. The logic of the progressives with regard to the consequences of their prescriptions has an enviable simplicity: If we only agree in advance of any reputable research that these bad effects do not exist—and the Americans, at least, always have the Guttmacher Institute of Planned Parenthood to vouch for their non-existence—well, then, they do not exist.

Again, Dalrymple puts the indulgent view of illegitimacy taken by progressives into proper perspective, seeing it as part and parcel of the progressive readiness to destroy the family, which progressives have always regarded as an undesirable rival to their Servile State. Accordingly, for Dalrymple, "The destigmatization of illegitimacy went hand in hand with easy divorce, the extension of marital rights to other forms of association between adults, and the removal of all the fiscal advantages of marriage.

---

[22] B. Harrison, *Finding a Role? The United Kingdom 1970–1990* (Oxford, 2010), p. 214.

Marriage melted as snow in sunshine. The destruction of the family was, of course, an important component and consequence of sexual liberation, whose utopian program was to have increased the stock of innocent sensual pleasure, not least among the liberators themselves. It resulted instead in widespread violence consequent upon sexual insecurity and in the mass neglect of children, as people became ever more egotistical in their search for momentary pleasure."[23] What Dalrymple, however, does not sufficiently register is the abuse this "destigmatization of illegitimacy" has visited on children, which can be seen in the soaring rates of abortion to which it has given rise.

The progressive contention that real evils can be charmed away by simply refusing to regard them as real evils is emblematic of the intellectual chicane that suffuses the pro-abortion case. Indeed, in America, historical accounts of abortion are continually skewered by a pro-abortion lobby that falsifies the facts of abortion with cynical pertinacity. As Justin Dyer points out, "Forty years after the Supreme Court's landmark decision in *Roe v. Wade*, prominent historians and lawyers continue to rely on a narrative history that is based on two demonstrably false premises: (1) abortion was a common-law liberty at the time of the American founding and (2) the primary purpose of anti-abortion laws in the 19th century was to protect women rather than the lives of unborn children. In the 1960s and 1970s, lawyers trying to build a case against century-old state abortion statutes trumpeted these two claims, all the while knowing they were false."

Dyer corrects this mendacious history by calling out the men who fabricated and disseminated it. "The scholarly pedigree for these claims," he writes, "can be traced

---

[23]   T. Dalrymple, *Life at the Bottom: The Worldview That Makes the Underclass* (New York, 2001), p. 254.

back to Cyril Means, the New York Law School professor
and counsel for the National Association for the Repeal of
Abortion Laws (NARAL), who took the lead in drafting
the new abortion history in the 1960s.

> In a 1968 article published in the *New York Law
> Forum*, Means set out to reveal "for the first time"
> that the true purpose of 19th-century abortion laws
> was to protect women, not unborn children. In a
> follow-up article published in 1971, he purported
> to uncover a related "story, untold now for nearly
> a century": that "English and American women
> enjoyed a common-law liberty to terminate at will
> an unwanted pregnancy, from the reign of Edward
> III to that of George III," and that this "common-
> law liberty endured ... in America, from 1607 to
> 1830."

> The practical purpose of Means's abortion history
> was clear. Writing on the cases of *Doe v. Bolton* and
> *Roe v. Wade* (both docketed at the Supreme Court
> in 1971), Means concluded: "Should the merits be
> reached in either case, counsel and the Court may
> find the present conspectus of the Anglo-American
> legal history of abortion of assistance; for, only if
> in 1791 elective abortion was a common-law
> liberty, can it be a ninth-amendment right today."

Dyer stresses just how consequential this false history has
been by pointing out to his readers that this was the history
invoked by Roe's attorney, Sarah Weddington, who, as
Dyer remarks "submitted copies of Means' articles as
supporting documents for the case and then relied heavily
on his history during oral arguments. The effort seems to
have paid off: Justice Harry Blackmun cited Means seven
times in his *Roe* opinion. Recounting her reaction when
the opinion was released, Weddington wrote, "I had not
been reading the extensive footnotes at the bottom of each

page closely, but sure enough, when I did I found several referring to Cyril Means's writings; I knew he would be pleased."

But the determination to falsify the record was worse. As Dyer explains, "The problem (as Weddington almost certainly knew) is that Means's central claims were not true. In a memo circulated among Roe's legal team in the summer of 1971, a Yale law student named David Tundermann warned that Means's 'conclusions sometimes strain credibility.' Even so, Tundermann tellingly concluded:

> Where the important thing to do is to win the case no matter how, however, I suppose I agree with Means's technique: begin with a scholarly attempt at historical research; if it doesn't work out, fudge it as necessary; write a piece so long that others will read only your introduction and conclusion; then keep citing it until the courts begin picking it up. This preserves the guise of impartial scholarship while advancing the proper ideological goals.

Dyer's conclusion is one that those committed to presenting the truth about abortion will find heartening, if only because it exposes so much influential falsehood. "The suggestion—still made today by credentialed historians, legal scholars, and respected journalists—that protecting the lives of the unborn was *not* the purpose of the abortion statutes overturned by the Supreme Court in 1973 is absurd. Although the role of history in abortion litigation has quietly faded to the background in the Court's most recent abortion cases, it bears noting that the politically motivated abortion history crudely constructed by activists and academics in the 1960s and 1970s has enjoyed a remarkable shelf life. Forty years after Roe v. Wade, as we debate the legacy of the decision and consider the state of abortion politics, it is time to lay to rest this fraudulent history—a history that would be far less tragic if it did not involve matters of life and death."[24]

Dr. Bernard Nathanson (1926–2011), the former abortion doctor and abortion rights activist who became an impassioned pro-lifer, admitted that he and the abortion lobby deliberately fed the media carefully crafted lies in order to sway public opinion in favor of legalized abortion.[25] Thus, before Roe v. Wade, as Nathanson recalls, "The number of women dying from illegal abortions was around 200–250 annually. The figure constantly fed to the media was 10,000 …

> Another myth we fed to the public through the media was that legalizing abortion would only mean that the abortions taking place illegally would then be done legally. In fact, of course, abortion is now being used as a primary method of birth control in the U.S. and the annual number of abortions has increased by 1500% since legalization. We systematically vilified the Catholic Church and its "socially backward ideas" and picked on the Catholic hierarchy as the villain in opposing abortion. This theme was played endlessly. We fed the media such lies as "we all know that opposition to abortion comes from the hierarchy and not from most Catholics" and "Polls prove time and again that most Catholics want abortion law reform." And the media drum-fired all this into the American people, persuading them that anyone opposing permissive abortion must be under the influence of the Catholic hierarchy and

---

[24] J. Dyer, "Fictional Abortion History," *National Review Online* (24 December 2012).

[25] In 1984, Dr. Nathanson directed and narrated the film, *The Silent Scream* in conjunction with the National Right to Life Committee.

that Catholics in favour of abortion are enlightened
and forward-looking.[26]

President Barak Hussein Obama and his Democratic Party
have been particularly successful with the anti-Catholic
tactic described here, though if America's bishops spoke
with a louder and more consistent voice in defense of life,
this tactic could be turned against the abortionists and
their political myrmidons. Still, no one should blame the
Catholic priests of America for the abortion industry.
There are many Catholic priests who have shown exemplary courage in this fight and their example should be
celebrated. Their witness to the categorical evil of abortion
is a commendable rebuke to the moral blindness of most
of our historians.

In his great encyclical, *Humanae Vitae* (1968), affirming the Church's rejection of artificial birth control, Pope
Paul VI conceded that in taking the stand he took on behalf
of the Church, he was not taking what would be a universally popular stand. "It is to be anticipated that perhaps
not everyone will easily accept this particular teaching,"
he admitted, with what now seems comic understatement.
"There is too much clamorous outcry against the voice of
the Church, and this is intensified by modern means of
communication." Yet, for so faithful a pontiff, and one so
steeped in history, this was not in itself surprising, for "the
Church ... no less than her divine Founder, is destined to
be a 'sign of contradiction.' " About this, the pope could
not have been clearer: the incidental unpopularity of the
Church's position would never cause the Church to "evade
the duty imposed on her of proclaiming humbly but firmly
the entire moral law, both natural and evangelical." And
this followed from the fact that, "Since the Church did not

---

[26] "Confessions of an Ex-Abortionist," *Catholic Education Resource
Center* (1997).

make either of these laws, she cannot be their arbiter—
only their guardian and interpreter. It could never be right
for her to declare lawful what is in fact unlawful, since that,
by its very nature, is always opposed to the true good of
man." [27]

Now, when public authorities around the world
"declare lawful what is in fact unlawful" with blithe
indifference to the "true good of man" with respect to
contraception, abortion, euthanasia and the redefinition
of marriage, the pope's words can be seen to have exhibited a terrible prescience. They also place the issue of
contraception where it belongs, in the most fundamental
of contexts, for "In preserving intact the whole moral law
of marriage, the Church is convinced that she is contrib-
uting to the creation of a truly human civilization. She
urges man not to betray his personal responsibilities by
putting all his faith in technical expedients." Thus, the
pope defended "the dignity of husband and wife" and
encouraged married couples "to share God's life as sons
of the living God, the Father of all men."[28]

If in affirming these truths, the pope realized that many
of the Catholic laity would not follow his lead, he was
equally realistic about the clergy, to whom he wrote
directly: "And now, beloved sons, you who are priests, you
who in virtue of your sacred office act as counselors and
spiritual leaders both of individual men and women and
of families—We turn to you filled with great confidence.
For it is your principal duty—We are speaking especially
to you who teach moral theology—to spell out clearly and
completely the Church's teaching on marriage." And in
order to accomplish this, the pope recognized that priests
"must be the first to give an example of that sincere

[27]   Pope Paul VI, *Humanae Vitae*, 9.
[28]   Ibid.

obedience, inward as well as outward, which is due to the magisterium of the Church."[29] As it happened, this obedience was not entirely forthcoming and there was a good deal of dissension among the clergy. Indeed, "To [Pope Paul VI's] horror," as Eamon Duffy wrote in his history of the popes, "instead of closing the question [of artificial birth control], *Humanae Vitae* provoked a storm of protest, and many priests resigned or were forced out of their posts for their opposition to the Pope's teaching."[30]

One priest who appreciated the profound rightness of the pope's response to this vexed issue was the Reverend Monsignor Austin P. Bennett, a priest of the Diocese of Brooklyn, who, although charged for decades with overseeing the Archdiocese's financial, medical and insurance affairs, has nothing of the ecclesiastical bureaucrat about him. On the contrary, this energetic, engaging, deeply practical man epitomizes the good shepherd—one who may be steeped in history, law, and languages, but who nevertheless serves his flock unstintingly, young and old, rich and poor, faithful and not so faithful, with Christ-like solicitude.

My wife Karina and I first met Monsignor Bennett at St. Rita's Church in Astoria, Queens, where he has been celebrating Mass since 1958. That he should have such a long history with this wonderful church is apt, for Saint Rita (1381–1457) is an emblem of patient obedience, a patroness of mothers and children. What immediately drew my wife and me to Monsignor Bennett is his wonderfully staunch commitment to the unborn. In his intercessions, he has his parishioners pray for the repeal of all laws legitimizing the killing of the unborn child in the womb, and in many of his sermons he deplores the

---

[29] Ibid., p. 14.

[30] E. Duffy, *Saints and Sinners: A History of the Popes* (New Haven, 1997), p. 281.

savagery that has led to the murder of over 50 million children in America alone since the passing of Roe v. Wade. Here is precisely the sort of obedient, faithful, conscientious priest that Pope Paul VI had in mind when he exhorted the clergy "to proclaim with humble firmness the entire moral law, both natural and evangelical."

Monsignor Bennett is not alone in his pastoral defense of the unborn. In a moving eulogy for Dr. Nathanson, Father Gerald Murray of the Church of St. Vincent de Paul in Manhattan declared how "I am not exaggerating when I say that Dr. Bernard Nathanson is a towering figure in the history of the United States because he was an unflinching witness on behalf of those millions who have been killed, or are threatened to be killed, by abortion. He was a witness who spoke out against what he himself had helped to bring about, namely the legalization of abortion in our country, along with his fellow founders of NARAL, the National Association for the Repeal of Abortion Laws. He broke with this evil movement, and repented of his sins. His epiphany came when he saw ultrasound images of the developing human being in the womb. He wrote: 'Ultrasound opened up a new world. For the first time we could really see the human fetus, measure it, observe it, watch it, and indeed bond with it and love it. I began to do that.' He continued 'Having looked at the ultrasound, I could no longer go on as before.' " Father Murray's final comments about this inspiring life will move all those who have had a similarly painful conversion after having their eyes opened to the full horror of abortion.

> Our life indeed is meant to be lived in intimate union with the crucified Lord. Golgotha, Calvary is indeed the place where we learn to be wise. The pain we experience, if united to Christ's pain, is then understood to be a blessing that opens our

hearts to the only Love that can take away that
pain. That Love is Christ, and the gift of eternal life
wipes away all pain and suffering. To live and to
die in hopeful expectation of that redemption is
God's great gift to us fallen creatures here below.
That gift was joyfully received by Dr. Nathanson
in this very Cathedral fourteen years ago.[31]

Father Gerald Murphy is one of the most charming,
capable, incisive priests that one could encounter. Yet in
addition to falsifying the facts of abortion, pro-abortion
activists and their historians seek to discredit opponents
of abortion by characterizing them as paranoid. James T.
Patterson, whose surveys complete the Oxford History of
the United States, resorts to this dismissive ploy with the
equanimity of a man who cannot conceive of anyone in
his audience disagreeing with him.

Roe v. Wade especially aroused religious conservatives. The decision, some of them exclaimed,
amounted to 'child murder' and the 'slaughter of the
innocent.' Others saw the ruling as a sinister step
towards state control of personal beliefs. As *Christianity Today*, a leading evangelical journal, editori-
alized in 1973, "Christians should accustom
themselves to the thought that the American state
no longer supports in any meaningful sense, the laws
of God, and prepare themselves spiritually for the
prospect that the state may one day formally repudiate them and turn against those who seek to live
by them." Statements such as this revealed a key fact
about cultural conflict in the United States for the
remainder of the century and beyond: Abortion,
more irreconcilable than any other social issue,
incited all manner of fears among conservatives.[32]

---

[31]   G. Murray, "The Witness of Bernard Nathanson" in *First Things*
(8 March 2011).

Whether these fears have proven warrantable is not something Patterson or other progressive historians are prepared to say. Certainly, there are grounds for asking such a question in light of the mandate issued on January 20, 2012 by the United States Department of Health and Human Services, under Secretary Kathleen Sebelius. This now infamous mandate would require nearly all private health insurance plans to include coverage for all FDA-approved prescription contraceptive drugs and devices, surgical sterilizations and abortion-inducing drugs—drugs that prevent implantation in the womb and consequently destroy the human child at his or her earliest stage of development. When a list of the "preventive services" that would become a mandatory part of the Affordable Care Act, commonly known as "Obamacare," were being drawn up in 2010, there was naturally a fair amount of concern about who would be deciding this list, especially after several religious groups urged that sterilization and abortion drugs be excluded. To no one's surprise, every member on the Institute of Medicine (IOM) charged with making up the list was an avid supporter of abortion—some were even in the employ of abortion advocacy groups. The upshot is that all health plans in the United States are now required to cover these "preventive services," irrespective of whether the insurer, the employer or other plan sponsor or even the woman herself objects to the coverage. The object of the mandate on the part of the State is threefold: to demonstrate complete disregard for any religious objections to such "preventive services," to make the State, and not the individual citizen, the arbiter of what is morally acceptable and unacceptable, and to force the Catholic Church out of the social services arena

---

[32] J. T. Patterson, *Restless Giant: The United States from Watergate to Bush v. Gore* (Oxford, 2005), p. 136.

as a first step to forcing them out of the public square altogether. In this regard, it is interesting that most progressive historians link abortion rights with homosexual rights because once the right to 'homosexual marriage' is established it will only be a matter of time before the Catholic Church's opposition to sanctioning such 'marriages' will be criminalized. In light of these developments and however they are finally resolved, the *Christianity Today* editorial begins to look a good deal more prescient than paranoid, even if progressive historians refuse to acknowledge the true tyrannical character of the mandates that give these prognostications their point.

The deliberate flouting of reality on the part of abortionists and their progressive advocates calls to mind some passages from Henry James' great travelogue, *The American Scene* (1905), which he composed to memorialize an extensive visit he made to his native land after an absence of over twenty years. In one passage particularly, he described the way that Richmond, Virginia seemed to encapsulate the mind of the Confederate South:

> Well, I scarce remember at what point of my peregrination, at what quite vague, senseless street-corner it was that I felt my inquiry—up to that moment rather embarrassing—turn to clearness and the whole picture place itself in a light in which contemplation might for the time find a warrant and a clew. I at any rate almost like to live over the few minutes in question—for the sake of their relief and their felicity. So retracing them, I see that the spring had been pressed for them by the positive force of one's first dismay; a sort of intellectual bankruptcy, this latter, that one felt one really couldn't afford. There were no *references—that* had been the trouble; but the reaction came with the sense that the large, sad poorness was in itself a

reference, and one by which a hundred grand historic connections were on the spot, and quite thrillingly, re-established. What was I tasting of, at that time of day, and with intensity, but the far consequences of things, made absolutely majestic by their weight and duration? I was tasting, mystically, of the very essence of the old Southern idea—the hugest fallacy, as it hovered there to one's backward, one's ranging vision, for which hundreds of thousands of men had ever laid down their lives. I was tasting of the very bitterness of the immense, grotesque, defeated project—the project, extravagant, fantastic, and to-day pathetic in its folly, of a vast Slave State (as the old term ran) artfully, savingly isolated in the world that was to contain it and trade with it. This was what everything round me meant—that that absurdity had once flourished there; and nothing, immediately, could have been more interesting than the lesson that such may remain, for long years, the telltale face of things where such absurdities *have* flourished.

Since the American Civil War had played so memorable a part in his own youth—James was 18 when hostilities broke out after confederate troops under Pierre Gustave Toutant Beauregard bombarded Fort Sumter in South Carolina on April 12 and 13, forcing its surrender—he was always fascinated by the intellectual tradition that had made the war inevitable by attempting to justify and perpetuate the institution of slavery—"the hugest fallacy," as he called it, which has so much in common with the fallacy that animates those who contend that killing unborn children somehow redounds to the dignity and health of women. Once James returned to the place where the tradition of the Old South had taken root, he saw its full enormity as for the first time.

Here, obviously, would be the prime source of the
beauty; since if to be sad was to be the reverse of
blatant, what was the sadness, taken all round, but
the incurable aftertaste of the original vanity and
fatuity, with the memories and penalties of which
the very air seemed still charged? I had recently
been studying, a little, the record, reading, with
other things, the volume of his admirable History
in which Mr. James Ford Rhodes recounts the long
preliminaries of the War and shows us, all lucidly
and humanely, the Southern mind of the mid-
century in the very convulsions of its perversity—
the conception that, almost comic in itself, was yet
so tragically to fail to work, that of a world rear-
ranged, a State solidly and comfortably seated and
tucked-in, in the interest of slave-produced Cotton.
The solidity and the comfort were to involve not
only the wide extension, but the complete intellectual, moral and economic reconsecration of slavery, an enlarged and glorified, quite beatified,
application of its principle.

Here the similarities between slave drivers and abortionists are patent. Just as the Confederate South was committed to defying history to uphold the interests of the slave
trade, the abortion lobby is similarly committed to uphold-
ing the interests of the abortion trade, the only difference
being that whereas the advocates of abortion plead their
case before a liberal establishment that promotes abortion
at every opportunity in return for the immense political
support it receives from the abortion lobby, the advocates
of slavery had to make their case before a social order that
could still consider such moral issues with some moral
probity. The Cambridge intellectual historian Michael
O'Brien, in his entertainingly revisionist way, might try to
persuade us that there was really no difference between
the slave-owning South and the abolitionist North when

it came to their respective biases but James knew otherwise.[33] He was particularly witty about the response the slave drivers and their sympathizers received from the wider culture beyond the plantations and their counter-response.

> The light of experience, round about, and every fingerpost of history, of political and spiritual science with which the scene of civilization seemed to bristle, had, when questioned, but one warning to give, and appeared to give it with an effect of huge derision: whereby was laid on the Southern genius the necessity of getting rid of these discords and substituting for the ironic face of the world an entirely new harmony, or in other words a different scheme of criticism. Since nothing in the Slave-scheme could be said to conform—conform, that is, to the reality of things—it was the plan of Christendom and the wisdom of the ages that would have to be altered. History, the history of everything, would be rewritten *ad usum Delphini*— the Dauphin being in this case the budding Southern mind. This meant a general and a permanent quarantine; meant the eternal bowdlerization of books and journals; meant in fine all literature and all art on an expurgatory index. It meant, still further, an active and ardent propaganda; the reorganization of the school, the college, the university, in the interest of the new criticism. The testimony to that thesis offered by the documents of the time, by State legislation, local eloquence, political speeches, the "tone of the press," strikes us to-day as beyond measure queer and quaint and benighted—innocent above all; stamped with the inalienable Southern sign, the inimitable *rococo*

---

[33] See M. O'Brien, *Conjectures of Order: Intellectual Life and The American South, 1810–60* (North Carolina, 2003).

note. We talk of the provincial, but the provincial-
ity projected by the Confederate dream, and in
which it proposed to steep the whole helpless social
mass, looks to our present eyes as artlessly per-
verse, as untouched by any intellectual tradition of
beauty or wit, as some exhibited array of the odd
utensils or divinities of lone and primitive islanders. It came over one that they *were* there, in the
air they had breathed, precisely, lone—even the
very best of the old Southerners; and, looking at
them over the threshold of approach that poor
Richmond seemed to form, the real key to one's
sense of their native scene was in that very idea of
their solitude and their isolation. Thus they
affected one as such passive, such pathetic victims
of fate, as so played upon and betrayed, so beaten
and bruised, by the old burden of their condition,
that I found myself conscious, on their behalf, of a
sort of ingenuity of tenderness.[34]

The bowdlerization that James describes here eerily resem-
bles how historians like Morgan, Harrison, McKibbin and
Patterson treat abortion, omitting any mention of the
destruction of human life from their accounts and focusing
instead on abortion as an abstract right, an admirable
advance in what they insist on regarding as the altogether
salutary progress of feminism. In this regard, the interpretation of this tragic history mounted by these eminent
historians corroborates the interpretation offered by Gloria
Feldt, a popular abortion advocate, who, after taking over
the presidency of Planned Parenthood in 1996, insisted that
the abortion provider be more aggressive in "leading the
charge for reproductive rights and reproductive health" and
combatting the "conservative onslaught" against legalized
abortion. For Feldt, the fight to perpetuate abortion was

---

[34] H. James, *The American Scene* (New York, 1907), pp. 358–360.

"about when we're going to be a nation that embraces knowledge and education about responsible sex, as opposed to trying to keep people ignorant about it. I think abortion is not about abortion at all ... it's more about the future of women and children and families in this country."[35]

The only way to put that stunning piece of bowdlerization into perspective is to imagine what histories of America would look like if the South had won the Civil War and their glorification of slavery had somehow carried the day. This is the sort of rigging of reality that we actually behold in the accounts of pro-abortion historians—a rigging of reality that is of the very essence of political correctness. Then, again, there is another kind of bowdlerization common to the accounts of abortionists and it is a refusal to acknowledge the real life that is under assault by the crusade to kill children in the womb. A peculiarly distasteful instance of this can be found in Roy Jenkins' political autobiography, where he remarks how "We took the abortion bill from 10:15pm on Thursday, June 29, to 10:15am on Friday, June 30, and then returned to it on Thursday-Friday, July 13–14, starting at 10:15pm and completing it only just before noon.

> In my third-reading speech I paid the first of what was to turn out to be a series of warm tributes to David Steel, although he had to wait nearly fifteen years for most of them. His steering of this difficult bill, at the age of twenty-nine, had been notably cool and courageous. We aborted (if that is the appropriate term) the fourteen-hour filibuster only by making it clear that we were prepared, if neces-

---

[35] G. Feldt, quoted in D. T. Critchlow, *Intended Consequences: Birth Control, Abortion, the Federal Government in Modern America* (Oxford, 1999), pp. 234–235.

sary, to keep the House sitting throughout Friday
night and Saturday to get the bill.[36]

The praise of Steele is bad enough but to write "We
aborted" in this context is odious. Obviously, it meant
nothing to Jenkins that the bill he so zealously sponsored
would amount to a death warrant for millions of children.

If the Confederate South defied what James calls "the
reality of things" by giving out that the institution of
slavery was actually an honorable thing and beneficial to
those hapless enough to be enslaved, our pro-abortion
historians have improved on this by contriving to argue
that the immensely lucrative abortion trade, which gener-
ates $90 billion annually in the United States alone,
somehow serves not only the dignity and well-being of
women but the wider interests of society as a whole. Yet
whereas the unreality of the South led to a war that killed
700,000 Confederate and Unionist soldiers, the unreality
of our abortionists and their sympathizers has resulted in
the death of 70 million unborn children worldwide since
Roe v. Wade. So while parallels exist, they only go so far.
After all, the Old South could not have known that their
defense of slavery would issue in a war as bloody and
destructive as the American Civil War.

One cannot make the same allowance for the abortionists, who have waged their war against unborn children in
the wake of the Holocaust. After the passing of Roe v.
Wade, many in favor of abortion adopted the same
rationale for the killing of unborn children that the Nazis
used to justify the killing of Jews—the rationale that the
human beings they were killing, human beings created in
the image of God, were subhuman and, as such, justly
unentitled to legal protection. Of course, with the arrival
of sonogram technology, this rationale has had to change:

---

[36]   R. Jenkins, *Life at the Center* (New York, 1991), p. 199.

now the pro-abortion argument is that unborn children can be killed, not so much because they are subhuman, as because their right to life is subordinate to the more pressing and peremptory 'reproductive rights' of their mothers, which are held to conduce somehow to their well-being, even though numerous studies now show verifiable links between abortion and breast cancer, post-traumatic stress, infertility, depression and obesity. But this is a distinction without a difference. In effect, the advocates of the 'reproductive rights' of women still treat the unborn child in the womb as subhuman, even if they hide their indifference to the inviolability of life behind the threadbare cant of feminism.

The 'reproductive rights' argument is nicely exemplified by Dr. Katherine Hancock Ragsdale, President and Dean of the Episcopal Divinity School in Cambridge, Massachusetts, who testified before Congress on March 8, 2012 that if Congress were to outlaw the transporting of a minor without her parents' consent across state lines to get an abortion, she would continue to break the law by helping girls destroy their unborn children. At a hearing of the House Judiciary subcommittee on the Constitution, the Dean recalled how she helped a 15-year-old girl she had never met before obtain an abortion: "Although New Hampshire was closer to that girl's home than Boston, as it happened, I did not take her across state lines. Nor did I, to my knowledge, break any laws. But if either of those things had been necessary in order to help her, I would have done them," she explained. "And if helping young women like her should be made illegal I will, nonetheless, continue to do it." Her rationale for these views was instructive; she cited the vows she took as an Episcopal priest; it was these that impelled her to break the law, to help teenage girls kill their unborn children without their parents' knowledge.

Here, Ragsdale was citing the ruling of the Lambeth Conference of 1930, which held that: "Where there is clearly felt moral obligation to limit or avoid parenthood, the method must be decided on Christian principles. The primary and obvious method is complete abstinence from intercourse (as far as may be necessary) in a life of discipline and self-control lived in the power of the Holy Spirit. Nevertheless in those cases where there is such a clearly felt moral obligation to limit or avoid parenthood, and where there is a morally sound reason for avoiding complete abstinence, the Conference agrees that other methods may be used, provided that this is done in the light of the same Christian principles." After opening the door to contraception and abortion, the Conference attempted to extenuate its connivance in these matters by expressing "its strong condemnation of the use of any methods of conception control from motives of selfishness, luxury, or mere convenience," but, of course, the damage was already done. Dean Ragsdale may not be the most lucid of women but she knows her Church's moral judgment on this issue, and it does indeed offer clear sanction for the killing of unborn children.

A striking aspect about the Ragsdale episode is the light it sheds on how our age regards clerical authority. When Roman clergy oppose abortion, they are denounced as extremists; when liberal Protestant clergy defend abortion they are treated as oracles of enlightened good counsel. Indeed, many in the American Democratic Party regarded the Dean's moral authority as irreproachable. The subcommittee's ranking member Rep. Jerry Nadler (D-N.Y.), for example, wholeheartedly agreed with Ragsdale and called the Child Interstate Abortion Notification Act (H.R. 2299), which would make it illegal to "circumvent parental consent laws in a state by, without the parents' knowledge, taking a minor girl across state lines for an abortion" an "assault on the reproductive rights of women." Dean Ragsdale, however, goes much further than Representative Nadler; for her, abortion not only ensures the "reproductive rights of women," it is a "blessing."

> When a woman gets pregnant against her will and wants an abortion—it's the violence that is the tragedy; the abortion is a blessing. When a woman might want to bear and raise a child but fears she can't afford to because she doesn't have access to healthcare or daycare or enough income to provide a home—it's the lack of justice that is the tragedy; the abortion is a blessing. When a woman has planned and provided for a pregnancy, decorated the nursery and chosen a name, and, in the last weeks, discovers that her fetus will not live to become a baby, that it has anomalies incompatible with life, and that preserving her own life and health, and sparing the fetus suffering, require a late-term abortion—it's the loss of her hopes and dreams that is the tragedy; the abortion is a blessing. And, and here's one that really gets me in trouble, when a woman simply gets pregnant unintentionally and decides this is not a good time for her to bear and care for a child—there is no tragedy. The ability to enjoy healthy sexuality without risking a pregnancy that could derail her education or career, the development or exercise of the gifts God has given her, is a blessing.[37]

Here, it is important to stress that Dean Ragsdale makes no attempt to claim that the child in the womb is unreal; instead, she goes out of her way to consult the feelings of

---

[37] P. Starr, "Priest Who Calls Abortion a 'Blessing' Tells Congress She'd Break Law to Help Minor Cross State Line to Get One" in *CNS News* (8 March 2012).

the unborn child; indeed, she advocates abortion because, as she says, she is in favor of "sparing the fetus suffering." This same factitious pity leads her to argue that special-needs children should also be killed in the womb because, as she says, their "anomalies" make them "incompatible with life." This is the post-sonogram defense of abortion in all its remorseless inhumanity: inexpedient children are not entitled to life because they are threats to the 'reproductive rights' of women; they are "incompatible with life;" they are *Untermensch*.

That this post-sonogram defense of abortion is gaining ground is evident from an article entitled "After-birth abortion: why should the baby live?" by Alberto Giubilini of the University of Milan and Francesca Minerva of Oxford University, which recently appeared in the British *Journal of Medical Ethics*. There, the authors contend, as their abstract states, that "After-birth abortion (killing a newborn) should be permissible in all cases where abortion is, including cases where the newborn is not disabled." Their defense of their argument will surprise no one who has followed the defense mounted on behalf of abortion: "foetuses and newborns," the authors declare, "do not have the same moral status as actual persons" and therefore any law which permits abortion should also permit infanticide.[38] Moreover, the authors claimed that since newborns were not "actual persons," but only "potential persons" they did not have a "moral right to life."[39] Here the authors make no bones about the fact that they regard not only the child in the womb but the child outside of the womb as *Untermensch*.

---

[38] M. Teahan, "Ethicists call for killing of newborns to be made legal" in *Catholic Herald* (2 March 2012).

[39] "Killing newborns 'ethically permissible' says Australian philosopher Francesca Minerva," *The Telegraph* Sydney (2 March 2012).

At the height of the Nazi terror which, as we all know, ended very badly indeed for the *Untermensch* of European Jewry, Albert Einstein stood up and admitted how wrong he had been in his youth about the Roman Church. In 1940, he told *Time* magazine: "Only the Church stood squarely across the path of Hitler's campaign for suppressing the truth. I had never any special interest in the Church before, but now I feel a great admiration because the Church alone has had the courage and persistence to stand for intellectual truth and moral freedom. I am forced thus to confess, that what I once despised, I now praise unreservedly."[40]

In Britain and America, it is heartening to see faithful Catholics continuing to muster the necessary "courage and persistence to stand for intellectual truth and moral freedom" in an age of defiant unreality, in which the advocates of abortion, buoyed by political victory, seek to promote abortion on demand as the core of 'reproductive rights' around the world. In the years to come, the faithful can take heart from the fact that in the war between the forces of life and the forces of death, the Church never ceased to invoke the Giver of Life and to defend in prayer "the fruit of the maternal womb." In the prayer of Pope Benedict XVI, we can see the true respect for life that so many public authorities reject.

Lord Jesus,
You who faithfully visit and fulfill with your Presence
the Church and the history of men;
You who in the miraculous Sacrament of your Body and Blood
render us participants in divine Life
and allow us a foretaste of the joy of eternal Life;
We adore and bless you.

---

[40] Albert Einstein, quoted in M. Burleigh, *Sacred Causes: The Clash of Religion and Politics, from the Great War to the War on Terror* (New York, 2007), p. 213.

Prostrated before You, source and lover of Life,
truly present and alive among us, we beg you.
Reawaken in us respect for every unborn life,
make us capable of seeing in the fruit of the maternal womb
the miraculous work of the Creator,
open our hearts to generously welcoming every child
that comes into life.
Bless all families,
sanctify the union of spouses,
render fruitful their love.
Accompany the choices of legislative assemblies
with the light of your Spirit,
so that peoples and nations may recognize and respect
the sacred nature of life, of every human life.
Guide the work of scientists and doctors,
so that all progress contributes to the integral well-being of the
person,
and no one endures suppression or injustice.
Give creative charity to administrators and economists,
so they may realize and promote sufficient conditions
so that young families can serenely embrace
the birth of new children.
Console the married couples who suffer
because they are unable to have children
and in Your goodness provide for them.
Teach us all to care for orphaned or abandoned children,
so they may experience the warmth of your Charity,
the consolation of your divine Heart.
Together with Mary, Your Mother, the great believer,
in whose womb you took on our human nature,
we wait to receive from You, our Only True Good and Savior,
the strength to love and serve life,
in anticipation of living forever in You,
in communion with the Blessed Trinity.[41]

---

[41] See "Pope Benedict XVI composes prayer for the unborn" in *Catholic News Agency* (30 November 2010).

By and large, the historians in our midst have chosen to ignore this profound witness. Still, there are some historians who are recording the history of abortion with both fidelity to the often overlooked or distorted facts and critical insight. One can cite two books of exceptional distinction: Marvin Olasky's *A Social History of Abortion in America* (1992) and Joseph Dellapenna's *Dispelling the Myths of Abortion* (2006). Then, again, John Keown, Professor of Christian Ethics at Georgetown University put a good deal of the skewered rhetoric of pro-abortion historians in just perspective in his groundbreaking monograph *Abortion, doctors and the law* (1988). Regarding the claims of pro-abortion historians with respect to the dramatic rise of abortion since 1968, for example, he writes of the British experience.

> It is tempting to regard the evident increase in abortion since 1968, both numerically and conceptually, as evidence of a 'gap' between the letter of the law and the law in action. Certainly, the Act's sponsor would appear to be concerned at its current implementation for was recorded as saying, 'Abortion is, I am afraid, being used as a contraceptive. The present level is too high.' On the other hand, it is by no means clear that the broad terms of the Act do not allow for just this, for it conceded the profession's central demand for autonomy to decide when abortion is 'therapeutic.' It could be argued that it formally transferred the determination of what constituted therapeutic abortion from the courts to the medical profession, for it is difficult to envisage circumstances in which a doctor could not claim that the abortion he recommended was indicated in the interests of the patient's health, particularly if 'health' is given the sweeping definition in the World Health Organization's constitution as 'a state of complete physi-

cal, mental, and social well-being and not merely
the absence of disease or infirmity.'

Indeed, as Dr. Keown argues, one commentator maintained
that "the wording of the act is so vague as to be meaningless
and that both the scrupulous and the cynical doctor are able
to interpret it as they wish." [42] Dr. Keown is also astute on
the role that doctors have played in abortion. Referring to
the British abortion law, which requires that a "legal"
abortion have the consent of two doctors, Keown raises
issues which apply to the role of American doctors as well
in the acceptance and proliferation of abortion.

> The medicalisation of abortion raises several pro-
> found questions which are often overlooked, such
> as whether it really does eradicate stigma; whether
> social problems which underline requests for
> abortion come to be classified as individual medical
> problems and are thereby politically defused;
> whether it does not encourage the surrender of
> personal responsibility to medical experts; and
> whether these experts are really qualified to make
> decisions about abortion.

To make his point, Dr. Keown cites the New York University professor, Eliot Freidson, who remarked how, "If we
consider the profession of medicine today, it is clear that
its major characteristic is preeminence. Such preeminence
is not merely that of a prestige but also that of expert
authority. This is to say, medicine's knowledge about
illness and its treatment is considered to be authoritative
and definitive ... Medicine's official position is akin to that
of state religions yesterday—it has an officially approved

---

[42]   J. Keown, *Abortion, doctors and the law* (Cambridge, 1988), p. 164.
       The commentator to whom Keown refers is I. M. Ingram, "Abor-
       tion games: an inqury into the working of the Abortion Act" (1971)
       2 *Lancet*, 969.

monopoly of the right to define health and illness and to treat illness."[43] Now, of course, in America, where the state dictates to doctors on matters pertaining to abortion, this preeminence is being lost.

For Dr. Keown, one way that proponents of abortion have made abortion acceptable is by treating it as merely a medical matter. To make his point, Dr. Keown cites Thomas Szasz, who "stresses that the fact that the procedure of abortion is surgical no more makes it a medical problem than the use of the electric chair makes capital punishment a problem of electrical engineering. The question is, he stresses, what is abortion—the killing of a fetus or the removal of a piece of tissue from a woman's body?" Dr. Keown's conclusion is inescapable: the British Abortion Act of 1967 may be seen as "a medicalisation of deviance ..." [44]

Dr. Nathanson came to the same conclusion in 1974, nearly fifteen years before Dr. Keown, when he confessed to certain gnawing doubts about his pro-abortion stance in the *New England Journal of Medicine*, after which he entirely repudiated his former pro-abortion allies, including the unspeakable Betty Freidan. "Somewhere in the vast philosophic plateau between the two implacably opposed camps—past the slogans, past the pamphlets, past even the demonstrations and the legislative threats—lies the infinitely agonizing truth. We are taking life, and the deliberate taking of life, even of a special order and under special circumstances, is an inexpressibly serious matter. Somehow, we must not deny the pervasive sense of loss that should accompany abortion and its most unfortunate interruption of life. We must not coarsen our sensitivities

---

[43] Keown, p. 162. See also E. Freidson, *Profession of Medicine* (Chicago, 1988).

[44] Keown, pp. 165–166. See also T. Szasz, *The Theology of Medicine* (Oxford, 1979), p. 77.

through common practice and brute denial. I offer no panacea. Certainly, the medical profession itself cannot shoulder the burden of this matter. The phrase 'between a woman and her physician' is an empty one since the physician is only the instrument of her decision. Furthermore, there are seldom any purely medical indications for abortion. The decision is the most serious responsibility a woman can experience in her lifetime ..." [45]

Yet we can see the "medicalisation of deviance" recrudescing in Ireland, where abortionists are using the tragic death of an Indian woman, Savita Halappanavar, who died in childbirth after requesting and being refused an abortion, to try to force abortion on an Irish public that remains admirably pro-life. A brilliant ad now running throughout Ireland captures the bogus medical defense of abortion with brilliant unanswerable logic: "Mothers are safe. Abortion isn't needed to save women's lives; it just kills a baby." The Irish may not have quite the literary talent they had when the likes of Flann O'Brien and Lord Dunsany were going the roads but they retain their genius for advertising.

In a recent report, the American journalist, Christopher Caldwell praised John Waters, one of Ireland's most eloquent pro-lifers.

> Waters is one of the most interesting thinkers in Europe. He occupies a special role in Irish intellectual life. What Czeslaw Milosz did for a place (Cold War Poland), he has done for a generation (the baby boom). He has examined the new ideology that its ruling elites extol as a source of liberation and exposed it as a new form of servility. "This generation," he tells me, "has not been honest about its experience of freedom."[46]

[45] B. Nathanson, "Deeper into Abortion," *New England Journal of Medicine* (28 November 1974), Vol. 291, No. 22, pp. 1189–1190.

More than any of the other brave souls trying to dissuade the Irish from falling for the terrible cheat of "limited abortion," Waters urges his countrymen to realize what they are about when they contemplate abandoning their true traditions for the fads and follies of modernity or that even less reputable article, post-modernity. In defending the first of these traditions, the ancient Irish delight in God the Maker, he bases his defense of life on the firmest of foundations and in this he is a true heir of Pope John Paul II.

Another Irish pro-lifer, Mary Kenny, the journalist, biographer and historian who has been making the pro-life case in England now for decades with admirable élan, noted an amusing twist in the history of the "medicalisation of deviance" before drawing some important conclusions of her own. In a 2007 piece for the *Daily Telegraph* entitled "What Is Done Easily Is Done Frequently," she poured witty scorn on the notion, so beloved of the abortionists, that abortion somehow serves the interests of either children or mothers.

> When 10th Baroness Howard de Walden—described as "a devout Roman Catholic", which is media-speak for "dotty extremist"— let it be known this week that clinics in Harley Street are no longer to be allowed to perform abortions, the abortion rights lobby denounced her as a sinister opponent of "choice". But the lady is merely exercising her own choice—to do what she pleases with her own private property. The event is not without irony. Harley Street, part of the large swathe of Marylebone run by the Howard de Walden Estate, which owns the freehold, has been the site for "society" terminations since the time of Lillie Langtry. In the 1960s, when the Abortion Law Reform Association—the lobby

---

[46] C. Caldwell, "Changed, Changed Utterly?" in *The Weekly Standard* (1 April 2013), p. 30.

> that made David Steel's Abortion Act possible in
> 1967—was at its most energetic, some of its adher-
> ents regarded Harley Street as a deplorable example
> of hypocrisy and class bias. The rich went to Harley
> Street while the poor went to the back streets. I
> remember hearing the MP Lena Jeger make that
> point in an impassioned plea for abortion rights in
> 1966. Harley Street, she said, should be closed down
> because it provided abortions for the rich. Now it
> has been, thanks to Lady de Walden.[47]

It is interesting that Kenny should make these points
because, of course, the argument that the English abortion
bill was justifiable because it would reduce not only
back-street abortion but inequities of class is still trundled
out by historians. Addison, in fact, trundles it out in his
survey of post-war England, remarking how "Since wealthy
women could obtain abortions from Harley Street special-
ists, while the poor had to rely on the ministrations of
backstreet abortionists at whose hands about fifty women
a year died, the social injustice of the situation was glaring.
Given the shame that still attached to the unwanted
pregnancies of single women, the sufferings they endured
could be terrible."[48] If here Addison betrays the misplaced
compassion that is such a perennial feature of progressive
reformers, the journalist Andrew Marr provides some of
the history that inspired this bogus compassion in the first

---

[47] Regarding her grandfather, the 8th Baron Howard De Walden
(1880–1946), whom Max Beerbohm caricatured so amusingly, the
DNB noted how "The diverse talents of this versatile man were
matched by his noble generosity to many branches of art and
charity; hospitals, orchestras, and numerous individual
artists...benefited by his munificence and taste. In the breadth of
his patronage and in his own widespread activity, he epitomized
a splendid tradition of the English aristocracy, practicing as well
as stimulating the arts, sports, and learning which he loved."

[48] Addison, p. 207.

place, pointing out how "the abortion law reform movement can be traced to two unrelated, horrible stories.

> The first was the rape of a fourteen-year-old girl
> by some guardsmen in a West London barracks
> shortly before the war. After one doctor refused to
> perform an abortion, on the grounds that since her
> life was not in danger he would be breaking the
> law, another doctor, Aleck Bourne, stepped in. He
> performed the abortion and was duly prosecuted.
> Bourne defended himself on the grounds that the
> girl's fragile mental health meant that the abortion
> was, in practice, essential. He won and became an
> instant hero to the small female campaign which
> had been set up to reform the abortion law in 1936.
> (From their point of view, this was a mistake.
> Bourne would later recant, declaring that mass
> abortions would be 'the greatest holocaust in
> history' and in 1945 he would become a founding
> member of the anti-abortion group, the Society for
> the Protection of the Unborn Child.) The second
> event was much more widespread. It was the
> Thalidomide drug disaster of 1959–62. This
> alleged wonder drug, which helped sleeplessness,
> colds, flu and morning sickness, was responsible
> for huge numbers of badly deformed children
> being born, many missing all or some of their
> limbs. Opinion polls at the time showed favour of
> abortion when the foetus was deformed. This was
> far more influential than the actions of the Abor-
> tion Law Reform Association which had just over
> 1,100 members at the time.[49]

Aleck Bourne (1886–1974) was deluged so with unwanted
notoriety after his acquittal that he was passed over for
the high office in the Royal College of Obstetricians that

---

[49] A. Marr, *A History of Modern Britain* (London, 2007), p. 255.

he might have attained. Later, after retiring, he left the flat in Wimpole Street where he had resided for over twenty-three years and settled in Surrey, where he composed his autobiography, *A Doctor's Creed* (1962). In his excellent entry for Dr. Bourne in the ODNB Keown remarks how "He was remembered by his colleagues as a kind and compassionate man of courage and principle; a champion of the cause of women—as his role in securing the admission of women students to St. Mary's after the Second World War testified; a superb clinician and an outstanding, inspirational teacher."[50]

Like Dr. Nathanson, Dr. Bourne personifies the radical change of heart that will need to become general if we are to end the barbarity of abortion. Still, as John Newton, the wretch who composed "Amazing Grace" and the abolition movement to which he contributed so much proved, converts to a cause can be its most effective advocates.

Apropos the role that social pressure has played in the acceptance and the entrenchment of abortion, it is amusing that Bourne should refer to "the moral code of a people" in his memoir as "the line of conduct which is found to be most compatible with the tribal or national social convenience necessary for a gregarious existence."[51] That he was first the darling and then the bane of this "tribal or national social convenience" gives his witness a peculiar authority. In his memoir, Bourne corroborated Keown by calling into question whether doctors truly possess the authority to be final arbiters on matters relating to abortion. In one unforgettable passage he relates how "Those of us who are young in years do not realize the tragedy of stillbirth ... I have often been

---

[50]   See J. Keown's entry on Aleck William Bourne in ODNB.

[51]   A. Bourne, *A Doctor's Creed: Memoirs of an Obstetrician* (London, 1962), p. 91.

surprised to hear the almost casual remark of an obstetric student that the baby was dead—but the mother is all right. It is not a grief the mother can easily express for she cries for one that has not been. She cries for the keenest expectation, a hope in which for months she has centered all her future imagined years. If we can enter into the tragedy of stillbirth ... it will give a new meaning to the practice of obstetrics."[52] The same could be said for the tragedy of abortion—abortion not as an abstract 'right' or counter in the culture wars but as an irreplaceable human loss, which no conscionable mother can suffer without remorse. In another passage, Bourne takes the obstetric profession to task for lack of imagination—something abortionists suffer from as well. "Immediately our works bring us into close association with people," Bourne writes, "we need more than technical knowledge, and that is something that can only be derived from a wider culture of the mind than that which comes from the study of a pure technology." Here Bourne implicitly rejected the culture of knowledge.

> It is therefore more than ever necessary to guard ourselves from the mental sclerosis that awaits us should we fail to employ the mind in all its capacities. In education most of us have done with the influence of our home-life and school. We are technicians in hospital and laboratory. But even the things we learn there should be an inspiration to the imagination. It is wrong to regard our learning as only a process for collecting scientific facts. In every branch of our training, be it embryology, physiology, or clinical medicine, we are in the presence of such stupendous mystery that it should be possible to turn aside occasionally and ponder on its origins.

---

[52] Ibid., pp. 122–123.

> We have made a great step forward when we have
> learnt the sense of wonder ...[53]

In retrospect, we can see that Bourne's imagination was changed forever in 1967, when an earnest young Scottish Liberal named David Steel, who had just been elected to the Commons in a by-election, took it into his head to champion the cause of abortion. Risibly enough, it was a Church of England report that persuaded him of the virtues of abortion. Before composing the 1967 Abortion Bill, however, Steel attended an abortion himself to satisfy himself that it was something that he could morally promote. But as Marrs point out, Steel essentially was put up to writing and pushing the bill through by Roy Jenkins, the Liberal MP, who was in favor of so many of the progressive reforms that came to characterize the permissive '60s, from abortion to divorce to homosexual reform. "Like Silverman and Abse [two other prominent Liberal MPs], he had such expert opinion on his side—not a Wolfenden Report or the passionate books of philosophers, but the World Health Organization, which had declared in 1946 that health meant 'complete mental, physical and social well-being.' This implied that mental suffering to the woman could be grounds for abortion. It was written into the bill and today of the 180,000 abortions taking place each year in Britain, all but 2 percent of them are on just such grounds."[54] Taking up where Marr leaves off, Kenny briskly refutes this sentimental rationalization for the killing of babies in the womb.

---

[53]   Ibid., pp. 55–56.

[54]   Marr, pp. 256–257. See also N. Annan, *Our Age: English Intellectuals between the World Wars* (New York, 1990), p. 130: "Roy Jenkins was the politician of Our Age who did more than any other to increase personal liberty."

The original campaigners for abortion law reform emphasised the scandal of back-street abortions: they also claimed that legal abortion and better access to contraception would mean (a) no more unwanted children; (b) no more children in care; (c) no more cruelty to children; (d) a reduction in "teenage mothers"—the figures had reached a shocking 4,000 in 1966; (e) a reduction in all "illegitimacy"; (f) a reduction in "subnormal"—that is, low IQ, mothers—giving birth; (g) the disappearance of "subnormal" children; (h) a reduction in child murders and attacks on children.

In the mid-1960s there were some 5,000 children abandoned to local authority care. Access to abortion would solve all that, campaigners believed. Forty years on, there are now some 50,000 children in care, and 40 years after the Abortion Act was supposed to decrease "illegitimacy", Britain has the highest rate of single teenage mothers in Europe, and a third of all births are now out of wedlock. As for improving conditions for children, a report from Unicef this week put the UK bottom of the developed nations' league for child wellbeing.[55]

If the primary rationalization for abortion in England was to make the world safe for skilled, as opposed to unskilled abortionists, the rationale in America was to combat the fear of overpopulation, which William Vogt, the research director of Planned Parenthood fomented in the 1960s. "If the United States had spent two billion dollars ... developing a contraceptive, instead of the atomic bomb," Vogt contended, "it would have contributed far more to our national security."[56] G. K. Chesterton noticed a similar

---

[55] M. Kenny, "What is Done Easily Is Done Frequently" in *The Daily Telegraph* (16 February 2007).

[56] Vogt quoted in Critchlow, p. 19.

concern with overpopulation among the English, ι.
it was compounded, as so many things in English life aι
with considerations of class. "Birth-controllers," Chesterton noticed, "never … talk about a danger from the
comfortable classes, even from a more respectable section
of the comfortable classes. The Gloomy Dean [William
Inge, Dean of St. Paul's, a notorious proponent of birth
control in the years between the wars] is not gloomy about
there being too many Dukes; and naturally not about there
being too many Deans.

> He is not primarily annoyed with a politician for
> having a whole population of poor relations, though
> places and public salaries have to be found for all
> the relations. Political Economy means that every-
> body except politicians must be economical. The
> Birth-Controller does not bother about all these
> things, for the perfectly simple reason that it is not
> such people that he wants to control. What he wants
> to control is the populace, and he practically says
> so. He always insists that a workman has no right to
> have so many children, or that a slum is perilous
> because it is producing so many children. The
> question he dreads is "Why has not the workman a
> better wage? Why has not the slum family a better
> house?" His way of escaping from it is to suggest,
> not a larger house but a smaller family. The landlord
> or the employer says in his hearty and handsome
> fashion: "You really cannot expect me to deprive
> myself of my money. But I will make a sacrifice, I
> will deprive myself of your children."[57]

Now that the Servile State is beginning to take full control
of its tragically docile citizenry, this attitude has only grown,

---

[57] *The Collected Works of G. K. Chesterton, Vol. 4: What's Wrong With
the World, Superstition of Divorce, Eugenics and Other Evils* (San
Francisco, 1987), p. 438.

though it is not only the life and death of children that this tentacular State means to control. It also has its eye on the old and the infirm, the disabled and the unproductive. That Chesterton saw this coming so clearly in the early twentieth century confirms his ungainsayable prescience. One of the most clear-sighted of our twenty-first century pro-lifers is Mary Ann Glendon, Learned Hand Professor of Law at Harvard University, for whom "the most ominous development" in our increasingly unconscionable culture "is the growing normalization of the extermination of persons who become inconvenient and burdensome to maintain at life's frail beginnings and endings.

> To state the obvious: If the outlook for dependences is grim, the outlook for everyone is grim. Despite our attachment to the ideal of the free, self-determining individual, we humans are dependant, social beings. We still begin our lives in the longest period of dependency of any mammal. Almost all of us spend much of our lives either as dependants, or caring for dependants, or financially responsible for dependants. To devise constructive approaches to the dependency-welfare state crisis will require acceptance of those simple facts of life.[58]

This sounds a sensible response but whether the cheese-paring bureaucrats of the NHS or the US Department of Health and Human Services will ever prove capable of "constructive approaches" to this looming problem is dubious, especially given their readiness to confuse the healthcare at their disposal with sterilization, abortion and euthanasia.

In commending the society that has made abortion its moral hallmark, progressive historians characterize those who do not share their commitment to killing children in

---

[58] M. A. Glendon, *Traditions in Turmoil* (Ann Arbor, 2006), p. 141.

the womb as reactionaries and obstructionists. Sir Noel Annan was particularly guilty of this when he referred to Evelyn Waugh as "the real deviant of my generation" because he "deviated from the values we esteemed." (Annan could never forgive Waugh's converting not only to Catholicism but to what he called "Augustinian Catholicism.") [59] Frances Donaldson—Freddie Lonsdale's daughter—attested to this provocative deviance in an amusing memoir that she wrote of Waugh after his sudden death in 1966, when he dropped dead in his bathroom after Easter Mass. When Waugh "motored round the countryside in company with his children," Donaldson recalled, "he taught them to recite benedictions or maledictions to his neighbors as he passed their houses. One of these owned a factory that made rubber goods and Evelyn insisted on regarding him as responsible for the control of birth throughout the country. Imprecations greeted his house ..." By the same token, when the car passed the houses of those of whom Waugh approved he would lead his children in a refrain based on the words of the 122nd Psalm—"God bless Colonel Brown. 'They shall prosper that love him. Peace be within his walls and prosperity within his palaces.' "[60] Among these beneficent souls, Waugh would doubtless include not only Mary Kenny, John Keown and Justin Dyer but all those who denounce the evil of abortion.

In conclusion, I shall end with the greatest historian of abortion, even though he was not an historian by profession. As I have endeavored to show, too many of our professional historians grossly misrepresent abortion by

---

[59]   N. Annan, *Our Age: English Intellectuals between the World Wars* (New York, 1990), p. 158.

[60]   F. Donaldson, *Evelyn Waugh: Portrait of a Country Neighbor* (London, 1967), pp. 40–41.

deliberately ignoring its savage destruction of innocent
life. By contrast, in his indispensable *Evangelium Vitae*,
Pope John II never flinches from calling a spade a spade.

> The moral gravity of procured abortion is apparent
> in all its truth if we recognize that we are dealing
> with murder and, in particular, when we consider
> the specific elements involved. The one eliminated
> is a human being at the very beginning of life. No
> one more absolutely innocent could be imagined.
> In no way could this human being ever be consid-
> ered an aggressor, much less an unjust aggressor!
> He or she is weak, defenceless, even to the point of
> lacking that minimal form of defence consisting in
> the poignant power of a newborn baby's cries and
> tears. The unborn child is totally entrusted to the
> protection and care of the woman carrying him or
> her in the womb. And yet sometimes it is precisely
> the mother herself who makes the decision and
> asks for the child to be eliminated, and who then
> goes about having it done ...[61]

However, as John Paul II made clear, mothers are not the
only ones to blame for the destruction of unborn children,
especially in a society whose first response to life at its
most vulnerable is often to fetch the abortionist. "In the
first place, the father of the child may be to blame, not only
when he directly pressures the woman to have an abortion,
but also when he indirectly encourages such a decision on
her part by leaving her alone to face the problems of
pregnancy: in this way the family is thus mortally wounded
and profaned in its nature as a community of love and in
its vocation to be the 'sanctuary of life.' "[62] Then, again,
Pope John Paul II does not ignore the grave part that

---

[61] Pope John Paul II, *Evangelium Vitae*, 95.
[62] *Evangelium Vitae*, 96.

historians play in deceiving the general public about the evil of abortion. By defending the destruction of human life and justifying it in the name of feminism, historians add the authority of their voices to what John Paul II characterizes as the "culture of death."

> This culture is actively fostered by powerful cul-
> tural, economic and political currents which
> encourage an idea of society excessively concerned
> with efficiency. Looking at the situation from this
> point of view, it is possible to speak in a certain
> sense of a war of the powerful against the weak: a
> life which would require greater acceptance, love
> and care is considered useless, or held to be an
> intolerable burden, and is therefore rejected in one
> way or another. A person who, because of illness,
> handicap or, more simply, just by existing, com-
> promises the well-being or life-style of those who
> are more favoured tends to be looked upon as an
> enemy to be resisted or eliminated. In this way a
> kind of "conspiracy against life" is unleashed.

Historians, especially those avid to win the favor of the powerful, are necessarily sensitive to offending the powerful. And thus they come to the defense of "legislators who have promoted and approved abortion laws ..." They encourage "the spread of an attitude of sexual permissiveness and a lack of esteem for motherhood ...," especially overtly feminist historians like Amanda Vickery. Yet, as John Paul observed, "one cannot overlook the network of complicity which reaches out to include international institutions, foundations and associations which systematically campaign for the legalization and spread of abortion in the world. In this sense abortion goes beyond the responsibility of individuals and beyond the harm done to them, and takes on a distinctly social dimension. It is a most serious wound inflicted on society and its culture by the very people who ought to be society's promoters and defenders. As I wrote in my Letter to Families, 'we are facing an immense threat to life: not only to the life of individuals but also to that of civilization itself.'"[63]

And it is important to stress that this threat confronts many individuals and many institutions, especially those of a religious character, which, if left to themselves, would never have anything to do with abortion. This is why pro-life education is so necessary—to counter the false information peddled by the abortionists, especially those working under the auspices of the State and its agents, and to reassure those that do defend life that their work is of inestimable value, for as John Paul II assured his readers, their "deeds strengthen the bases of the 'civilization of love and life,' without which the life of individuals and of society itself loses its most genuinely human quality. Even if they go unnoticed and remain hidden to most people, faith assures us that the Father 'who sees in secret' (Mt 6:6) not only will reward these actions but already here and now makes them produce lasting fruit for the good of all."[64]

Mrs. Oliphant once said of the French Catholic hagiographer Comte de Montalembert, that "he had a fine way of picking one up as on some polished pair of tongs, and holding one up to the admiration of the world around, in all the bloom of one's foolishness."[65] This is what our historians ought to have been doing with the abortionists in our midst, though *foolishness* is much too mild a word

---

[63] *Evangelium Vitae*, 97.

[64] *Evangelium Vitae*, 49.

[65] Mrs. Oliphant, *The Autobiography* (Chicago, 1988), p. 99. In the Chamber of Deputies, the exemplary Montalembert (1810–1870) never hesitated to present himself as a Catholic, at a time when, as he said himself, "to profess or defend the Catholic faith one had to face marked unpopularity." See the *Catholic Encyclopedia*.

to describe the evil of which those who deliberately kill children in the womb are guilty. Instead, by ingratiating themselves with a culture of death that cares for nothing but its own sordid perpetuation, they connive in the very moral decline which they should be working to expose. Fortunately, despite the wreck of culture that we see all around us, seeds for renewal are ready to hand, as Pope John Paul II so eloquently reminds us.

> The angel's Annunciation to Mary is framed by these reassuring words: "Do not be afraid, Mary" and "with God nothing will be impossible" (Lk 1:30, 37). The whole of the Virgin Mother's life is in fact pervaded by the certainty that God is near to her and that he accompanies her with his providential care. The same is true of the Church, which finds "a place prepared by God" (Rev 12:6) in the desert, the place of trial but also of the manifestation of God's love for his people (cf. Hos 2:16). Mary is a living word of comfort for the Church in her struggle against death. Showing us the Son, the Church assures us that in him the forces of death have already been defeated: "Death with life contended: combat strangely ended! Life's own Champion, slain, yet lives to reign."[66]

Here are the ancient truths that no amount of falsehood from pro-abortion historians can diminish. "The Lamb who was slain is alive, bearing the marks of his Passion in the splendour of the Resurrection. He alone is master of all the events of history: he opens its 'seals' (cf. Rev 5:1–10) and proclaims, in time and beyond, the power of life over death." And this is the hope that we must revive in our own hearts as we continue our fight to protect the life not only of unborn children but of the sick, the disabled, and

---

[66] *Evangelium Vitae*, 95–97.

the elderly, for all of whom Pope John Paul II wrote his incomparable encyclical.

> And as we, the pilgrim people, the people of life and for life, make our way in confidence towards "a new heaven and a new earth" (Rev 21:1), we look to her who is for us "a sign of sure hope and solace".

O Mary,
bright dawn of the new world,
Mother of the living,
to you do we entrust the cause of life.
Look down, O Mother,
upon the vast numbers
of babies not allowed to be born,
of the poor whose lives are made difficult,
of men and women
who are victims of brutal violence,
of the elderly and the sick killed
by indifference or out of misguided mercy.
Grant that all who believe in your Son
may proclaim the Gospel of life
with honesty and love
to the people of our time.
Obtain for them the grace
to accept that Gospel
as a gift ever new,
the joy of celebrating it with gratitude
throughout their lives
and the courage to bear witness to it
resolutely, in order to build,
together with all people of good will,
the civilization of truth and love,
to the praise and glory of God,
the Creator and lover of life.[67]

---

[67] *Evangelium Vitae*, 165–167.